Special dedication to Mr. Mehdi Khachlouf

I dedicate this work to my dear friend who well supported me throughout the work period, which I find the origin of the young student who believe in a prestigious future of our continent, a real man of business encourage the young people: affairs are directed to the young talent, so far the tendency of the younger market support that seems so far of being real and relevant, big thanks.

"Just after our last three years, two business magazines, here we start pedaling; assuming responsibility and conquering determined objectives, let's get "busy ".

- Neili Belhassen -

African whispers

Labels the world leaders

By Neili Belhassen

The African history

The story of Africa is the set of past facts about Africa, from prehistory to today. The term "Africa" meant to the Romans only the northern part of the continent. Africans were those who believed in goddess "Ifri" (Berber goddess), then the term encompassed the entire continent.

The East Africa is probably the place where the human species have emerged; there are about 2.5 million years. Thereafter, peoples were formed, grew, and were spread on the African territory. Towards the end of prehistory, the Sahara was then formed large lakes became dry and "cut" Africa in two. The history of North Africa then mingled with that of the Mediterranean Sea, and sub-Saharan Africa grew on his side.

The history of Africa is experiencing the same three "technical revolution" than the rest of world history, each deeply upsetting previous mode of life Among them the "Revolution of fire" took place (depending on assumptions) there 800 000 to 400 000 years, Which has given the human race way to modify the natural environment. (In favor of his own: the savanna and grassland) to be a much more effective predator and feed nutrients cooked, The "Neolithic revolution" took place (according to geographical areas) there are 8 000-2 000 years BC, marked by the settlement and agriculture and the "Industrial revolution" occurred for about two centuries, and gave mankind access to energy (electric) and fossil and fossil fuels.

Before the Roman Empire, Ancient Egypt was one of the wealthiest and most advanced civilizations of the world. The port of Alexandria, founded by Alexander the Great in 334, was a hub of commerce in the Mediterranean for centuries.

The conditions were different south of the Sahara, where the density of forests and deserts formed as barriers to trade. Only Nubia, Ethiopia, Mali and Ghana Empire had channels of communication to the Mediterranean and the Middle East.

Throughout the first millennium, the Kingdom of Aksum dominated the Horn of Africa. He had a navy and traded with the Byzantine Empire, India and perhaps China. The introduction of the camel by the Arabs in the tenth century made it possible to cross the Sahara. Revenue from gold and salt led to the emergence of many powerful empires in the western Sahel, including Ghana, Mali and Kanem-Bornu kingdom.

The Arabs also developed maritime trade along the eastern coast, where Swahili civilization prospered by exporting ivory and slaves across the Indian Ocean. Further south, traces of empires or kingdoms traders are much rarer, except Great Zimbabwe and in the Great Lakes region, Rwanda, Burundi and Buganda.

In the fifteenth century, Portuguese merchants are freed roads Sahara to join the Guinea directly by the sea. Other European nations followed and West Africa is rich quickly.

That's when we celebrated the kingdom of Benin, Dahomey and the Ashanti Confederacy, Decentralized federations of the city states were common, such as those of the Yoruba and Hausa, Mainly based on the slave trade with Europe, this prosperity collapsed with the abolition of slavery in the American colonies.

The story of Africa is the set of past facts about Africa, from prehistory to today. The term "African" meant to the Romans only the northern part of the continent. Africans were those who believed in the goddess Ifri (Berber goddess), then the term encompassed the entire continent.

The East Africa is probably the place where the human species have emerged; there are about 2.5 million years. Later, people were formed, grew, and were spread on the African territory. Towards the end of prehistory, the Sahara, then formed large lakes became dry and "cut" Africa in two. The history of North Africa was then mixed with that of the Mediterranean Sea, and sub-Saharan Africa grew on his side.

The history of Africa is experiencing the same three "technical revolution" than the rest of world history, each deeply upsetting previous mode of life : one, the "revolution of fire" took place (the assumptions) there 800 000 to 400 000 years, which gave mankind the way to modify the natural environment (in favor of his own: the savanna and grassland) of be a much more efficient predator ,two ,the "Neolithic revolution" took place (according to geographical areas) there are 8 000-2 000 years before our era, marked by the settlement and agriculture , three , the "industrial revolution" occurred for about two centuries, and gave mankind access to electric power, fossil and fossil fuels.

Development of agriculture and metallurgy

At the end of the last glaciations, there are about 10,500 years; the Sahara was a fertile and populous region. However, it gradually dried up as a result of global warming 5000 years later. Its inhabitants now began to ascend the Nile Valley in search of more hospitable lands, beyond the second cataract.

In Africa, the domestication of cattle above agriculture and seems to have existed at the same time that the tribes of hunter-gatherers, the farming was practiced in North Africa from 6000 before Jesus Christ (Jc).

The first traces of rice and sorghum date back to 5000 before Jc in the Sahel region, from 4000 before Jc. The advance of the Sahara desert intensified rapidly, drying lakes and rivers, which caused the migration to West Africa, more humid.

Toward - 3000, agriculture grew almost simultaneously in West Africa, with the culture of yam and oil palm, and Ethiopia, with coffee.

Ironworking appears early in Africa since the third millennium BC.

(Current territories Gabon, Cameroon and Republic of Congo) and in the Great Lakes region.

The first traces of writing in Africa dating back to ancient Egypt, the timing is still used to date the cultures of the Bronze Age and Iron Age history of the region. The Kingdom of Egypt reached its peak during the New Kingdom, between -1567 and -1080.

In regions bordering the Mediterranean counters were created by the Phoenicians before -1000. The latter founded Carthage -814.

To the east, the Greeks founded the city of Cyrene to -631. Cyrenaica became a flourishing colony, albeit isolated by deserts around him. The Greeks also exerted a powerful influence in Egypt. The foundation of Alexandria and is attributed to Alexander the Great and the Ptolemaic dynasty tried to expand its territory to the south, bequeathing papers on Ethiopia.

However, the Romans come to the end of the three powers shared Cyrenaica, Egypt and Carthage. The latter fell -146 after centuries of rivalry, followed in less than a century by the other two.

They reached into Nubia and Ethiopia, but ordered by Emperor Nero to discover the sources of the Nile expedition was a failure. The writings of Ptolemy, can be inferred from the extent of the known world (directly or testimony) of the Romans mention the Great Lakes reservoirs of the Nile, of trading posts along the coast of the Indian Ocean to Rhapta in Tanzania now and the Niger River.

The invasion of the Vandals in the fifth century brought an end to the presence of classical civilizations in Africa.

Vandals briefly occupied North Africa and there founded a kingdom in 429, which fell to the Byzantine Empire in 533.

Introduction of Christianity

According to legend, St. Mark brought Christianity to Alexandria in 60 and became its first bishop. It's more likely that the Jerusalem Church sent missionaries. To 200, Alexandria was the seat of a Church officiating in Greek; in 325, Egypt had 51 bishops and the Bible circulated in Coptic. 400, 90% of Egyptians were Christians.

In Carthage, it was reported running in 180 twelve Christians who refused to practice the imperial cult.

In 203, Perpetua and Felicity are condemned to death and executed in the arena. First sporadic persecution becomes more frequent under the emperor Decius between 249 and 251 Christianity still continues its southward expansion, especially in Numidia. Persecution under Diocletian show that attempts to destroy the religious texts. Thereafter, Donatus Magnus, Bishop of Carlyle nigrae, refused to admit traitors who had given the books to the Roman authorities and causes a schism in 305 Donatism that emerged was predominant in the Maghreb through the fourth century until dissolution of the movement in 412 after the Council of Carthage. However, he survived the repression until the seventh century and the invasion of the Arabs.

Ethiopia is Frumentius of Axum, trader captured and first Bishop of Axum, who converted King Ezana would in 333 after he became his tutor. In fact, many religions coexisted in the Ezana court and traces of other religions remain at least until the fifth century. The scriptures were translated into Ge'ez and Christianity spread to Adulis. At the breakup of their kingdom in the seventh century, the Aksumite populations would close the "Cushitic" peoples established further south to anchor the Church and kingdom of Ethiopia.

Islamization

From the seventeenth century, Arab armies conquered North Africa. In 639 "Amr ibn al-As" entered Egypt at the head of 4,000 soldiers. Four years later, in 643, he succeeded in Libya, then the gates of Sbeïtla in 647 After a brief interruption due to quarrels of succession, conquest resumed in Oqba Ibn Nafi in 665 Al Fihri, nephew of Amr ibn al -As. He founded Kairouan in 670 and made it the capital of Ifriqiya, a former Roman province newly Islamized; this was during the same year (670) is founded the Great Mosque of Kairouan considered the oldest mosque in North Africa. From there, he joined the coast of West Africa but faces on the way back to a strong Berber resistance led by Koceila. It ended up taking Kairouan and, after his death, the Arabs cannot settle in western Algeria in alliance with the Berbers.

Egyptian Christians have the choice between conversion and the "dhimmi" status for a tax on land. Most chose the second option and retained significant administrative responsibilities to the eighth century, when they lost gradually their power.

Arabic became the official language and Coptic was relegated to a liturgical language. In the fourteenth century, Christians accounted for only 10% of the Egyptian population.

For five centuries, several powerful dynasties succeeded in North Africa. In 910, the family of the Fatimids took power in Kairouan and stretched as westward as eastward, taking Egypt from the Turks in which it had fallen in the meantime. Severe famines between 1062 and 1073 and its decline amorcèrent Saladin overthrew the kingdom in 1171.

In the nineteenth century, after the abolition of slavery, European states invaded North Africa and sub-Saharan thanks to their technological lead and despite the resistance of African peoples Africa.

The colonial period in Africa extends from the Berlin Conference (1884-1885) at independence in the 1960s and was the founding

act of the current African States: the colonial powers then share Africa at the Berlin Conference 1884-1885.

The Battle of Adwa, where the Italians were defeated by the troops of "Menelik"in 1896, marks a historic turning point in the colonization of Africa.

Colonization has shaped space and economic orientations of the countries. Initially, the colonizers did not intend to share the territories but they only want to protect their companies against foreign intervention. Therefore, the settlers share space as meridians, latitudes, rivers and rarely between populations.

Ethiopia is the only African state with Liberia, which was not colonized by a European power; the country enjoyed a brief tenure of five years (1936-1941). Liberia was colonized by the United States to install the released slaves. One reason is that, like the few African countries (Egypt, Morocco), Ethiopia is a country historically constituted (the land of Cush described in the Bible). She was not "invented" because of European colonization in the nineteenth century. This explains, at least in part, the

choice of Addis Ababa to host the headquarters of the African Union in 1963.

African nationalist aspirations led to independence that bleeds from 1910 to 1975 by country.

Plans were not settled democratically and toiled to develop their country.

Africa until the 1990s was manipulated by the powers of the Cold War. Since the fall of the Berlin Wall, African countries have ranged from civil wars and democratization process.

During the partition of Africa in the late nineteenth century, the European powers divided Africa and its resources policy areas the Berlin Conference of 1884-85.

In 1905 African territory is completely appropriate by European nations, with the exception of Liberia and Abyssinia. Britain and France have the largest possessions, but Portugal, Germany, Spain, Italy and Belgium and are also more or less widely owners of portions of the African territory. Africa has suffered one side, short and long term effects of colonization and imperialism, with the exploitation of its natural resources such as gold and diamonds and hand-d 'work, economic dislocation, social and cultural, geopolitical division, and political subjugation.

On the other hand, the transfer of elements of European civilization and the creation of larger political units has opened new perspectives.

On the African level, the Second World War saw the colonies help their colonizers in the process of war, but without mention of independence for African nations. The dominion of Union of South Africa led by Jan Smuts entered the war on the Allied side, is committed in Egypt and Madagascar and participated in the liberation of Ethiopia. Most French colonial governors showed their loyalty to the Vichy regime until 1943 German propaganda during the war is no stranger to this mistrust of British rule. Because the Japanese imperial conquest began in the Far East, it faces a shortage of raw materials such as rubber and various minerals. Africa was then forced to compensate for this shortage and has greatly benefited from this change. Another key issue that the Europeans faced was the presence of U-boats (German submarines) patrolling the Atlantic Ocean, This reduced the amount of raw materials transported to Europe and led to the creation of local industries in Africa. These industries, in turn, caused the expansion and creation of new districts. With the growth of urban areas and industry came the unions.

In addition to unions, urbanization encouraged reading and writing, which led to the appearance of pro-independence newspapers.

In 1941, Roosevelt and Churchill met to discuss the postwar world. This results in the Atlantic Charter. One of the clauses of this document, introduced by Roosevelt, was the autonomy of imperial colonies. After the Second World War so there was pressure on the UK to comply with the terms of the Atlantic Charter. When Churchill introduced the charter to the parliament, he expressly transposed colonies in newly conquered Germany to be able to pass the country. After the war, African colonies are still considered "infantile" and "immature", democratic governments have been introduced at the local level.

During the 1930s, the colonial powers were careful to maintain elite minority leaders, educated in Western universities and familiar with ideas like self-determination. These leaders, including some major nationalists like Kenyatta (Kenya), Kwame Nkrumah (Côte-de-Gold, Ghana), Léopold Sédar Senghor (Senegal) and Felix Houphouet-Boigny (Côte d'Ivoire), led the battle for independence.

In most British and French colonies, the transition to independence was relatively peaceful. However, some settlers disapproved the introduction of democratic governments.

Following decolonization, Africa has shown a political instability, economic disaster and an addiction to debt. Political instability has arrived with the introduction of Marxist and capitalist as well as ongoing frictions due to inequality between races influences. This led to the Civil War; the Black Nationalist movements have been involved in violent attacks against white settlers, trying to end the "domination of the white minority" in government.

Other violence occurs because of disagreement over geography did during colonization. Despite widespread acceptance of this division, border conflicts such as those between Chad and Libya,

Ethiopia and Somalia and Nigeria and Cameroon have emerged, sometimes even today.

Another result of colonialism, followed by decolonization, was the depletion of natural resources of the African economy without the possibility of diversifying the export of cash crops to the settler's countries. Suffering from famine and drought, Africa has struggled to industrialize its workforce hit by poverty, with insufficient funds.

In an attempt to influence the Third World to adopt either the ideology of capitalism, or of communism, the United States and the Soviet Union lent food and money to Africa. To feed, educate and modernize its population, Africa has borrowed large sums to various nations, banks and companies.

In return, creditors forced African countries to devalue their currencies and attempted to exert political influence in Africa.

However, the money borrowed does not lift the devastated economy. The huge debt capital is usually wasted by poor management of corrupt dictators; social problems such as education, health, and political stability have been ignored.

Derivatives of decolonization, political instability, border disputes, economic collapse, and enormous debt continue to gnaw Africa today.

Because of the current military occupation, the Spanish Sahara (now Western Sahara), has never been fully decolonized. The majority of the territory is under Moroccan administration, the remainder being administered by the Sahrawi Arab Democratic Republic.

The resources of the Afro - Geography & demography

With a land area of 30 million square kilometers, Africa is the third continent in terms of area; this represents 7% of the land surface and 20.3% of the land surface. Separated from Europe by the Mediterranean Sea, it is attached to Asia at its northeast extremity by the Isthmus of Suez (passing through the Suez Canal). Since its northern extremity at Ras ben Sakka in Tunisia at its southern end to Cape Agulhas in South Africa, the continent extends about 8000 km; from Cape Verde, to the extreme west to Ras Hafun in Somalia, in the Far East, it stretches over 7,400 kilometers.

His ribs, straight, are 26 000 km long. The absence of deep indentations of the shore is remarkable; Indeed, by comparison, Europe, which covers 10.4 million km, or about one third of the area of Africa, has a coastline of 32,000 km, longer than 6 000 km.

The largest country in Africa by area is the tenth in the world, Algeria, while the Seychelles archipelago, off the east coast of Africa, is the smallest. The Sahara Desert alone covers an area of 8.6 million km.

Africa has a wide variety of climates, equatorial center, warm temperate in North Africa and Southern Africa. The northern plains and desserts are very hot due to the great distance that separates them from the ocean. The temperature differences between summer and winter, and between day and night, are the most important. Further south, the heat is tempered by the moisture provided by the ocean and by the altitude, especially in the highlands of East Africa. Vegetation is also thicker. Finally, the northern and southern extremes both know a temperate climate, while cooler and wetter in the south.

The "official" record of temperature is 55 ° C measured July 7, 1931 at Kébili, Tunisia.

  Africa faces three major phenomena that are drought in the states of the Sahel and the Horn of Africa (Ethiopia, Somalia, Eritrea, Kenya, Djibouti) causing many episodes of hunger in these regions, desertification due to over-farming and the population growth finally deforestation caused by extensive slash and burn agriculture and many armed conflicts including the eastern Democratic Republic of Congo.

A study by researchers at the British Geological Survey and the University College London, the African continent has abundant water in the basement. These researchers believe that African waters are a hundred times more abundant than water renewed annually surface and twenty times greater than the supply of fresh water of all lakes in the continent that's why the challenges of Africa multiplies.

Africa is the continent with a population percentage has increased since the early twentieth century and the rate of natural increase, with 2.6% in 2013 is the highest estimated at 133 million in 1900 8.1% of the world population, the population of Africa increased in 1950 to 228,000,000 or 9.1% and then to 808 million in 2000 or 13.2%, to $

1.1 billion in 2012 16% of the world population and could be 2.4 billion in 2050 or 25.0% of the world population.

The fertility rate in Africa is the highest in the world with 4.8 children per woman in 2013, against a global average of 2,539. If the majority of African countries have a high birth rate, they also face a very high infant mortality. In 2013, two African countries had infant mortality rates above 100 ‰ 34 and above 50 ‰ 41 rate.

In addition, four countries with the hope of lower life in the world in 2012 were all African.

AIDS has become the leading cause of death in Africa in the late twentieth century. This was the case in 2007, UNAIDS estimated that 22 million the number of people infected in Africa. HIV was 1.3 million deaths on the continent in 2009, but it was 1.4 million in 2001 over the same period (2001 to 2009), cases of new infections, themselves, are down 25% in 22 countries in sub-Saharan Africa.

Malnutrition (vitamin deficiency or caloric), starvation, lack of water or poor water quality, disease are all important causes.

Infant mortality has fallen by 30% in 20 years and life expectancy increased from 15.4 years since 1950, but in sub-Saharan Africa, 1 in 8 children dies before his 5 years against 1 143 in developed countries threatening the strength of the work involved and the human conditions for development.

Africa has different vegetation types that correspond to distinct climatic zones.

When rainfall is plentiful and south of the Equator, the forest is covered with ferns, mosses and trees in tropical timber. In Savannah, there are tall grasses, shrubs and large trees.

In the Sahel region, which lies between the Sahara to the north, the wetter south tropics, living conditions are difficult.

In this landscape of bush, people lack water for their crops and are struggling to feed their animals.

Mineral resources are not lacking in contrast. There are in fact a large amount of coal, oil, gold, diamond, iron, zinc, and also clay, salt and sulfur. The exploitation of natural resources is sometimes so strong that we neglect the environment. Men build massively many roads through the forest to access these resources, a source for them a better life.

In Africa, men are dependent on the climate. When rainfall is low, it borders drought; this dry weather led to the desertification of the Sahara. People must leave this arid area for other regions to better climate.

Survivals matter. These forced migrations led to divide the peoples of sub-Saharan African and North Africa; them with horses and camels moving across the desert.

North Africa and the Atlas region, including the Sahara, we note the presence of the Berber people, which is the oldest North African community; and the Arabs come from the Arabian Peninsula.

South of the Sahara, it is mostly blacks who live in this region. As for the Indians, they are grouped in the cities of East Africa and South

Africa; where we also note the presence of Europeans. In the South, there are ethnic groups like the Bushmen who were nomadic hunters, ancient people in the desert "Nabib." Finally, the Pygmies live in the Congo Basin and the live logging. It originated in African rain forests.

The most populated areas of the continent are in the Nile, Niger, Congo and Senegal in the Great Lakes region. Nigeria is the most populous country. The African population is urbanizing especially in North Africa. The continent has the world's fastest population growth and saw its population consist mostly young; those over 60 years are scarce and life expectancy is around 47 years. Infant mortality is very high; diseases and malnutrition are the daily lot more than one family.

Bringing together the various dimensions of Africa North Africa; is one of the five major regions of the African continent.

It is bordered to the south by the Sahara and includes the Great Maghreb which brings together five countries. The Morocco whose capital is Rabat is bordered to the north by the Mediterranean Sea, on the west by the Atlantic Ocean and to the south by Mauritania. The country has an area of 706,550 km2 eroded in part by the Sahara. Here we admire the mountains of sand dunes of Erg Chebbi in the Sahara near Merzouga, the highest in North Africa Morocco. Various reliefs consists Morocco as the Rif are a low mountain range or the Middle Atlas reaches 3,000 meters. The resort Agadir is a delight for Europeans in winter; Casablanca, Fez or Marrakech are the most visited cities in the country. The second country Algeria's capital Algiers; it is bounded on the north by the Mediterranean Sea. It is the second largest country in Africa with its 2,381,740 km2 also occupied by the Sahara much. One can discover the Atlas Mountains to the south and north.

Carthage, Tunisia, Algeria is also considered the second Francophone country in the world with cities such as Tlemcen, Oran and Constantine.

The third zone is Tunisia, which includes cities such as Sousse, Sfax and Carthage; the latter is known for its magnificent archaeological sites. As for the island of Djerba, European tourists flock to the beautiful beaches all year; Tunis is the capital.

The last two countries that are part of the Grand Maghreb are Mauritania and Libya. The first capital Nouakchot and charm you with its houses and mosques of the 13th century found in Chjinguetti.

When the second, which its capital is Tripoli, overlooking the Mediterranean Sea and is located between Morocco to the north and south Senegal. The history of the Great Maghreb was dominated by the French colonization.

the West Africa; are countries such as Gambia, Ghana, Burkina Faso, Cape Verde, Niger or Sierra Leone are all part of West Africa. Senegal, the country that is familiar with the Dakar rally is bordered by the Atlantic Ocean; covers 196,700 km2 and its main cities are Kebemer, Kolda, and Ndar Tivaouane. Its capital is Dakar is also the country's main port. She is a member organization of the World Heritage Cities; that is to say cities that have inscribed by UNESCO on their territory site. Second city of Senegal, St. Louis is classified to this directory heritage.

"Cote d'Ivoire» it is famous for its beautiful beaches south of the country. Its capital is Yamoussoukro. It is bounded on the north by Mali and Burkina Faso, to the south by the Atlantic Ocean, on the east by Ghana and to the west by Liberia and Guinea. Its main cities are Abidjan, Bouaké, Man, Danané marked by little relief. Note the presence of hills and mountains that's highest: Mount Tonkoui with its 1180 meters.

Mopti, Mali The largest state in West Africa is Mali with its 1,240,000 km2. Many ethnic groups make up the country as the Moors, the Tuareg, Bambara, Peul, the Songhai, Soninke and Voltaics. Its capital is Bamako and its major cities are Segou, Mopti, Sikasso and Kayes.

Ethnic groups in Benin are both present, there are about forty. Fons account for almost 50% of the population; followed by the Yoruba, the Gouns the Baribas and Sombas. This country located on the Gulf of Guinea capital Porto Novo; Cotonou is one of the most populous cities and wants to be the political and economic heart of Benin.

Central Africa: includes Burundi, Rwanda, Cameroon, Gabon, Equatorial Guinea, Sao Tome and Principe, Central African Republic and Chad. Not to be confused in the region, the Democratic Republic of Congo also called Congo Kinshasa, with the Republic of Congo Brazzaville Congo named.

One of the most populated areas is that of the Great Lakes region which includes four countries; Burundi and Rwanda are two countries on the border of East Africa. ; Democratic Republic of Congo and Uganda, which is part of East Africa.

Found in this region of Lake Victoria which is the third largest lake in the world. And another beauty of nature, the Congo with its 4,670-km is the longest river in Africa Central Africa after the Nile.

Virunga Mountains of the borders of Rwanda, Congo and Uganda Forests of the Congo Basin with more than two million km2 is the largest after the Amazon; but maybe not for long; massive deforestation is raging in this region. This tropical wood is a gold mine for Africans. They exploit and commercialize massively endangering this magnificent forest.

To avoid this problem, an economic community comprising eleven states of Central Africa was founded in 1983, manages various issues such as security, environment, health, trade and new technologies. Help children and women in Central Africa has become possible thanks to the national priority ECCAS and contributions to the United Nations Children's Fund, UNICEF. Shares of ECCAS for peace and security are also numerous; Central Africa has had many armies in most of its states and conflict in 1999 was created a Council for Peace and Security.

The East Africa; includes the countries of the Rift Valley that extend more than 6000 km and that of the Horn of Africa that stretch to the Arabian Sea. Kenya making party is well known among tourists for quality safaris; it is washed by the Indian Ocean. Its capital, Nairobi is one of the largest cities in Africa. The highest peak in the country is Mount Kenya with its 5199 meters. One can see many lakes like Turkana in the Rift Valley and if you like the seaside, you will not be disappointed with over 500 km of sandy coastline where you can see off the islands and Funzi Mombasa known for its port.

Other countries bordering the Indian Ocean, Tanzania whose capital is Dodoma. Local pride is of course the Kilimanjaro with its 5895 meters to the delight of hikers from around the world. This summit is protected by national who is visited by thousands of people every year.

Huts and landscapes in Ethiopia Located in the heart of the Horn of East Africa, Ethiopia's capital Addis Abeba and has over 2 million inhabitants. It has more than 80 ethnic groups; the Oromo are the largest group followed by Amhara and Tigray. This country is notorious for its high rate of infant mortality. Wars and famines were awarded the prize for one of the world's poorest countries.

According to statistics of 2005, life expectancy did not exceed 50 years. The fight against poverty and hunger comes to the forefront of the international agenda. One child every five seconds starve in the world. We remember the "Live 8" event organized by singer Bob Geldof who was born in France by Jack Lang. This concert had a mission to educate people worldwide on the Ethiopian position.

Southern Africa; the countries south of the equatorial forest and islands like Mauritius and Reunion are Southern Africa; Madagascar is the fourth largest island in the world. Formerly inhabited by Bantu and Khoisan peoples, there are countries such as Botswana, Comoros, Lesotho, Malawi, Mozambique, Namibia, Swaziland, Zambia and Zimbabwe.

South Africa extends over 1,219,090 km2. To the east of the country, you can admire the magnificent Drakensberg Mountains.

The city of Pretoria is the administrative capital and the Cape is considered the legislative capital; Johannesburg is one of the largest cities.

Slums of Soweto, South Africa unfortunately many slums invade the country and South Africans sometimes have no water or electricity to live. The black community is more than 70% of the population and whites at about 13%. We also note the presence of some ethnic groups such as the Bushmen, the Tsongas, Vendas and the Zulus; these are the most numerous and account for only 20% of the population.

Another major problem in South Africa, the population is becoming poorer; solely responsible for AIDS is coupled to a crime that is ravaging the country. Nevertheless, the economy remains stable thanks to the industries in Africa South such as mining or oil.

In 1992, a treaty establishing the Community for the Development Southern Africa, SADC was signed in Windhoek, Namibia. Its objectives are to free trade, free movement of people and respect for human rights. The national priority is to fight against poverty, promote peace and security in South Africa. Hopefully this treaty is respected to avoid policies such as apartheid.

African giant natural resources (oil, natural gas, coal, uranium, cobalt, precious stones, gold, zinc ...) are used mainly by large multinationals. These are often accused of contributing to the impoverishment of the people.

In recent years, we have witnessed the exploitation of natural resources by new players, especially Asian countries, including China and India and the oil states in lack of space; of agricultural land is purchased, and the areas covered are very important for a continent that suffered malnutrition and regular famines. Some speak of re-colonization of Africa on it.

Demographics: the new population-Bomb

The sub-Saharan continent will have nearly 2 billion people by 2050, a fifth of humanity. Corollary of this population explosion is a fast urbanization that mainly affects 16 countries in West Africa. An opportunity for economic and social conflict sources development?

When we will celebrate the fifty years of African independence, Africa, more than ever, "is there", as they say over there: Saharan Africans were 180 million in 1950 they are currently 860 million and be of 1.8 to 2 billion into forty. One century, Ten-fold increase in the local population.

"The never-seen in the history of mankind", a confusing comparison: "If France had experienced the same growth as the Ivory Coast between 1960 and 2005, it is now estimated 250 million people, 60 million foreigners who" wrote Jean-Michel Severino - until to it a few days ago Director General of the French development Agency - and his adviser Olivier Ray, who made this demographic emergence cornerstone of their recent book "Time for Africa". A human swelling "beyond belief," admitted an expert. And a surprise for all those who imagined that continent still empty and suddenly find full sacred. On the field, Africa gives yet for years of false air of populated Bangladesh. It actually feels the multitude. Lagos (Nigeria) has long been the image of the famous "go-slow", the insane traffic jams, and Kinshasa (Democratic Republic of Congo) choked by human tides rose every morning at the elbow to elbow to centers and flow to the suburbs in the evening. Small countries are housed in the same boat: in Benin, the hundred thousand "Zemidjans" these motorcycle taxis that flood and smoke out the streets, give Cotonou looks like a nest. Apart from the desert, the campaigns they either are not left out: there always someone crosses.

Most Niger

On paper, the statistics speak for themselves. Some examples: one in four births in the world today occur in Africa; a human being in five will be African in the middle of this century; is born each year in Nigeria as more children throughout the European Union; Niger, where it has the highest fertility rate in the world (more than 7 children per woman), will see its population almost quadrupled between 2000 and 2050 to reach 50 million ...; by forty years, Nigeria's population will exceed that of Pakistan, Bangladesh, Indonesia and perhaps even the United States, says Gilles Pison, research director at the National Institute Demographic Studies (INED) while the DRC Congo and Ethiopia are likely to overtake Russia and Japan. Africa is now on the mainland population of all records and the global supply of the future population growth: its fertility rate is twice the world average growth rate of the population at least twice and also its birth rate to 2.5%, at least double again emphasizes INED. Not surprisingly, the corollary is his youth: 45% of its population is under fifteen. Uganda, for example, is considered the youngest in the world. Even the ravages of HIV in Southern Africa cannot do anything about this dynamic.

The reasons for this flight?

An "African singularity," says Gilles Pison: its late demographic transition. This historical movement, which companies move from a model of birth and high mortality in a model of low birth rates and mortality, is already completed or under construction around the world, even in developing countries. In Africa, there is still at the first phase of this "transition" because if we live longer with health and medicine, social inertia that we always do many children: 4.6 children per woman. "Contraception is shy and there is no political will in terms of family planning," says Dakar Philippe Antoine, director of research at the IRD (Research Institute for Development). "We do not have staff to manage that! Our emergency is drinking water ... "confesses Nicephore Soglo, former president of Benin and mayor of Cotonou. While some countries, such as Ghana and Kenya have started to decline in fertility in the 1980s, the United Nations (UN) estimates that the total African demographic transition will not be a reality until 2035-2040. On the scale of humanity, but we can see a shift in the catch. Bleeding by the slave trade and imported by colonizers epidemics, Africa was depopulated four centuries and it is only now finding the relative share of the world population ... it was in the 1500s.

Worrying population boom? "This has blown up in our faces: demography is actually the unifying feature of the continent, from the conflict in Chad to the growth of cities, through emigration to Europe," said Jean-Michel Severino. "She will submit the complexity of African societies to unprecedented changes, not just transform the African continent, but the entire planet. There are risks, but also many opportunities. "

Mirror of this powerful demographic intensification, urbanization is explosive, note experts. In Africa, the growth of urban population is the fastest in the world and has been multiplied by 11 in fifty years. In 2030, one in two Africans will be city and nearly two out of three in 2050, a move that affects the continent, having developed in Southern Africa around industrial and mining centers, but today especially the 16 states of 'West Africa. As Northern Europe or the eastern seaboard, thus the next night will see from space flicker of a major coastal megalopolis of more than 1,000 kilometers and some 100 million people from Douala (Cameroon) to Abidjan.

Encouraged by decentralization almost everywhere at work, this urban continuum weaves at speed. "From Lagos to Abidjan, we do not drive half an hour without seeing a city. Those with more than 20,000 inhabitants are separated by less than 25 km, "said John Igué scientific director of Lares (Laboratory of Regional Analysis and social expertise) in Cotonou. In Benin, one can easily see model things rolling. The cities will be spread and affect and are parties to make only single agglomeration between the border with Nigeria and that of Togo. Swallowed up by the city, the port and a cement factory and found today in the center of Cotonou, and wetland lagoon areas were populated confines of his inexorably towards the capital Porto Novo, east, and to the Togolese border to the west. The future is written in the eye, signs stuck into the shallows waterlogged brackish and named after the owner of the parcel announce future construction. And on all roadsides, are made of concrete blocks and sell sand and cement with a vengeance.

In Nigeria, the Governor of Lagos (14 million inhabitants) has launched the construction of a highway to five lanes twice - with a tram in the middle -reliant capital in Benin, his true port open to the world.

Disappearance campaigns

In urbanization, Africa is very strange. If today there are about 40 cities with over 1 million inhabitants booming "African megacities are not made elsewhere by concentration, and vertically, but spread into space, into the countryside, in a form of "suburbanization" in European style. Rural-urban migration itself is suddenly there, in a sort of in situ urbanization, "says François Moriconi-Ebrard, a researcher at CNRS. Northwest of Cotonou, Abomey, its new suburbs, and thus extends inexorably out of sight, without individual houses. "In 2002, nothing existed. The city gained 300,000 in five years, "says Monica Coralli, geographer at Paris West Nanterre. "The border often becomes increasingly blurred between the rural and the urban. There is a dilution "semblance of cities," without large intermediate cities. This is worrying, "adds François Moriconi-Ebrard.

This model of "country town" dear Alphonse Allais, knitted with high population growth and a tradition of habitat storey space eater, could lead to extreme situations: "One day in Burundi, there will be only one city "is concerned the researcher.

But this "urban tilt" of Africa can be an opportunity for the continent, experts say.

"Cities are engines of development"

"Around the world, urbanization has been accompanied by economic growth" and development aid, to be massive to meet its huge demand for services and infrastructure, "is more effective in densely populated areas" , said the FAO (Food and Agriculture Organization). "If urbanization and land use are well managed and consistent, Africa will have here a huge boost. Otherwise, it will be a source of problems and equally huge "conflict, says Jean-Michel Severino.

With its population, Africa now has a fast-growing domestic market and, thanks to urbanization, industrialization and significant productivity reservoirs. She was already interested in the world for its agricultural land, raw materials, its carbon sinks and world premieres of hydropower reserves, but its "demographic bonus", this huge battalion of young urban professionals, who begins to seduce emerging countries. China, Brazil and India, which, by fifteen years, will reduce their competitiveness, could be relocating their industries workforce. Cities, where the demand for education is higher and raising the level of palpable life, then certainly reduce the African fertility: "Economic and social development is the best contraceptive", likes to say the World Bank and ... the loop of the demographic transition is complete.

African population is a Joint

African demography is strictly joint, according to a report presented at the International Conference on Population and Development (ICPD), held in Addis Ababa (Ethiopia), women represent 50% of an estimated one African population 02 billion people in 2010.

To take advantage of the demographic dividend, the study advocates including the promotion of gender equality, strengthening the empowerment of women, improving access to care, family planning services and security food.

The demographic profile of the continent provides an opportunity to seize in order to encourage a sustainable economic growth, says the report of the African Union (AU) on the population that establishes a link between demographic and socio-economic development.

"This dividend is not something that will take place automatically, policies should be adopted to make Africa an integrated region, peaceful, prosperous, driven by its citizens and ensuring an influential role on the world stage" continues on.

Highlights of the document indicate that Africa continues to have a population growth rate among the highest in the world, from 1950 to

2010, the continent's population increased from 234 million to 1.02 billion in 2050 will reach 1.7 billion people to 2.5 billion by 2100.

Of the 20 countries with the highest population in the world, Africa has 5 states namely Egypt, Ethiopia, the Democratic Republic of Congo (DRC) and South Africa.

According to a breakdown by age, the study shows that the continent has the youngest population in the world, with 200 million people whose age ranges between 15 and 24 years.

Africa is experiencing "an explosion of the youth population" in the sense that 42 pc of the population is aged 15 months, it added; noting however that the number of elderly (over 65 years) represents 5% of the total population, and this figure will rise to 7% in 2050.

Regarding mortality, the report welcomes the decline of African countries in recent decades, regretting however that the continent has not reached the targets set in the Millennium Development Goals (MDGs).

ICPD, initiated from September 30 to October 4 by the United Nations for Africa (ECA) Economic Commission, aims to highlight the need for state and non-state actors to re-engage at the highest level to implement a Plan of Action on population and development at national and regional level.

Under the theme "Harnessing the demographic dividend: the future we want for Africa", the forum will examine among other regional population report especially its conclusions as a basis for the development of the development agenda in Africa post-2015.

The challenge of urbanization

Over 78% of the urban population in the least developed countries lives in slums like Kibera (Kenya) next to Nairobi. Half are under 20 years. Which future if not revolt?

"My mother, like her mother, her grandmother and so on, was born in poverty in the rural village of Rarieda, Kenya. I too was born in this village and I lived there until he was hit by a brutal famine when I was two years old. Without food, money or opportunities, my mother did what thousands of African villagers every day: she moved with us to the city in search of a better life. But given the lack of jobs and housing in Nairobi, we met in Kibera, one of the largest slums in Africa.

Located just a few miles from downtown Nairobi, Kibera is heavily polluted camp, the densely populated, with its roads and makeshift shacks with corrugated iron roofs. The Kenyan government does not recognize Kibera, there is no sewerage system, no electricity grid or regulated. Its inhabitants, estimated at a few hundred thousand and over a million, have no official existence. Kibera is just one example of the consequences of rapid urbanization that is gaining ground worldwide. Over 44% of people in developing countries already live in cities.

The Population Reference Bureau estimates that by 2050 only 30% of the world population will remain in rural areas, but few people took the time to consider the implications of this change for families like mine.

When you think of Africa, is often focused on the difficulties of life in the villages: a visible perception through these iconic images of African women in their daily trips to fetch water. But a growing number of people (already nearly 300 million) is faced with the harsh reality of the slum, where resources are scarce and elusive economic opportunities. Over 78% of the urban population in the least developed countries in the world and one third of the world's urban population live in slums.

Nairobi is a dynamic growing city, with its shopping centers, restaurants and catering company's Western style for the emerging middle class in Kenya. Yet no one knows how many people live there. According to the last census (highly politicized) conducted in 2009; Nairobi has a population of over three million. But this figure is probably closer to five million, much of which lives in slums.

These are the people, the poorest residents of Nairobi, who build buildings, serve in restaurants, driving taxis and are the lifeblood of this city (from age 12 until I was 22, I 'belonged to this group, I worked on building sites and in factories.) Indeed, without the poor Nairobi would not work one day.

Yet they remain almost invisible, without political clout. The continuing global perception of Africa as a village for aggravating the situation of slum dwellers and excludes them from the agenda of global development.

Every day, more people arrive in Nairobi, attracted by the promise of a job, resources and a better life, only to realize that they are not equipped to survive and that their children will grow up in a slum. (Half of those live in urban slums under 20 years). Without access to education, the generation that will soon be the largest, has little hope of escaping these precarious conditions.

But how long will he serve a majority minority? How long will he accept the lack of water, sanitation, education and dignity?

Urban slums around the world will soon reach a critical point when the younger generation will reject such a lifestyle. Their strength lies in their numbers: More than half of young people around the world sharing their fate and anger. They will rise up and they refuse to accept their status as second-class citizens in urban centers constantly expanding; they will destabilize countries like Kenya and undermine efforts to build more stable prosperous societies.

Cities are not just the future of Africa: they are the present. Without collective action initiated now to transform cities like Nairobi into engines of economic development and sources of opportunities they should be, they will become a tinderbox of perpetual inequality.

For millions of people like my mother, and more importantly, for the good of their children and grandchildren, we must first fulfill the promise that attracts the poor to the cities. "

An opinion of Kennedy Odede, president of Shining Hope for Communities a social service organization in Kibera, researcher and New Voices Fellow 2013 the Aspen Institute.

Doubling of the population by 2050

With a population that is expected to double by 2050 and a growth rate of GDP is more than 5% per year, Africa is the continent

That is the second fastest in terms of population growth in the developing world. It is expected that, in any case, the UN agency specializing Population Reference Bureau in a new report on job creation in Africa.

The size of the African population of working age is expected to grow, for its part, to 442-1400000000 between 2000 and 2050 over the past 10 years, Africa has created more than 37 million paying jobs, but the pace of job creation must be accelerated to track the number of people who need a job and maintain a high level of economic growth.

Similarly, between 1970 and 2010, the working age population in Africa has increased by 92 million to nearly 575 million and will continue to grow over the next 40 years. As young as age between now and 2050, the size of the population of working age is expected to increase significantly over the group size of the dependent population (below 15 years), contributing and pave the way for a demographic dividend.

Another point raised by the Population Reference Bureau is the average official unemployment rate in Africa, which is 9%, does not reflect the fact that many are involved in subsistence agriculture or in informal self-employment to survive.

During the last decade, only 37 million were paid stable jobs, while 52 million were subsistence workers or involved in other informal activities to earn an income.

The agency also notes that the economic sectors identified in development plans, such as mining, oil and gas, contributing significantly to GDP, but require fewer workers and focus more on capital goods and machinery to produce goods. Accordingly, the expansion of these sectors added few jobs in the labor market.

On the other hand, the public service and jobs in the social sector accounted for the largest share of employment growth in Africa over the past 10 years, but account for a smaller share to the GDP growth.

This reality should not, however, lead to pessimism. According to the Population Reference Bureau, Africa has made significant progress in the education of its workforce. In the last decade, the proportion of Africans who today completed secondary or higher education has increased by 32% to over 40% and expected to rise to 48% in 2020.

However, there is still a lot of investment needed to improve the quality of education and provide more vocational training to help develop key professional skills.

The agency also notes that many African businesses remain, despite more than a decade of economic growth, concerns about political instability, corruption and the threat of inflation. Similarly, many companies have a lack of adequate infrastructure, including access to them electricity and reliable transportation. Companies continue to lose opportunities for growth and expansion because of the risks of corruption.

According to the Population Reference Bureau, the extent to which Africa can take advantage of its young population and reap the benefits of demographic dividend depends heavily on a favorable political environment. Good governance is important, along with a strong macroeconomic management, a well-functioning financial and labor markets, and efficient investment in health and education. Only by considering all these factors that African countries can achieve a dividend changing age structure of the population and ensure sustainable levels of economic growth, productivity and development, says the agency.

More than 2 billion people by 2050

By 2050, Africa's population will exceed 2 billion people, according to data from Nkosazana Dlamini-Zuma, President of the Commission of the African Union, to visit Moscow.

"The African population of over 1 billion people, has she said on Monday after talks with Foreign Minister Sergei Lavrov. More than half of people aged fewer than 20. Therefore, the African population will exceed 2 billion people by 2050. "

"We need to work with partners such as Russia to improve our infrastructure, develop the transport system, the energy sector," noted Ms Dlamini-Zuma, responding to a question from ITAR-TASS on the achievements of African Union for half a century of its existence.

"There's 50 years, Africa was colonized continent, and now we are free, she has said. In 50 years, we will work for the prosperity of Africa, to bring peace on our continent. I hope that in 50 years, whoever travels to Moscow, no more talk of crisis or conflict, but integration. "

The continent will have 2.08 billion people in 2045

In four international organizations, Africa will have 2.08 billion people in 2045.

Africans account for 20% of the world population in 2045 This is what reveals the economic outlook in Africa 2012 report produced jointly by the African Development Bank (AfDB), the United Nations Program for Development (UNDP), development Centre of the Organization for economic Cooperation and development (OECD) and the Economic Commission of the United Nations for Africa (ECA).

This was driven by lower mortality rates and by maintaining a moderate birth rate. With some 200 million 15-24 years, Africa has the youngest population in the world. A figure expected to double by 2045 in 2011, the total population of the continent stood at 1.04 billion people. The report also notes that "Africa has as many men as women, with a ratio of 100 males per 100 females."

Following the uprisings in North Africa, the continent's growth was lower in 2011, 3.4%, compared to 5% in 2010, but with the recovery of the economies in North Africa and sustained improvement in other areas, Africa's growth is expected to accelerate to 4.5% in 2012 and 4.8% in 2013, according to the report. But internal and external risks remain especially due to the continuing economic crisis in the euro zone or political unrest in some countries that could affect neighboring countries.

Moreover, the prices of food and fuel are the main causes of inflation in Africa increased from 5.8% in 2010 to 7.9% in 2011 Gradual slowdown is expected in 2012 and 2013.

Finally, employment in Africa remains a priority. Despite the many new jobs in the last decade, the pace must be accelerated to meet the demand for African future generations. Neither the public nor the large companies will have the ability to absorb the flood of young jobseekers. According to the report, governments will have no choice but to acknowledge that "the informal and rural sectors will create the bulk of new jobs and [they will] remove barriers to growth." As for the education and training system, they will be better articulated to meet the needs of labor markets.

Africa, a young continent towards aging

A study by the National Institute of Demographic Studies (INED), the number of people aged 60 and over to Africa should increase from about 50 million today to 200 million by 2050.

Titled "Africa, a young continent cope with aging," the study explains that the rapid aging of the population in Africa is linked to longer life expectancy and falling birth rates on the continent. According to Laurent and Muriel Sajoux Nowik, authors of the study, the rapid aging of the African population will mainly the problem of care for the elderly.

They maintain that the needs of people aged 60 and over in Africa are currently covered by family solidarity, not the welfare system restricted to public sector employees and agents of private companies and parastatals.

In the future, families will find it increasingly difficult to secure properly the specific needs of seniors, says the study also points out that in Africa most of the population lives below the poverty line defined by United Nations.

The study warns that African states will be forced to make painful choices between essential expenses such as children's education, and the organization of social protection that takes into account the specific needs of a large population aged.

Africa has since 1 January 2010 more than one billion people including 40% of young people under 25.

The African Union (AU) was dedicated in July 2011 in Equatorial Guinea a Special Summit on Youth and Employment in Africa.

The number of elderly people will increase by 4 in 2050

Although its population is still young, Africa will not escape the aging, a process which should be much faster than in developed countries and will pose challenges to care for older people, says a study published Thursday 2013.

Today the age of 15 represent 40% of the population in Africa, against 27% in the total world population, says the study from the National Institute of Demographic Studies (INED).

But in the next forty years, the proportion of 60 and over (5.5% in 2010) should "double in many African countries if fertility continues to decline at the current rate," says the study. INED notes that "this aging will occur much more rapidly than has been the case in developed countries speed."

Thus, the number of seniors is expected to quadruple in Africa between 2010 and 2050, from 56 to 215,000,000, almost as much as in Europe (241 million). The African continent would then have 22.5 million people 80 years and older, five times more than today.

Among the challenges that an aging it, INED notes that "less than 10% of seniors are eligible for a pension" in Africa, mainly officials or employees of large private companies.

The Institute also points out that in terms of health, "The vast majority of older people do not have insurance coverage."

Finally, while the old Africans can generally count on the "family network" to meet their needs, the study notes that "major social and economic changes are observed across the continent and affect the family "organizations.

In particular, "the younger generations everywhere want to break free from the tutelage of elders" and "social status" of the elderly is "less valuable than before."

"The decrease in land resources" also leads from the city, where "the units are smaller and more expensive." Increased opportunities for women, diplomas, studies are also changing lifestyles and contribute to weakening support for seniors.

It is therefore necessary for African countries to conduct "appropriate public policies" (social protection, retirement ...) to meet the challenge of aging concludes INED.

Calls to control the population

The director of the population and planning of human development in Senegal, Bakary Djiba, called Dakar African countries more to the population control in Africa.

Djiba speaking ahead of World Population Day (WTD) on July 11 in St. Louis, in northern Senegal, said the jump in population in developing countries, particularly in Africa south of the Sahara, was accompanied by profound social and economic changes that have a negative impact on the living conditions of the populations.

The theme of the 2012 edition focuses on "universal access to reproductive health services."

The purpose of the JMP is to inform, educate and advocate for universal access to reproductive health, but also carry out advocacy towards policy makers and donors to increase funding for health reproduction.

"For this reason, sensitive to issues related to this problem governments have early taken the full measure of the degree of worsening incurred to demonstrate the importance they attach to issues of population," he said, noting that his country had always been there and has demonstrated its commitment to respect for economic, social and cultural rights of the people.

He said the Senegal plays a pioneering role in population policy which is one of the illustrations in the development and implementation of population policy statement as a framework, crystallizing the strategic directions of the state in dealing with the issues of population, noting that the goal is to improve the level and quality of life and promote the establishment of a well being.

However Djiba said that as part of maternal health and family planning, Senegal has made sufficient efforts to promote awareness and facilitate access to reproductive health services.

World Population: growth of the urban population in Africa and Asia

Africa and Asia are the continents that will experience the fastest growth in urban population over the next forty years, according to a UN report released Thursday2013.

The population of African cities will increase from 414 million to over 1.2 billion by 2050, while Asian cities will host 3.3 billion people on the same date against 1.9 billion today, said the report of the Department of economic and Social Affairs of the United Nations.

Together, Africa and Asia account for 86% of the increase in urban population in the world during this period, the report entitled "Prospects for urbanization in the world" (World Urbanization Prospects).

According to the report, this rapid urbanization should enable the African and Asian population better access to education and some services, but poses new challenges in terms of housing, employment, energy and environment.

The largest increase in urban population by 2050 is expected in India (497 million increases in population), China (341 million) and Nigeria (200 million). The United States is far behind with 103 million, followed by Indonesia (92 million).

The urbanization is accelerating especially in Nigeria, where the urban population grew by only 65 million between 1970 and 2010.

The report also warns of a danger to the large population concentrations. Over 450 cities and conurbations of more than one million people studied (comprising 1.4 billion people in 2011) 60% (890 million) are located in regions exposed to at least one major risk natural disasters (earthquakes, hurricanes, floods, etc).

Cities in Africa and Europe are the least exposed, unlike Asian cities or North and South America.

How to manage the growing number

The elderly are increasing in Africa. This was the finding of a report by the African Development Bank (AFDB), released last Wednesday. But the paper's authors report that African authorities will struggle to cope with the increase of the aging population.

Although the proportion of older people is still low in Africa, it will see growth in the coming years. This is one of the conclusions of a report by the African Development Bank. According to this, seniors could "represent 4.5% of the population of the continent" by 2030 and nearly 10 percent in "2050." In some countries, the proportion of older people will, "in 2030 and 2050, close to that of developed countries," write the reports of the Bad. When the reporters are the recent history of the African population aging, they found that the percentage of people over 65 in Africa rose "3.3% in 2000 to 3.6% in 2010."

The progressive aging of the population will require the development of ways to support health in particular. And this is where will pose problems for the mainland authorities. The authors of the report, if the African population is "aging, just like the rest of the world," the continent's governments are "ill-equipped to handle the growing number of older people." The main concerns are the health benefits and pensions.

"In much of Africa, governments spend much less money on health care than in most developed countries. In 2005, 48 of the 54 African countries spent on average less than 26$ per capita on health care, "advised the Bad. Who believes that the deterioration of traditional modes of family support in Africa further complicates the situation "This deterioration is due to increasing urbanization and - in some African countries - the effects of HIV-AIDS.

Many older people are indeed overwhelmed by the burden of the care of children whose parents were swept away by the Hiv-Aids, "argue the authors of the report".

It is not only the consequences of AIDS that are singled out. There is the issue of health care is acute because of chronic diseases associated with aging, such as "heart disease, cancer, respiratory disease and senile dementia." While the reporters acknowledge that these problems are "the lot of the elderly to people around the world." The report mentions the Bad; however, they will become "increasingly severe in developing countries, where the system is less capable than in the developed world to take over."

As for the pension, few Africans benefit, which will reduce their income with a consequent purchase nearly enough powerful.

The other conclusion to remember is the increase in life expectancy of Africans. "In Africa," life expectancy at birth was 52.7 years in 1990, but increased to 56 in 2010 middle-income countries in Africa, such as Mauritius, South Africa, the Egypt, Morocco and Tunisia, have seen the largest increases in the number of elderly. Other countries, such as Libya, Botswana, Zimbabwe and Djibouti have also experienced rapid growth in the number of elderly people, "wrote the reporter. This goes against many ideas generally being in the Western world that see Africa as a continent where life expectancy is short.

"Life expectancy in Africa is even lower than in developed countries, but is increasing. It should be noted, "They argue.

The challenges of the demographic transition in West Africa

Countries in West Africa could benefit in the coming decades, a "demographic window of opportunity" to reduce poverty. The arrival on the labor market of 160 million young people between 2010 and 2030 can accelerate economic growth. But these countries will benefit from this "demographic dividend", as has been done for 40 years now emerging, provided lower their fertility rates, which will reduce the number of inactive dependents per worker. With more than five children per woman on average, these rates are the highest in the world.

An IRD researcher states in the synthesis just published by the French Development Agency (AFD), on an extensive study conducted in 12 West African countries, including family planning and contraceptive promotion are major drivers of sustainable economic growth. But to do so, these countries need to allocate to this policy means 3-5 times higher than today. Will they negotiate this critical demographic turning point?

Several countries in West Africa - such as Burkina Faso, Mali, and Ghana - have returned to economic growth since the mid-1990s, with rates of 4 to 6% per year. But with the high population, this increase is insufficient to meet the needs in health and education of the population, reduce food and nutrition insecurity and reduce poverty, which still affects between one and two thirds of their inhabitants.

The fertility decline, an economic lever

West African countries can not emerge economically if they seize a "demographic window of opportunity" by reducing their fertility, as was done in the 1970s to today termed emerging markets.

So says an IRD researcher in the synthesis just published by the French Development Agency (AFD), on a large study in 12 countries of the region.

With strong population growth, we should expect in the next 20 years to significant increases in the labor force. The arrival on the labor markets in West Africa many young - from 6 million per year in 2010 to nearly 10 million per year in 2030 can be disastrous if growth and jobs are not appointments you. But it can be an advantage if, thanks to the decline in fertility, the number of dependents (children and elderly) per worker (15-64) is reduced. With the decrease in this ratio, also called the "dependency ratio", the assets may reduce their spending on mostly children and devote a larger share of their income to savings and productive investment. In doing so, they will help stimulate economic growth.

Accelerate the demographic transition: an emergency

Reduce fertility to accelerate the demographic transition and thus reduce the dependency ratio is an essential process for sustainable economic growth. In fact, between 1970 and 2000, most developing regions, such as East Asia and South-east, where the demographic transition was smooth benefited from this "demographic dividend". Most, but not sub-Saharan Africa, precisely, because the birth rate remained very high. They remain the highest in the world, with an average of more than five children per woman. Therefore, in West Africa today, the ratio is always an inactive to an active or a dependency ratio of 100%. But with average 3-5 times greater than those currently allocated to family planning, the countries of the region could halve this report within 20 years, reaching levels close to those observed dependence today emerging countries.

Priorities dictated by the urgency

So far, the financial and human resources allocated to the control of population growth fell short because of the weakness of political commitment and Africa, the lack of data and research in this area. Indeed, faced with major public health problems, policies, plans, programs and strategies implemented over the past 20 years have been the emphasis on prevention and care for people with HIV / AIDS and the care of pregnancy and childbirth, and obstetric and neonatal emergencies. Along with these interventions, access to family planning services and the promotion of contraceptive use were not sufficiently encouraged.

Today, only 10% to 20% of African married women are using contraception. Yet there is a strong demand for family planning: between 30% and 60% of these women would have access. The development is not only to control the birth rate, but accelerating the demographic transition through the increased use of contraception - which responds to the needs expressed by women is one of major levers that would allow the West Africa to address the socio-economic challenges it faces and will.

Recall that nearly half of the high economic growth in East Asia and South-east between 1970 and 2000 is attributable to demographic changes caused by governments. Like the latter, the West African countries must increase over the next 10 years the resources allocated to family planning to stabilize the number of births by 2030 and hope to benefit from the demographic dividend. Will they in turn negotiate this watershed.

Overpopulation is a myth

For a long time the idea has emerged that the population hinders the development of African countries. According to the Malthusian theory, population growth exceeding that of resources, people will be condemned to a subsistence economy.

The only way to break this vicious circle and leave African countries out of poverty is to reduce the population. What is it really?

Ndaba Obadias, Regional Director of the World Youth Alliance Africa, revived the debate on the issue by offering arguments are not in line with mainstream thinking, thus calling into question the relevance of the theory of overpopulation as responsible for the underdevelopment in Africa.

Development policy in Africa assumes that "less population means more development." The idea was born in the West and was repeated several times by African leaders and the media, to the point that everyone seems to accept it without questioning its relevance.

Recently, the National Coordinating Agency for Population and Development (NCAPD) in Kenya warned that "Kenya's population is growing too quickly and may become unsustainable in the near future." This is a typical statement that reveals the mindset of many people, particularly policy makers in developing countries and Africa.

The idea behind this statement is too simplistic to be valid: at least it has people in a country, the best the government can take care of them. Human beings have been reduced to what the respective governments can manage, at a "manageable" population.

In other words, people are perceived in terms of problems & mouths to feed. They are not seen as capable minds to think and innovate for a better future.

According to the UN report "The global population in 2008," there are 170 people per square kilometer in Western Europe compared to 33 h / km² in Africa.

The UK for example, 253 h / km² while Kenya has only 69 h / km.

Where is the population? In Africa? Kenya? Although the population of Africa increased by five times compared to what it is now, the countries of Western Europe such as France, Germany and Switzerland will always be more "overcrowded" than African countries. Despite these figures, the myth continues to associate the size of the population and development in Africa and other developing regions.

What is preached today in Africa has been in Hong Kong in the 1950s, when she was still poor. The forecast indicated that Hong Kong has no natural resources crowded a bleak future. One newspaper even proclaimed that the country was "dying". His government lamented that "the problem of rapid population growth is at the heart of the problems facing the country."

No relationship between the size of the population and development.

The Apocalypse predicted never materialized. Instead, Hong Kong has achieved an economic miracle, and today boasts a population of 7,026,400 inhabitants with 6,460 inhabitants per sq km (2009 estimate). Furthermore, according to IMF estimates in 2009, the per capita income is USD $ 42,748 (the country with the eighth highest income in the world, if separated from the mainland). However, its population has increased by about six times its level in the 1950s, when it was said that it had a population beyond its ability to support.

There is no relationship between the size of population and development.

When people are educated and earn higher incomes, authentic development occurs. However, today we teach illiterate people in villages throughout the developing world, through various programs financed by the government or by donors, that birth control is the way to development. We unfortunately divert attention from where it should.

When people can educate, benefit security, access to quality health care to reduce infant mortality, and opportunities to exercise their talents, they will make free choices. And as history has shown elsewhere, their children will have access to their needs, their desires, their hopes and dreams.

This mentality of "population management" has diverted attention from more pressing issues such as education, health services and the transfer of technology that could boost the economies of poor countries. This is easily achieved by combining population growth with other problems, food shortages to environmental degradation. While global population has more than doubled since 1950, the food supply has more than tripled worldwide during the same period.

In developed countries, everyone's life has been improved through education and medical care, and this was followed by a trend or a preference for small families. In fact, the economic boom requires a large labor force to take off. If current trends continue, Africa can end up with a negative population growth. If this happens, Africa will have the dual problem of a hand of reduced work and underdevelopment.

The African -bounce- by "Time for Africa"

Fifty years after African independence, time to take stock rang. Curiously, many analysts blow a wind of this jubilee reasoned optimism.

Simply fashion-editorial? Will be convinced that this is not the invigorating reading test has delivered Jean-Michel Severino just before Nicolas Sarkozy decides not to renew the mandate of the latter at the head of the French Agency development (AFD).

Not only Africa is condemned nor its geography or its history or its culture to remain mired in a "poverty trap," say the former Director General of AFD and his co-author Olivier Ray, but the transformation of the continent is on track. Not only "Africa's entry into the world", contrary to what had firmly told the president in 2007 in Dakar (Senegal), but "the world enters in Africa," they argue.

The continent, stronger of the two "growth drivers" that are its huge land reserves and the dynamism of its demographics, is now devoted to economic expansion and hence development, say the authors. The statement takes on the Coue method. It results from a series of analyzes supported by a wealth of data and enhanced portraits.

To believe Jean-Michel Severino and Olivier Ray, the downward spiral experienced by many African countries since independence and especially since the 1990s first result of tragic errors of economic and international financial institutions cycles.

Today, the emergence of a middle class, the liveliness of civil societies, the influx of international investment, loosening the stranglehold of debt are all encouraging signs. The continent is not it committed in recent years, on a slope of 5.5% annual growth?

If the profile of the authors exclude the naive elements of their demonstration of African "bounce" may be blended or dispute: presented as an asset, demographics can also be seen as a terrible burden; the book slides over the brake endeavor, the African family model; it barely scratches the role of some African elites in predation of wealth.

Good students

The most compelling chapters are those in which the book takes readers on a tour with the "good students" of Africa. Botswana Mozambique and Burkina Faso to Tanzania, Jean-Michel Severino and Olivier Ray show that "no recipe" is unique, but "just good cooks."

Common to these countries "earning" is to have "a proactive state" able to "drive economic choice," instead of the "shadow state" or the "predatory state" prevailing among many their neighbors.

The authors note that "good students" are variously distinguished in terms of democracy. And "good governance" is it not necessarily the condition of development, it may be the consequence. A note to meditate at a time when the West Africans require mechanical adoption of rules and behaviors they themselves have taken centuries to conquer and adopt.

According to the report, in the same period, the average age of Africans will increase from 19 to 28 years. The document notes that the population of Europe will decline from the current 725 million people to 630 million in the same period, as well as its birth rate.

Europe will also have a longer life expectancy; the average age of the population will increase significantly, from 39 in 2005 to 48 in 2050.

The report estimates that the world population, estimated at 6.4 billion, will increase by almost 2.7 billion people from 2005 to 2050, this growth will be concentrated in developing countries, 1.3 billion in Asia One billion in Africa and the rest in Latin America and in other regions of the world, the report said.

A risk to the environment

According to specialists of the population growth will increase pressure on the environment, renewable and non-renewable.

This study adds that population pressures and rising incomes lead to rapid desertification, reduced the fishing tape, land degradation, habitat destruction and the extinction of many species.

According to the document the act of launching in Luanda was chaired by the Angolan Minister of Planning Ana Dias Lourenço, 81.3 percent of the world's population is concentrated in less developed regions of the world.

ECONOMY

The country's economy depends mainly on exports but also economic systems established to promote trade between the states. We find three who manage to make things happen in a country ravaged by poverty, drought and diseases such as cholera, malaria and AIDS. Good point so for the Economic Community of West African, the Economic Community of Central African States and the Organization of African Unity.

The extraction of minerals alone represents the majority of export earnings of the country. South Africa produces almost half the income of minerals and three-quarters of the world's gold; followed by Zimbabwe, the Democratic Republic of Congo and Ghana. Nigeria,

Libya, Algeria and Angola are among the world's top oil producers. Coal is mined in Zimbabwe and South Africa; Exports of natural gas are limited to Algeria.

Africans engaged in farming and ranching forever. It provides more than half of the global demand for coffee, cocoa, peanuts. In the north and northwest of the continent, is grown wheat, oats, corn and barley.

Cereals, such as millet and sorghum are the main crops of the savanna. Cattle farming are very difficult in Africa; it almost made impossible since many areas are infested with tsetse flies that kill animals. Fishing side, the coasts of the Atlantic have the reputation of being the richest in the world, but the fishermen do not have enough material to exploit this natural resource extensively. Where the foreign investors are is the question facing many Africans.

Africa is economically the poorest continent in the world: the global gross domestic product of Africa's 1 621 billion dollars in 2008 (according to the official exchange rates of the currencies of 2008 - double if is calculated by purchasing power parity), or 2.62% of world GDP, estimated in 2008 at 62,250 billion, or the equivalent of Canada's GDP for the same year. However, this comparison has limits because the GDP of African countries is highly underestimated forty countries on the continent have not updated their statistical tools for fifteen to twenty years.

GDP per capita is on average $ 1,636, while the world average out of Africa is at $ 10,460 per capita and the world average in Africa included $ 9,170 per capita (still the official exchange rate 2008, not adjusted for purchasing power).

In 2008, according to the official exchange rate, the country with the largest GDP of the continent is South Africa with 300.4 billion dollars and the country with the largest GDP per capita Equatorial Guinea with 31,848 dollars. In 2013, after review of statistical tools, the country with the largest GDP of the continent appears to be Nigeria with $ 510 billion. In 2007, Libya is the most developed countries in Africa if we refer to the HDI (Human Development Index) established by the United Nations Program for Development (UNDP).

Many governments are experiencing a marked fiscal imbalance; some countries are on the brink of bankruptcy. He is regularly carried out debt forgiveness. Total external debt is 255 billion. The relief debt agreements have reduced the public debt of 205.7 billion in 1999 to 114,500,000,000 in 2008 Private debt is itself increased from 92.4 to 110,200,000,000 $.

Southern Africa, particularly South Africa and the Maghreb countries are more economically prosperous as Central Africa and West Africa. The continent is rich in natural resources, but the income from the marketing of its resources are often diverted by managers, and are among the factors that explain some internal conflicts. The institutional framework (rule of law, financial markets ...) useful for economic development is unstable in many countries. The services sector accounts for the largest share of GDP with 44.7%, followed by industry (41.5%) and agriculture (13.8%). In 2006, the industrial and agricultural sectors we recorded the highest growth with 5.7 and 5% respectively.

For 2007, the average growth was 5.8%, against 5.2% in 2005, the global average of 3.7% (2007). This average hides significant disparities: hydrocarbon exporting countries grew faster than the others, as a result of rising oil prices; others have declined, particularly Zimbabwe, which experienced a severe crisis. The oil exporting countries recorded a surplus of 5.3% of GDP while importing countries have a deficit of 1.2%, the continental average of 1.7%. Inflation was 7% on average between 2002 and 2007 in 2007, 60% of African countries have experienced an inflation rate equal to or greater than 5%.

Africa is considered to have extremely rich subsoil. It contains a rich diversity of natural resources, of which approximately 30% of all minerals in the world, 40% gold, 60% cobalt and 90% of the platinum planet.

This is only partially true because resources are concentrated in a few regions (gold and diamonds in South Africa, copper in the Democratic Republic of Congo and Zambia). However, the continent served as a source of raw materials to the West during the Cold War. After a surge in commodity prices in the 1970s, the fall in prices in 1982 and the new geopolitical situation has slowly eroded the market share of Africa against exports from Canada, the United States, Australia, Russia and Ukraine. The effects were even more sensitive than the government had failed to build up reserves during periods of rising prices and invest in infrastructure transformation into finished or semi-finished, resulting in a loss of competitiveness.

During the Cold War, several European countries including France, Britain, the Netherlands and Italy turned to Africa for oil supplies to bypass the priority enjoyed by the United States in the Middle -orient.

After a significant decline in demand in the 1990s, the continent once again draws the attention of the industrialized countries to meet their growing needs for hydrocarbons.

In 2004, Africa reported 90 billion barrels of proven reserves, 29.5 billion and 11.3 billion in Libya in Algeria. Production increased by 40% since 1990, reaching 10.6% of world production, Nigeria leads with 2 million barrels per day. In 2003, the United States imported 14.5% of its oil from Africa.

Road transport

Africa has about 2 million kilometers of roads, of which 27.6% are paved. The density and distribution of the road network are low, with respectively 12 km and 2.71 km per km2 per capita. Road traffic accounts for 90% of long distance transport.

Rail transport; the rail network is 89'380 km of rail, or 2.96 km to 1000 km.

Maritime transport

International trade in Africa is by the sea at 97%. The tonnage increased from 7.3 million tons in 1990 to 6.1 million in 1999, representing 0.8% of the world total, which increased in the same period from 618.4 to 799 million tones. Only container ships have increased their share to 15% of the global market in 1997, with a mean age (11 years) is also closer to the world fleet (10 years), while the rest of the merchant fleet is older an average of 19 years (global average: 14 years). Liberia alone accounts for 94.4% of deadweight tonnage.

Air transport

Africa accounts for 1% of global air traffic. 286 largest airports or land for African aviation included in the accreditation report and restriction of aviation May 2000 Air Mobility Command, only 84% of military airports identified the most important land can support aircraft operations -cargos C-130 and less than 65% of C-17. Fill rates for the transportation of people and goods are lower by 12 and 20% to the global average.

The Yamoussoukro Declaration adopted in 1999 by the Assembly of Heads of State and Government accelerated market liberalization and reforms in the management of airports.

Telecommunications

Africa's population has access to fix telephone lines 3.21 and 28.44 cell phones on average per 100 inhabitants.

In general, the mobile network is better developed and more efficient than the wired network, in poor condition and expensive to maintain.

The total number of mobile phone users has increased by 40 between 2000 and 2007 to reach 274 million subscribers and a penetration rate of 28%.

Energy

The electricity produced in Africa is essentially thermal (80.2%), followed by hydropower (16.3%) and nuclear (3.5%). Biomass is the largest part of energy consumption, mainly as a cooking fuel for almost all sub-Saharan African countries.

African dams produce about 87 TWh of electricity per year. The total capacity of the continent is estimated at over 1,000 TWh / year.

African Economic Community

At the continental level, the African Economic Community aims to improve economic integration by promoting intra-regional trade and to diversify sources of income. Founded in 1991 and entered into force in 1994, it is based on seven key organizations:

The Arab Maghreb Union (UMA):

The Common Market for Eastern and Southern Africa (COMESA), including the countries of East Africa with the exception of Tanzania, and seven southern African countries:

-The Community of Sahel-Saharan States (CEN-SAD)

-the Economic Community of Central African States (ECCAS)

-the Economic Community of West African States (ECOWAS)

-the Intergovernmental Authority on Development (IGAD)

Community Development (SADC) And seven more local communities:

-Economic and Monetary Community of Central Africa (CEMAC), whose six members are all part of ECCAS;

-Community of East Africa (EAC), bringing Kenya and Uganda (COMESA) and Tanzania (CDIC member)

-The Economic Community of Great Lakes Countries (CEPGL), three members are members of ECCAS

-The Indian Ocean Commission (IOC), including four members of COMESA and Reunion

-The Mano River Union (MRU), composed of three members of ECOWAS

-Customs Union (SACU), bringing five members of SADC

-The West African Economic and Monetary Union (WAEMU) which comprises eight members of ECOWAS.

The agenda of the CEA is lined with six stages through 2028, from the existing building to the realization of the African Economic and Monetary Union regional communities, and the creation of a Pan-African Parliament. However, the goals are slow to be realized and are only poorly integrated into national development plans. The trade is principally directed at developed countries, in particular to the European Union.

Merchandise

In 2007, Africa exported $ 422 billion worth of goods, an increase of 16% since 2000, the same time; it imported $ 355 billion (up 15% since 2000). The oil-exporting countries account for 58.5% of exports and 27.3% of imports.

Primary products are on average 80% of African exports; conversely, the imports are mostly manufactured goods. African countries are trading mainly outside the continent (Europe, Asia and North America) for both imports and exports. The will of diversification of production and trade are facing tight local and regional as well as the low purchasing power of the population markets.

Trade with Asia is intensifying in both directions since 2000 between 2000 and 2005, exports to China have quadrupled to $ 19.5 billion and 7% of total exports, 14.9 billion imports (6%). China is now the third largest trading partner on the continent after the United States and the European Union. Nigeria is Africa's main partner in India, with oil accounting for nearly all of its exports (96%) to that country. Chinese demand for cotton was grown producer exports by 41%, increasing GDP by 1.1%.

African countries import from Asia mainly manufactured products but also rice and grains from India. China exports electronics and household items cheap.

Trade in services

Trade Service reported $ 84 billion in 2007, 21.4% for Egypt and 15.4% for South Africa. Imports increased by the same amount, 97 billion went to.

Foreign investment

The PRC has been interested for several years in the economic potential of the African continent. The first countries receiving investment from China is Sudan: oil in 1994, bank 2000.22 in 2005, there were officially 820 Chinese companies operating in Africa. Chinese investments have increased sharply to exceed those on the South East Asia. Trade amounted to 29 billion Euros.

China's Sinopec seeks oil in Gabon. November 3, 2006 held the China-Africa Forum in Beijing that brings together the heads of state of the Dark Continent. China has become the second largest trading partner in Africa, with $ 39.7 billion in 2005.24 The African continent has officially 130,000 Chinese living (2006) and accounts for China a tremendous source of raw materials and energy and a market for its products.

Evolution and post-differences

As is known, output per person employed in sub-Saharan Africa is the lowest of all major regions of the world and, on average, progressed slowly and haltingly since 1960 but the political and the results have been significant developments and large variations in space. In the area of Policy, structural adjustment in the 1980s marked a turning point: a fundamental change, the administrative allocation of resources has been replaced by a market allocation of resources. However, the change was less dramatic in most former French colonies, where (except in Guinea) a convertible currency allowed governments to avoid some additional checks on prices and quantities, which were becoming more frequent in the former colonies, mostly British, outside the franc zone. Regarding performance, the overall growth rates of the economy of the region were quite respectable until the years 1973-1975 (Jerven 2009). Ironically, they have stagnated or even became negative in ten years, within a few years, following the adoption of structural adjustment; the boom in global commodity prices, led by China, then made the region into a twelve-year GDP growth of 5% per year on average, until the crisis of 2007 (with rising fuel prices and food prices and the onset of the global financial crisis) and 2008 brought about a "Great Recession" in 2009 (IMF 2009).

The general growth trends were notable exceptions, both before and after the turn of the first five years of the 1970 Côte d'Ivoire and Ghana, neighboring countries of similar size, marked by factor endowments and relatively similar geographic characteristics but different colonial legacy, have an attractive contrast. Côte d'Ivoire suffered what could be described in broad terms as a magnified version of the standard growth trajectory. From 1960 to 1978, it has experienced an average GDP growth of 9.5% (Barthelme and Söderling 2001, 324-325), but then had several years of stagnation and a civil war. Meanwhile, Ghana did almost the opposite. GDP per capita was only slightly higher in 1983, when the country began the "structural adjustment", that upon gaining independence in 19572.

But Ghana, one of the two most successful cases structural adjustment in Africa (the other being Uganda), had an average annual growth of nearly 5% for a quarter of a century from 1983 basically, we can say that the Ivory Coast was progressing while Ghana was falling, and vice versa. One economy in sub-Saharan Africa, Botswana, sustained growth over three decades - four in fact - since independence in 1966, with an average annual growth of 9.3% (Barthelme and Söderling 2001, 324-325).

Opposing perspectives on the colonial legacy

In the theoretical and ideological debate on the history of economic development in Africa, we see that it is possible to arrive at very similar conclusions starting from very different academic and political positions. About the colonial impact, the charge that there is a generation was mainly driven by dependency theorists and radical nationalists (Amin 1972; Rodney 1972), today emanates from growth economists the "rational choice". Daron Acemoglu, Simon Johnson and James Robinson (2001, 2002a, 2002b) indicated that the relative poverty of Africa in the late twentieth century was primarily the result of the form taken by European colonialism on the continent, that is - dire installing Europeans for extraction, while the installation of many European populations have led to the creation of certain types of institutions - private property rights and governance systems that support them - that according to these authors, helped the economic development of North America and Australasia.

In Africa, colonial extraction was manifested in the most indisputable way through the appropriation of the land to the European settlers or European plantations, a strategy implemented not only to give investors and European settlers a safe and inexpensive control of the land, but also to force Africans to sell their labor to farmers, growers and owners of European mines (Palmer and Parsons 1977). Even in the "peasant" colonies, where land is predominantly remained African ownership, we will see that significant parts of the services sector were in fact monopolized by Europeans. Colonial administrations then proceeded to coercive recruitment of labor, which was to work either for the state or for private European companies (Fall 1993 Northrup 1988). The refusal to accept the colonial governments, and more to promote the emergence of markets for property rights on land occupied by Africans in the settlements or colonies in operating, had a potentially great importance long-term (Phillips 1989). According to the theory of dependence and institutionalism as "rational choice", the original sin of colonialism in Africa is not to have introduced true capitalist system based on private property and would have created incentives for competition and accumulation needed to stimulate self-sustaining economic growth.

In the years 1950 to 1970, the group, then small liberal development economists held a significant but less ample reasoning. At a time when development economists (including, but not limited to those who wrote in French) tended to give the state a leading role in the pursuit of development in mixed economies (Hugon 1993; Killick 1978), Peter Bauer (1953, 1972) attacked the colonial state fire by criticizing it for having created offices of state and, thus, have opened the way for state interventionism he saw as a brake.

Explicitly positive outlook on the colonial government in Africa are rare (but see Duignan and Gann 1975). Yet many studies mention the end of intra-African wars, the abolition of the slave trade and domestic slavery, the introduction of mechanized transport and infrastructure investment, and the development of modern industry economies "settler" and the Belgian Congo. Exalted by the wave of "globalization" of the economic end of the twentieth century, some economic liberals have argued that the British Empire was a pioneer in the process by objecting generally to protective tariffs (1846-1931) and taking other pro-market measures (Ferguson 2003, Lal 2004). The argument tariffs would apply less to French colonies because of protectionism of the French empire. It applies also much lower in the last thirty years of the British government in Africa that have emerged not only tariffs but also of state offices in some branches of the economy. From the perspective of institutional change, John Sender and Sheila Smith (1986) made an important observation for the area in general. Being in the tradition "tragic optimism" of Marx's writings on the British government in India, they emphasized the fact that wage labor was scarce at the beginning of the colonial government and increasingly common at the end of the period. According to these authors, such as Bill Warren (1980), imperialism was the "pioneer of capitalism."

Beyond optimism and pessimism, a third perspective on the colonial government, and therefore his legacy is to say that its importance is overstated. Different thoughts come to that conclusion. Many historians are struck by the brevity of the colonial government south of the Sahara - about sixty years in most of tropical Africa (Ajayi 1969) - and the weakness of the colonial state (Herbst 2000). In this context, it is logical to say that Africans, by economic rationality and entrepreneurship are the main responsible for everything that went well in the "peasant" economies (and economies of cultures annuity have greatly increased); is Polly Hill (1997/1963) that best illustrates this position. Jean-François Bayart (1989, 2000) takes a more ambivalent reasoning. Starting from the well-known observation that governments in Africa have struggled to draw significant revenue in the domestic sources, Bayard says that during the colonial period and since then African elites were clients of colonial states or metropolitans. They thus forged a relationship that, though uneven, their advantage as they took advantage to foreigners. While dependency theory emphasized the primacy of the foreign action in determining the historical developments, Bayart repeat that African elites have played a computer and crucial role in the establishment of the "extrovert" model of African Political Economy.

A pre-colonial perspective on colonial legacies

To assess the colonial legacy, we must distinguish what is the status and trends that existed on the continent at the beginning of the colonial government, which dates back, in most of sub-Saharan Africa, the "race" European, which took place from 1879 to about 1905. At this time, as before, the area was characterized in general (but not everywhere all the time) by an abundance of arable land relative to labor available for work (Hopkins 1973; Austin 2008a). However, one cannot speak of resource abundance because most of the endowment of mineral resources in Africa was either unknown or unreachable with the pre-industrial technology, or it had not yet value even in France. For example, many of the most important discoveries (including oil in Nigeria and diamonds in Botswana) should only be made during the period of decolonization. In addition, the fertility of most of the land was relatively small or at least random, making any costly or difficult intensive culture, particularly the lack of animal manure.

Sleeping sickness prevented the use of large animals for plowing and transport in forest areas and most of the savannah. The extreme seasonality of the annual distribution of rainfall made it really impossible agricultural work during much of the dry season. Therefore, the opportunity cost of labor in the dry season was low and the interest of progress of labor productivity in the small craft. Conversely, the choice of farming techniques typically moving towards extensive use of land and minimal use of labor, the fine layer of arable soil limited the returns to labor (Austin 2008a). All these factors help explain why, for centuries, the productivity of the African labor seemed highest outside Africa, an idea that is found in the economic logic underlying bills Foreign slaves who finally and ironically, have compounded the lack of manpower in Africa itself (Austin 2008b; Manning 1990).

In Africa, the incentive structure encouraged a strong and self-sufficiency in the mid-twentieth century, it was often said that the pre-colonial economies had always been predominantly subsistence-oriented. Searching for the last half-century allowed returning gradually to this statement, especially for West Africa where, in the sixteenth and seventeenth centuries, a strong tendency to productions other than subsistence emerged prominently. Although compounded by the effects of "Dutch disease" related to the transatlantic slave trade (Inikori 2007 Austin forthcoming) this trend has recovered strongly from the first decade of the nineteenth century, when the deals started to be abolished and the West Africans produced on a larger scale for the domestic market but also outside. Because of the relative scarcity of labor, and in the absence (usually) significant economies of scale in production, it was rare that the reservation wage (the minimum wage from which it is possible to convince a person to sell his labor instead of working for herself) is low enough that a potential employer can pay. The majority of the labor markets of pre-colonial Africa are summarized in the slave trade.

Given the abundance of land, political centralization was not practical and just as hard to maintain. Political fragmentation facilitated the transatlantic slave trade in the sense that larger states would have more interest and ability to refuse to participate (Inikori 2003). The same fragmentation then facilitated the European conquest. Ethiopia was the exception that proves the rule: with its fertile central provinces and large agricultural surplus supporting a former state and being upgraded, it is the only African to have had a sufficient economic base to resist "race".

Much of sub-Saharan Africa was colonized at a time when the industrialization of Europe created or expanded markets merchandise that could be profitably produced in Africa, and it has nothing of coïncidence4. The ratio of land / labor, the environmental constraints on intensive agriculture but also the specific qualities of various types of land in different parts of the continent of Africa detained at least a potential comparative advantage in primary production by extensive cultivation. At the time of colonization, particularly in West Africa, indigenous peoples, drew increasing profits from the combination of these elements and provides access to external markets expanding. From Senegal to Cameroon, thousands of palm oil and peanut tons, from the 1880s, rubber were produced to be sold to European traders (Law 1995).

Colonial regimes: similarities and differences

The colonial government in Africa should be inexpensive for European taxpayers. British doctrine was that each colony is financially independent. Any increase in government spending would be financed by an increase in revenue, as was the case in Ghana in the 1920s when Governor Guggisberg managed to fund the creation of what would become the hospital and school the best known of the country, but also of a new port and new roads and railway tracks by customs revenues fueled by the growth of exports of cocoa beans by the colony. In practice, the French were just as eager to cover their costs. French West Africa has also been a great public works program in the 1920s, although, as in Ghana, spending had to be reduced drastically after a few years when export prices fell and revenue continued to increase.

After their withdrawal during the depression of the 1930s and especially during the Second World War, the colonial administrations (for various reasons) entered the post-war with a new public commitment: to be considered actively promoting the development of savings they presided. The "developmental" language was reflected in part by an increase in spending, which in principle partially came from the Metropolitan taxpayer. But Patrick Manning (1988, 123-125) has calculated that in the case of France, tax revenues from Africa continued to exceed government spending in Africa. In British West Africa, new public offices export accumulated substantial surpluses maintaining a substantial margin between the prices at which they bought from the producers and those to whom they sold on the world market for agricultural products. The surpluses were kept in London by the British government securities, forced savings of African farmers (Rimmer, 1992, 41-42) who helped the British metropolitan economy recover from the shortage of dollars in the postwar period.

Depending on the particular identity of the colonial power, persons subject to the Government of Europeans have had different experiences. Traditionally, the contrasts between the two largest empires in Africa is built around the fact that the British were based more on African leaders acting as intermediaries (indirect rule), while the French doctrine assimilated a small minority of Africans culture and French citizenship. Overall, we can say that, in the economic field, the similarities were far greater than the differences, except for differences in the composition of the respective African empires of the two powers. The French government, like the British government relied on African intermediaries, including heads, although France has many more sought to abolish African monarchies (as in Dahomey, as opposed to treating the British structures and dynasties of Buganda states, Botswana, Lesotho and - after a failed attempt to abolish - the Asante kingdom). In West Africa, the French have much more used forced labor, but mainly because the French territories were the outset, relatively free of revenue potential liquidity and thus possibility of resorting to paid employment. This particular policy - the chore, and its use for the benefit of white farmers than for the benefit of African farmers - conveyed a different colonial legacy in Ghana and Côte d'Ivoire. It explains why the African cocoa farming has taken off much faster and more dramatically in Ghana, which was found as a result much more successful at independence, while Côte d'Ivoire, after a late start, was being catching up (and exceeded) (Hopkins, 1973, 218-219), a process which results in the 1980s.

So if we argue here that the differences between the legacy of the British and French governments in Africa are primarily attributable to differences in the composition of African empires of these powers, it is possible that this idea should be seen in the light of results a very good recent research by Thomas Bossuroy Cogneau and Denis (2009). The authors studied social mobility in five African countries and found that in the former British colonies considered, Ghana and Uganda, "the links between origin, migration, education and vocational destination appear much looser" than in former French colonies studied, the Ivory Coast and Guinée5 (Bossuroy Cogneau and 2009, 2). To explain this finding, the authors emphasize the importance of investment in education; the amounts were higher in the British colonies in the French colonies in their sample. Here we find an important new line of research. I think the successful conclusion to the former British colonies also partly reflects the fact that Ghana and Uganda, for reasons that are only partly and indirectly to do with their colonial legacies, were two great successes of structural adjustment in Africa in terms of growth; These achievements have improved the chances of educational, physical and occupational mobility from the 1980s, that is to say soon enough for this trend to be reflected in the figures - and also when the Ivory Coast knew economic stagnation and civil war. Finally, it is possible that the contrast also translated in part the legacy of the period of the drudgery and agriculture "settler" in Côte d'Ivoire, before the takeoff of the economy in 1950-1960. A study of 26 former British and French colonies in tropical Africa (thus excluding Southern Africa) showed that since 1990, thanks to the legacy of the "miracle" Ivorian former French colonies were those income per capita highest in terms of purchasing power, with a difference of over 30% (and Bossuroy Cogneau 2009, 45, citing data from the World Bank).

The colonial government and the specialization of Africa in the export of primary products

Is often deplored extraversion "and" monoculture "practiced in African economies and they are condemned as signs of the victory of the colonial interests of African interests? Yet it is necessary to compare the risks of extreme specialization gains with long-term income that can be expected from the exploitation of comparative advantage. But again, even if we could identify and locate a comparative advantage of the colonial economy, it was necessary sooner or later, to capitalize this advantage, knowing what investments would accentuate this advantage and, importantly, how costs and benefits would be distributed. Ideological, and especially the balance of power between the various interest groups conflict, had different effects in the African colonies. The most fundamental difference is made between "peasant" economies and "settler". Let's look at two opposite cases of export agriculture, particularly in West Africa, and mining, the most obvious being that of the South African example.

We noted that on the eve of the partition of the continent of Europe, Africa had already revealed a primer of comparative advantage in export agriculture. In West Africa in particular, population, European and colonial administrations merchants had all interest to accentuate this advantage. In Ghana, the British planters were allowed to enter at first to grow cocoa beans. But that did not receive selective support that the government had given to their counterparts in Kenya and southern Africa, they lost commercial competition which opposed African producers (Austin 1996a), as later the French planters would overwhelmed by African farmers in Côte d'Ivoire after the abolition of forced labor. The colonial practice of relying on the efforts of African farmers and small capitalists in the field of culture and local marketing of export crops has been very successful in what became Ghana and Nigeria: the real value of foreign trade has increased 20-fold between 1897 and 1960 (Austin 2008a, 612), benefiting both the British commercial interests that colonial treasure (through tariffs).

From 1906 to 1925, WH Lever, soap manufacturer, sought to be authorized by the government (and its necessary support coercive) to create large oil palm plantations in Nigeria but his requests were all rejected because they preferred Africans continue to occupy almost all the farmland. Ultimately, this choice was based on the finding that African producers showed the height (Hopkins, 1973, 209-214) by well suited to factor endowments extensive methods. They rejected the advice of the colonial agricultural officials when such advice was inconsistent with the requirements of effective adaptation (Austin 1996a). The positive contribution of government was to authorize and strengthen the exploitation of comparative advantage of economies in export agriculture, partly by investing in transportation infrastructure - investments that will be seen, were also the fact of African entrepreneurs (Austin 2007). Another equally important is that the colonial administration, even though it never really established a system of land titles, for example, Ghana maintained the native customary rights of farmers to own the trees they had planted regardless of the consequences of subsequent disputes over the ownership of land where there were trees. African producers have thus enjoyed a safe enough lease to invest confidently in tree crops on a scale that, in the case of Ghana, would create the largest economy in the world for almost seventy years.

South Africa had gold and diamonds, but to be beneficial, operation required a reduction in labor costs well below what was involved in the land / labor ratio physical. The quantitative exercise conducted by Charles Feinstein shows that without such coercive intervention in the labor market, the majority of South African mines were not profitable until the end of the period of the gold standard 1932 (Feinstein 2005,

109-112). If South Africa ended up getting a comparative advantage of "free market" in mining, it is only after several decades of use extra merchants means for compressing the wage of blacks, including ownership land and measures to prevent the Africans to use the land belonging to Europeans except as workers - but not as sharecroppers.

It is difficult to compare the legacies of European in poverty in economies "settler" and "exploitation" because there are many differences from one colony to another. However, we can draw some generalizations. It is clear that the distribution of wealth and income has been - and remains - much more unequal in economies "settler" in the "peasant" economies. The first results of a study of Sue Bowden, Blessing Chiripanhura and Paul Mosley (2008) had the idea that land ownership has created a floor on real wages in the "peasant" colonies and allowed workers migrating to agricultural export crop regions to share the benefits of exports that otherwise were divided between European companies, Asian and African intermediaries and African farm owners (see also Austin 2005). Bowden et al. (2008) found that real wages had increased in the "peasant" colonies of Ghana and Uganda from 1920 and 1930 respectively and were not then fell back to the floor level of 1914. Against, it was only in 1970 that the real wages of black gold miners in South Africa have experienced a prolonged growth to exceed the levels they had known in the early twentieth century (Lipton, 1986, 410). The study by Bowden et al. (2008, 1063), it is only in pure savings "settler", South Africa and Zimbabwe (Southern Rhodesia), and not in the economies 'exploitation' of Ghana or Uganda, nor even in the intermediate case of Kenya, the living standards of Africans living in rural areas declined over periods of more than fifteen years in the course of the twentieth century. This model of real wage growth, combined with the long-term expansion of the African agricultural exports that has underpinned the growth of real wages in the colonies "exploitation", resulting in an earlier decline in infant mortality in Ghana and Uganda and the Southern Rhodesia and South Africa (Bowden et al. 2008).

It should be added that many African colonies lacked both known mineral reserves and land for profitable export agriculture. Europeans did not retain these colonies to settle and economies have not been driven by strong African peasant capitalist production or rural. These colonies had to rely on seasonal exports of wage labor and masculine cultures less lucrative cash crops such as cotton; as these crops demanded of the workforce at the same times that food crops, food security was uncertain (Tosh 1980). A current trend in research, led by Alexander Moradi, used to measure the size of the physical well-being. The average size of the African population rose during the colonial period in Ghana and even in the partially populated economy of Kenya (Moradi, 2008, 2009). When this research will be extended to the poorest colonies like South Sudan, Tanganyika (mainland Tanzania) or colonies Sahel of West Africa, it would not be surprising to see slower growth of property -be in better endowed economies studied until now. This is particularly in the less well-endowed economies (and parts of these economies) that colonial governments sought to raise productivity through projects very large, authoritarian and capital intensive, particularly with the huge irrigation project of the Office du Niger in Mali and campaign mechanization of Africa project west for peanuts in Tanganyika. These two examples were spectacular failures in terms of production levels and productivity, especially because they had not properly taken into account the physical environment and the ratios of existing factors (Hogendorn and Scott 1981; Roberts 1996, 223-248, van Beusekom 2002).

25The settler colonialism has had poor results on the standard of living of the indigenous population but in colonies where Europeans have appropriated land on a large scale for the benefit of settlers or companies, that modern industry appeared as early and widely.

The road toward industry

where it occurred, the industrialization of Asia has generally followed a path requesting more manpower that industrialization of Europe and North America; she did instead was to longer working hours that increased mechanization where possible (Sugihara 2007) and, in general, she had a proportion work / higher at all levels of production capital. In the early twentieth century, in a region like sub-Saharan Africa where the work as the capital was scarce relative to land, both channels were also difficult.

Yet, South Africa, followed to a lesser degree by Southern Rhodesia, had acquired a large manufacturing sector at a time when much of the rest of Africa became independent. The cost "artificially" low black labor has contributed to this result, but only for unskilled jobs, skilled jobs were reserved for whites; In addition, the chosen techniques were generally capital intensive. The growth of manufacturing production was possible due to a customs protection where the advantage of the location (as in brewing and the cement industry) was not enough.

What was decisive is that mining has identified purchasing power and thereby acquire imports to meet the needs in equipment and, where necessary, in materials first. It was also the direct or indirect source of much revenue that governments have used to invest in the industry, either directly or through the construction of infrastructure. Major European populations have brought both educated workers and capital, but we can say that it is by their political support to the industrialization that contributed most to his development, even if it was through price the often higher than world market consumers (Austen, 1987, 181-187; Kilby 1975, Wood and Jordan 2000). Where they had control of the government, as in South Africa and after 1910, largely in Southern Rhodesia from 1923, numerous white voters fed ambition to move up the value chain; this ambition is also that of African voters since independence. In South Africa, the Government of the National Pact and Labour parties, elected in 1924, has implemented a policy of promoting import substitution industrialization with tariffs and public investment in the electricity and steel (Feinstein 2005, 113-135). Southern Rhodesia followed in the 1930s, partly in response to the challenge posed by the new customs regime of South (Phimister 2000) Africa. In addition to these settlements, there is a third case of early growth of modern industry: the Belgian Congo. The settlers there were neither independent nor autonomous. But as in southern Africa, mining has fostered the creation of conditions conducive to the emergence of an industry of import substitution, allowing the construction of infrastructure, purchasing power of imports and a partial opening the market. South Africa remained the flagship of the industry in the region, but expansion opportunities have been increasingly limited due to the high cost of skilled labor in an economy where only a minority of the population had access to secondary education and also because the low wages of black limited market size of products manufactured en masse. If the radical school was right to mention the contribution of repressive racial policies to economic growth in the early twentieth century (Trapido 1971), the Liberals were right when they evoked the period before the end of the apartheid system then became a hindrance, not an engine for economic development (Moll 1990; Nattrass 1991, Feinstein 2005).

In the 1960s, the modern industry was quite developed in South Africa but not competitive internationally. She was much smaller in the rest of sub-Saharan Africa. The industry accounted for over 10% of the GDP or estimé8 officially in only two countries: Southern Rhodesia (16%) and the Belgian Congo (14%). With 9.5% was the economy in part settlement of Kenya and Senegal (Kilby 1975, 472). The latter was a "peasant" economy, but, being the administrative and commercial center of French West Africa, he had an unusually large population of European residents who brought, more than elsewhere, management experience, a technical expertise and access to capital (Kilby 1975, 473, 488-490). In West Africa, the low level of industrialization in 1960 reflected a very late surge, driven by developmentalist of the post-war (in the case of Senegal, government subsidies for industry) and decolonization, which brought European companies to establish local factories to protect the markets they already had (Kilby 1975, 475, 490-507; Boone 1992, 65-77).

Given the scarcity of labor, the small size of the markets and the comparative advantage available to Africa for primary production by extensive cultivation, it is not surprising that the industry does has not been more developed at the end of the colonial period. Where it could take off, colonial governments were rarely interested in changing the status quo; they preferred that colonial markets for manufactured products continue to be supplied largely by a monophony where European merchants sold goods which were produced a disproportionate share in metropolitan European economies concerned (Brett, 1973, 266-282; Kilby 1975) . But knowing that, despite the increase in population, factor endowments of African economies, even the largest, were not adapted to industrialization in 1960, it is perhaps more important to investigate whether the colonial government, directly or indirectly, laid the foundation could then enable Africa to establish favorable conditions for accelerated growth of the industry.

If one believes the experience in Asia, the growth of the industry should probably be done through intensive use of labor. In the long term, the most fundamental change in the colonial period was probably the beginning of a sustained population growth that can be, on the whole, from the end of the influenza pandemic of 1918 although the exact dates may vary from one place to another. It is difficult to determine how population growth was due to colonial actions, such as removing slave raids, peace in Africa after 1918 and the public health measures that have reduced mortality crisis (Iliffe 1995, 238-241). It is estimated that the population of the sub-Saharan area doubled between 1900 and 1960, to around 200 million people (for references, see Austin 2008a, 591). The demographic context to have a cheaper labor thus beginning to develop, but it was only the beginning. Industrialization with intensive use of labor also calls for investments in energy supply and quality of labor. It requires disciplined workers and could also have specific training or to more easily learn new skills (Sugihara, forthcoming) skills. Enrollment rates increased during the colonial period that were previously low or zero, and in many countries they have doubled or tripled between 1950 and 1960, this increase was possible partly because African politicians began to control domestic budgets during the transition to independence, for example in Nigeria, where enrollment rose 971 000-2 913 000 primary and from 28 000 to 135 000 in secondary education (Sender and Smith 1986, 62). In 1957, the annual electricity production (in kilowatts) amounted to 2.75 billion in the Belgian Congo and 2,425,000,000 in the Central African Federation, the largest of which was produced in Southern Rhodesia. By cons, according to figures from the previous year, the French West Africa had produced a cumulative total of 138 million kilowatts9, Nigeria 273 million, and the rest of British West Africa 84 million (Kamarck 1964, 271) . Therefore, industrialization was favored nationalist but the newly independent countries were not well equipped to embark on industrialization with intensive use of labor in the 1960s when industrialization was chosen These are intensive methods of capital that were selected (subsidy to capital protection by tariffs) and factories rather gives rise to economic rents that have reported earnings per their competitive success (Boone 1992).

Markets and African entrepreneurship

African entrepreneurship led to changes in the choice of products and the means and the organization of production in different contexts before, during and since the colonial period. It is particularly noticeable in West Africa, where the pre-colonial economies of the nineteenth century were often considered more commercial than other major economies of sub-Saharan Africa (Austin, forthcoming). Again, this is often the existence or lack of ownership of land on a large scale by the Europeans, individual settlers or companies who impact of colonialism was determined on African entrepreneurship and its markets.

This known between, on the one hand, the colonies "settler" and "plantation" and the other division, the "peasant" colonies (and rural capitalists) is far from being purely exogenous in African economic history. Where African producers were able to penetrate the export early and large-scale markets, before European exporters are really enter, they have been quite successful so that in the debates between colonial policy makers, the balance tips in favor of those who thought wiser, the political as well as economic point of view, leaving the farming to Africans. As we saw in Section 6, the British West Africa has been the prime example. In South Africa, Southern Rhodesia and Kenya, African farmers have quickly seized the opportunity to grow more to supply domestic markets. But in response, governments have tried to push the Africans out of the market for agricultural products and to enter the labor market, reserving land for Europeans and Africans by prohibiting the lease or (as in Kenya in 'between the wars) by limiting the time that the "occupiers" African could devote to their own work in terms of working time they had their European owners (Palmer and Parsons 1977; Kanogo 1987). Yet the African market output resisted and governments have finally accepted; they have given up trying to move producers to introduce more controls on the marketing of agricultural products, controls that favored European producers. In Kenya, it is only in the mid-1950s, during the Mau Mau, the government lifted restrictions limiting cash crops with high value Africans (Mosley 1983). If at the end of the nineteenth century, the African commercial production was higher in what would become the "operating" agricultural export economies in what became plantation economies, this contrast was accentuated by actions of governments in the past over the following decades.

However, we cannot say that now owned for Africans there was necessarily supported the African capitalism. Certainly, we have seen that the colonial state in Ghana had protected ownership of agricultural investors in that it had preserved the property of the farmer or the farmer on the trees he or she had planted, regardless the potential consequences of this right in the case of legal dispute over the ownership of the land in question. But in economies "settler" as the colonies 'exploitation', colonial governments were hesitant and generally hostile to the development of land markets in African regions under control. This policy eventually changed in Southern Rhodesia and Kenya, where we made a selective promotion of land registration before the emergence, in fact, sales of land and private property (land cultivable being less numerous in the areas left to Africans) and because African landowners were considered politically conservative force in relation to Mau Mau (Mosley, 1983, 27-28; Kanogo 1987). In West Africa, the settlers had not lobbied to prevent the Africans access to land and cash crops have expanded in the early colonial period and again in the 1950s, the granting of land titles was called for or the politically nor economically view (Austin 2005).

African entrepreneurs, like their European counterparts, should be able to recruit labor. In this context, the colonial period was marked by a gradual innovation and usually imposed. Sooner or later, but often later, colonies have adopted laws prohibiting slavery. However, in West Africa - the region where it is known that the slave population was the largest in the early twentieth century - replacing the slave market by wage labor market was largely dependent on the progress of the African agriculture annuity (Austin, 2009). In the decades between the two world wars, colonial authorities, who continued to use forced labor, suffered a steady pressure from the International Labor Office in Geneva. Faced with the embarrassment caused by these pressures, further reforms were introduced gradually and reluctantly. At the end of World War II, as shown by Frederick Cooper (1996), the British and French authorities had agreed that the employee is working a normal job for Africans, not just a seasonal side business to supplement their agricultural activity. In fact, as Cooper then shows the tax implications in the long term of equal rights for workers in Africa and Europe contributed to London and Paris decide to withdraw from tropical Africa. In African societies, the end of slavery and the rise of wage labor were probably the condition of a large-scale participation in international trade.

In 1907, the chocolate manufacturer Cadbury had moved its cocoa purchases in Ghana after a bad press accused him of using cocoa "cultivated by slaves" in the Portuguese colony of Sao Tome, where he was previously supplied (Southall, 1975, 39-49). In 1960, slavery was generally more acceptable among trading partners. Colonial abolitionism, however gradual, has contributed to the "modernization" of labor institutions in Africa.

The colonial government promoted the import of capital in a continent where capital was scarce. But this influx has been widespread in mining and, to some extent, in agricultural colonies "settler" and "plantation". The study of Herbert Frankel (1938) on foreign capital investment in Africa ruled by whites remains the only major study of the colonial period. According to this author, crude and nominal terms, these investments amounted to a total of 1.221 billion USD between 1870 and 1936, of which 42.8% were from South Africa. This means an investment of £ 55.8 per person in South Africa, but only £ 3.3 in the French colonies and £ 4.8 in British West Africa. Public investments constituted 44.7% of the global total and nearly 46% of total non-Southern Africa (Frankel, 1938, 158-160, 169-170). Governments and, to some extent, mining and plantation companies have invested in transport infrastructure necessary for development, mainly the import-export. In Nigeria and Ghana, Africans have also played a leading role in the construction of motor roads and the creation of pioneer road transport services (Heap 1990). From the institutional point of view, the colonial period eventually see the abolition of the pledging of human beings, replaced by promissory notes and, where possible in West Africa, with loans with cover of cocoa farms. It also saw the introduction of modern banking, but banks received more willingly savings Africans they gave their lending - in part because the colonial governments did not submit the required credential recognition property (Cowen and Shenton 1991).

Such as shipping and import-export, banking in West Africa had a strong tendency to be cartelized (Olukoju 2001-2002 Austin and Uche 2007). Imposing rules and colonial borders at the start of the colonial period, has upset of intra-African networks and domestic presence increasingly strong European merchants relegated many African traders down the chain intermediary between carriers and farmers (Goerg 1980 Nwabughuogu 1982). This is especially later organized resistance to European cartels has grown and it is most often limited to certain colonies, such as the traditional "hold-ups" on cocoa, which saw farmers and agents African trading repeatedly come into conflict with European trade cartels in Ghana, and the movement of indigenous banks in Nigeria (Miles 1978, Hopkins 1966). Until independence, dominated by Europeans in the colonies markets "operating" were cartelized as markets invested by Africans were characterized by extreme competition (Hopkins 1978, 95). At least, African entrepreneurs could they act in the import-export and domestic trade, although more than they could do in the settlements. Although they were largely confined to the lowest levels of trade pyramids, they took advantage of the general expansion of economies, particularly in West Africa (Hopkins 1995, 44). Monopolistic arrangements were somewhat shaken by decolonization (Austin and Uche 2007) but the former African sector has become the "informal" sector, the former European sector becoming the "formal" sector (Austin 1993). At independence, the newly established governments have faced the familiar dualism of these financial problems, including lack of access to cheap credit granted by the formal to informal sector enterprises sector.

Despite an asymmetrical competition, "peasant" colonies of the most successful economically saw to continue a tradition of entrepreneurship and, most often (but not always), a modest accumulation in agriculture, crafts and trade. The result, as noted by John Iliffe, was "a very marked difference between West Africa, with its capitalist sector and its contractors artisans and merchants long established and East Africa and Southern Africa, where it was mostly by [...] Western education and employment in the modern sector entrepreneurs had emerged "(Iliffe, 1983, 67, our trans.). The first post-colonial policies have not always relied on these elements, for example in Ghana, and heavy taxation on agricultural exports was sometimes established and state-created monopolies in certain sectors.

The ability of the state

It is commonly accepted that States play a key role in economic development, at least because they ensure compliance with the rules of economic activity and provide physical public goods. We need to explore how the colonial government affected the historical barrier to political centralization in Africa: the challenge of increasing revenue. And beyond that, we must study the size of the state and the nature and legitimacy of authority, asking whether colonization caused the fragmentation of Africa, as is often said, or if colonial rulers, by their terms, have been a force for modernization that has given the state a "stateless" and replace patrimonial rule by bureaucratic authority.

Colonial administrations have themselves suffered heavy budgetary constraints. European empires in Africa have certainly brought the possibility of loan finance (at least in an impersonal way, obeying the law as undemocratic well) but the colonial government could use the money markets in a limited way because the city insisted that each colony is fiscally autonomous and balance its budget. The inclusion in each colony of a single legal tender is likely to have reduced the net transaction costs (although in some cases the demonetization of existing currencies has adversely affected their African owners). But the ministries of finance metropolis refused to subordinate their colonies independence that would allow them to coin money (Herbst, 2000, 201-213). The French colonies used the French franc. In British West Africa, colonial book was issued but the rules guaranteed convertibility at par with the metropolitan book. Only independence the new African governments were given the option of creating local currencies, a possibility that the former French colonies have mostly refused when the former British colonies have quickly accepted.

Face the same practical constraints that African states that had preceded them, colonial governments have generally maintained the tax system in force in the pre-colonial kingdoms, aimed trade and people rather than land and agriculture. It was during World War II that took place the main colonial innovation in taxation with the discovery that we have already mentioned the significant potential of export offices to increase revenues. Independence approached the unintended consequence of a war ship opened to African politicians unprecedented opportunities, for example, provide new educational opportunities for their people. The tax offices instrument was an important colonial legacy and we then only beginning to understand the opportunities it offered and its implications. In the 1980s, the limitations of the device became obvious: commercial agents and ordinary producers could indeed escape by trading in parallel markets.

With smuggling, we address one of the most famous colonial partitions of Africa legacy: the imposition of boundaries that separated people from the same culture, the delimitation of state so small that one could doubt their economic viability, and the creation of states so vast they became potentially ungovernable. These criticisms are very relevant but recent research has shown that the origins of these borders were not necessarily as arbitrary and that some of them at least had subsequently acquired a social reality or popular legitimacy (Nugent 2002). We repeat, colonization has left several very small states, but most colonies (even small ones) were larger than pre-colonial political entities that or instead of which they were imposed; In addition, some formed larger regional units (including the French West Africa). If colonial borders were largely preserved, attempts to introduce a Weberian bureaucracy revealed significantly less durable results (Bayart 1989). This is, or is manifested by the prominence of ethnicity in political competition for control of resources in most African countries.

From the late 1970s, a generation of historians and anthropologists tended to assert that ethnicity in Africa, far from being "paramount," was created, or at least established by colonial strategies division (the idea is part of the major contributions of Iliffe [1979, 318-341] and Ranger [1983], and was extended beyond those first cautious statements). Recent historiography shows that it was legitimate part to emphasize the ability of the colonial states had to invent and manipulate traditions, including those related to ethnicity and chieftaincy but also stresses that it has underestimated the ability of elites and African peoples themselves deal with the effects of these inventions and manipulations (Spear 2003). In any case we cannot say that all ethnic divisions have arisen from the colonial period (Vansina 2001), although they have so often been the most thorough and reified by the interaction of colonial and African elites (Prunier 1995). Whatever the precise division of responsibilities in this interaction, researchers generally agree that it is more from the colonial regime before it that ethnicity was a principle of political association and conflict. The distinction is important for economic development because ethnic divisions are often viewed by the public and by some economists (including Easterly and Levine 1997) as key policymakers annuity rather than growth implemented in Africa postcolonial. But this approach has been criticized for various reasons (including by Arcand et al. 2000) and the prominence of ethnicity in African politics and economic life is as much a reaction to the difficulty of expanding the pie of the economy the African context and the problem of the continuing weakness of the state that because of these obstacles.

In contrast and / or bad growth performance of African economies after decolonization balance, Botswana stands out. Daron Acemoglu, Simon Johnson and James Robinson (2002a) claim that this country is the exception that proves the rule: if Botswana has not benefited from the institutional legacy of characteristic colonies "purely settler" such as Australia, the government UK there was exceptionally small, so the country has escaped the worst mining trends, according to the authors, generally characterized colonialism other than "settler".

The conclusion I can personally is different, for two reasons. First, it is unclear whether the Botswana post-settlement would have grown dramatically faster than the Bechuanaland without the discovery of diamond growth. In fact, in the three decades after independence, the results of the Botswana mining sector, excluding diamond mining, were no better than those of Zambia (Jerven 2008). Then the British government was relatively heavy contrary to Bechuanaland. Taking the criterion of the number of Africans administrator, the country placed fifth out of 33 African colonies around 1937.

The limited potential of the African colonies for income generation (especially before have not made some of the most spectacular mineral discoveries) allows to explain the decisions of French and British governments to accept a deal with the early decolonization increasing popular in nationalist claims channeled increasingly present movements. At the same time, french companies apparently beginning to be less interested in saving the colonies (Marseille 2005). If this is true, it is ironic that the French government has kept a close proximity to its former colonies after independence, particularly through the franc zone. Similarly, in the 1950 British companies present on site were concerned about their future as independent African governments, but the authorities involved in the decolonization have not given their attention (Tignor 1998, Stockwell 2000). Here, the irony is that, a few years later, the attitude of the British government to the secession of Biafra was influenced by the interests of British oil companies.

the question of the colonial legacy in relation to the long-term dynamics of economic development in an area that was in 1900, extremely rich in land and which was characterized by a lack of both labor and capital by native market exchanges which perhaps surprisingly extensive, particularly in West Africa, and by varying degrees, but often weak political centralization. Colonial governments and European companies have invested both in infrastructure and (especially in southern Africa) in the creation of institutions whose purpose was to develop African economies export of primary products. In both cases, the old economic logic of use of forced labor continued with the maintenance of slavery in tropical Africa at the beginning of the colonial period and the use of land seizures extensively to support the flow migrant workers in the economies of settlement. But there have been changes and nuances. There were differences between the French and British policies, for example in West Africa, but it is in the "peasant" colonies "settler" that objections were strongest.

In British West Africa in particular, African farmers, European colonial governments and merchants had a real interest in strengthening and exploit the comparative advantage of West Africa in extensive farming. With the income thus generated, many slave owners could at least become employers. In these cases, the British government - and the French in Ivory Coast since 1945 - has seen their interests where they stood and supported the African investment in export agriculture. It is in these colonies "exploitation" better endowed with land suitable for the production of the most lucrative that African populations have experienced a substantial increase in purchasing power and improved physical well-being cultures. But in these colonies, colonial rulers, partly because of fiscal constraints, but probably after a realistic assessment of short-term economic prospects, have little directly incurred to prepare the economy to "move up the value chain ". The first generation of postcolonial leaders have presided over economies that lacked trained manpower (and cheap) and enough electricity (and cheap enough) to be able to engage and succeed in the way of industrialization. The countries of West Africa, and tropical Africa in general have had to invest in education and other public goods after independence to approach a prospect of significant growth in the industry with highly labor-intensive, assuming that international competition allows.

Colonies "settler" had worse results in terms of poverty reduction, especially if one thinks of the mineral resources of South Africa and Southern Rhodesia, but better outcomes structural change. The use of coercion scale has laid the foundation for economies with whites, who eventually, especially in South Africa, being profitable enough to bring some success to an industrialization policy substitution in part motivated by political considerations imports. Rents from the exploitation of African workers were thus channeled towards structural change, although continuing the process has ended up causing own downfall and contributed to the fall of apartheid.

In their role as promoters of market institutions, colonial regimes have had very mixed results; but in all countries of sub-Saharan Africa, hired labor was probably much more abundant, sales of many more land and more people dependent on the broader market in 1960 until 1890 or 1900 A last legacy of the colonial period was a rather vague relationship with the colonial policy, the continued growth of population (total) since 1918 has gradually transformed ratios factors and overall economic advances the long-term potential of the continent .

"Industrialize" to a structurally transform in Africa

African economies have sustained unprecedented rates of growth in the past decade. This growth was mainly driven by exports of natural resources and commodities, improved macroeconomic management, a growing middle class, and increased domestic demand fuelled by consumption and increased political stability. However, Africa's growth has not been inclusive, as poverty rates and inequalities remain high. In order to foster growth inclusiveness, African economies should shift from low- to high-productivity activities and sectors. Therefore, Africa needs to sustain a structural transformation from a resource-based economy towards an industry- or service-based economy. Only a few African countries, including Mauritius, South Africa and Uganda, have succeeded in structurally transforming their economies. Other African countries experienced some degree of structural transformation following different paths and at different speeds. Some countries may transform through low-wage manufacturing while others may transform through services or the agricultural sector. Africa has experienced a delayed structural transformation: labor is not moving out of agriculture to other more productive industrial or services sectors fast enough and the share of agriculture in GDP is declining too fast. This was mainly explained by the lack of inclusive agricultural policies and the non-effective industrialization strategies of most African countries.

Structural economic change is indispensable to achieve the desired progress of Africa and to bring prosperity to the continent's populations. In order to alleviate poverty and reduce income inequalities, Africa will need to embrace structural transformation while maintaining robust economic growth. Fostering diversification through transition to high-productive sectors will be a catalyst for industrial upgrading and technological innovation which in turn will increase job creation. The path toward obtaining the status of middle-income and high-income countries will necessitate diversifying African economies away from dominant sectors such as agriculture and commodities.

Fostering structural transformation in Africa

Achieving structural transformation will involve a greater degree of industrialization of African economies. The agriculture sector should remain central to African economies in any process of transition. Fostering innovation and regional integration would also be very important for an effective transformation of the continent.

Africa's industrialization: For a successful structural transformation, the African continent needs industrialization to create jobs, increase incomes and foster economic diversification. A commodity-based industrialization could be very useful in assuring the success of Africa's structural transformation. In fact, using the endowment and potential of Africa in terms of natural resources to foster the industrial sector could be a more effective way to structurally transform the continent than focusing only on diversifying the economy away from commodities.

Agricultural development: The agricultural sector is a dominant economic sector in many African countries and employs a majority of Africa's population. It is a major source of revenue for households as well for savings and investments. African policy-makers should be aware that the transition toward an economy based on industry or services does not mean neglecting the strategic agricultural sector. Developing agriculture in Africa by industrializing it or by making it more innovative and more competitive is essential for eradicating food insecurity and hunger on the continent. Growing domestic demand for food in Africa is an opportunity to foster the role of the agricultural sector. Authorities in Africa should lower agricultural taxation, encourage the development of large-scale farming, and strengthening regional agriculture institutions.

Fostering innovation: Structural transformation requires innovation to overcome deficiencies in what regard infrastructural development. Good knowledge of industrial value chains and structures are prerequisite for an effective transformation of African economies. Investing continuously in education, training, improvement of skills and technological innovation is imperative to prepare the ground for a successful industrial transformation.

Innovation will help build the capacity to produce more sophisticated products with high added value.

Regional integration: The process of transition towards an economy based on industry and services cannot meet its targets without the mobilization of substantial resources. Despite the fact that most African countries are well endowed in terms of resources, these resources will not be sufficient for structural transformation. In this context, regional integration among African countries would be essential to mobilize the needed resources for the whole region. Regional integration will accelerate structural transformation through achieving economies of scale and enhancing competitiveness of African economies.

Structural Transformation: The Implications for the African Development Bank

Structural transformation is a central theme for the African Development Bank. For the Bank, transforming the economy of the continent involves expanding sources of growth and productivity to achieve an inclusive economic development. Fostering employment especially among young people and women could be achieved through structural transformation of African economies. The acceleration of economic transformation in Africa would be achieved by unlocking the potential of youthful population and boosting investments in innovation and new technologies. In order to achieve a smooth structural transformation, human development through education and training should be among the top priorities for Africa.

Also, empowering women and youth and strengthening governance institutions could further promote a structural transition towards high productivity activities on the continent.

The rationale for much of the current discourse of the "African Moment" and "Africa Rising" is clear. Some of the fastest growing economies in the world are African. Africa has shown relative buoyancy in an era of economic crisis. While global growth declined by 2.7% last year, Africa bucked the trend and grew at 5%. Notably, all our sub-regions grew faster than the global average, with the highest rate being 6.3% and lowest one 3.5%. This performance was due to several factors including improved macroeconomic management, increased exports of natural resources and a rising middle class. Lagos now has a larger consumer market than Mumbai and spending in continental households exceeding those of India and Russia.

This growth experience is however not sufficient. It falls short of 7% which is the minimum required to double average incomes in a decade. This is partly due to the fact that far too many of our economies are dependent on the production and export of primary commodities. Far too many are highly unequal. As we celebrate the fact that seven of our countries are in the top ten of global growth we must also bear in mind that a similar number are in the top ten of global inequality. Indeed, far too many of our people remain in the grip of unrelenting hunger and poverty.

Let me take an unconventional excursion through Asia before coming back to the issues before us today. Although we are aware of individual conflicts in Asia we tend to look at them in isolation. Thus in the Philippines we know of the conflicts in Mindanao, in Malaysia there is the Sabah insurgency; there are the border clashes between Thailand and Cambodia, and many others. Even rising India has the "Naxalite" insurgency and issues of Kashmir to attend to while South Korea sits on the border of a belligerent sister state.

Despite the widespread nature of these conflicts in Asia the region is not branded as unstable but rather seen as a dynamic contributor to global growth. It is true that in Africa we have conflicts such as exist in Mali, the Great Lakes Region, Sudan and Somalia but these are the remnants in a declining trend of conflict in Africa. In other words, though the trend of conflict in Africa is downward and the numbers are smaller than Asia, the global perception of Africa continues in many to be one of a continent beset by crisis and a risky place for making investments.

Let me give just two examples. There were about 29 piracy attacks in 2009 off the coast of Somalia as compared to 150 attacks in the Strait of Malacca in 2005. Yet this did not lead to generalized negative perceptions about Asia's economic prospects.

It should be noted in a similar context that despite its unstable business environment, Pakistan is the second largest textile exporter in the world.

There are many ways in which structural transformation can be defined but the sense in which I am using it here is the 'large scale transfer of resources from one sector to another due to changes in economic fundamentals and policies'. In an empirical sense, it means a significant change in the sectored composition of Gross Domestic

Product with the share of the primary sector in employment and output shifting to industry and modern services. It also implies a greater use of technology and increased productivity across sectors.

Africa desires structural transformation and not structural adjustment and industrialization is indispensible to this objective. Industrialization will help to generate employment, increase incomes and enable diversification, including their exports. This is evident from the experience of other regions.

Africa has attempted industrialization before. In the 1960s and 1970s, newly independent Africa emulated other regions of the world in undertaking import-substituting industrialization. It did lead to some remarkable progress but ultimately stymied by the limits of the model and global political economy. This is why Africa must today also be mindful of the current global context.

In this regard, one approach with prospects for success is commodity based industrialization. Thus, rather than exerting our energies on trying to diversify away from commodities, we should focus more on using them as effective drivers of industrialization. In addition to the broader benefits of industrialization, a commodity based approach offers immediate scope for value addition and plenty of opportunity for exploiting forward and backward linkages. Given the dominance of global value chains and intense cost competition in the trade in manufactures, Africa can gain entry into the industrial sector using its huge commodity and natural resources base. The fact that agro-processing is already one of the most developed manufacturing sectors in the continent is proof that this approach can work.

However, achieving success in this regard will not be easy. It will require innovation and the determination to overcome infrastructural deficiencies. It will require robust knowledge base of industry structure and global value chains. Indeed, our economies must continuously invest in knowledge, skills, technology and innovation. The trading landscape including barriers and preferences must be well understood. Above all, boosting intra-Africa trade remains imperative for creating the markets needed for successful industrialization.

As we celebrate the 50th anniversary of the establishment of the OAU, we must begin to ponder on the kind of society that we wish to bequeath to our children and grandchildren. Such clarity of vision must also be accompanied by a clear understanding of our historical experience, current context and policies required to attain our objectives in a rapidly changing global environment. It is in this regard that ECA is pleased to be working with the AU Commission and African Development Bank on an "Africa 2063" vision. It is our hope that this process will benefit from the insights of several vital constituencies including our leaders.

Needs & structural transformation in Africa

The starting point in my view is for a leadership that provides a clear vision and that mobilizes all sectors of society behind the development imperative. We have to change our approaches, attitudes, and priorities. We have to nurture a highly educated, healthy and skilled population that can imbibe the technology and build the infrastructure which is indispensable for progress. Our states must similarly strengthen bureaucratic capacity to undertake dynamic long-term planning and the coordination of economic activity.

For finance, we must begin to pay more attention to domestic resource mobilization while we accelerate the pace of regional integration to reap greater economies of scale. We will increasingly require more robust data and better statistical systems in order to better measure and monitor progress.

Indeed, the push for structural transformation will require that we make better use of Africa's economic strengths and enable all sectors of society, particularly women and youth to fulfill their role.

ECA's objective going forward would be to work closely with member States to achieve Africa's transformation agenda. ECA will undertake rigorous analytical thinking in areas of research where its research can make a difference. We will support member States in their efforts to implement growth oriented macroeconomic policies, and to restore development planning. This will be underpinned by the generation of high-quality data using latest technologies, including mobile and GIS.

ECA's mantra going forward will be 'Africa First'. By this we mean that we will put the interests of this continent first in all that we do. It also means that we will address emerging and other issues from the lens of their impact on Africa.

We must drive the process of structural transformation on the basis of our own vision and priorities. We must tell our own story and for this we must generate our own data and statistics.

This approach will define our partnerships across board as we seek to promote coherence and deepen the impact of our work. The time for action is now and if we do not take immediate steps, this window of opportunity may be lost for another generation.

Africa has been prohibited: industrial development

The first stage (1960-1970) saw the need for young African states to drive local firms producing consumer goods for the domestic market. This was the beginning of the industrialization of the continent.

Economic juggernaut created by former colonial powers discouraged this dynamic. Again, we had to import intermediate goods and capital goods that local industries need.

Whether bilateral or multilateral trade rules have significantly reduced the levers that could be used to promote industrial development in African countries, it does not belong to the group of least developed countries.

The fourth stage began in 2010 is that of the emergence of Africa. This phase is best summed up by Carlos Lopes, deputy secretary general of the United Nations and Executive Secretary of ECA: 'we must seize this opportunity to transform our continent as we have the wind in their sails.

Surveys of economic intelligence branch Knowdys show that manufacturing is the industry segment that offers the greatest number of opportunities in terms of exports, sustainable growth, employment and poverty reduction in Africa.

Afri-Industrialization

Africa has the means and resources to ensure its industrial, economic and social development. But the only problem is how.

But, fortunately for this Africa, there is an expert, who is now seen in the world of economists, as a scholar. This is the expert economist Consultant- Anikpo Daniel. His vision to transform Africa into an industrialized continent convinces many. The Malian government following recently, this proposed industrialization of the Ivorian expert, dispatched from Thursday, December 11, 2008, a delegation in Côte d'Ivoire.

'It is humiliating that young people die at sea', lamented Saturday, December 13, 2008, the Ivorian expert Anikpo Daniel, author of three publications (From challenge to African bet, the project company and participation) (the mega economy, Review development) and (household economy, the profitability of purchasing power (being edited)). Father PPDGA (First African global development program), the Ivorian Anikpo Daniel plans to build a set of industrialization programs. This is the result of 22 years of work and reflection.

This ambitious project aims to eventually create 150 national industrial captaincies producing capital goods and machinery for 1,000,000 small businesses cited business and household appliances to power households in villages and urban neighborhoods countries.

The PPDGA will, according to Daniel Anikpo terminate underdevelopment, unemployment and poverty and start a new era of prosperity. Animated by this hope of transforming Africa, mainly his country, Cote d'Ivoire, a city of industrial units, the expert continues to increase exchanges through conferences. All meetings with the population have always focused on the conditions to reach that machine vision dear to Africa. Considered as among economists as' the 21st century 'scholar', Daniel Anikpo whose theory of development does not move anyone in Abidjan, is courted. Become virtually a chartered economist Consultant-, the writings of the Ivorian constitute references.

Industrialization and development of "Côte d'Ivoire" & Africa.

In his theory, five (5) axes lead to the industrialization and development of Côte d'Ivoire and Africa. This is the Human Capital Formation, industrial takeoff, industrialization and agro-industrialization, Entrepreneurship, Shareholding, placement and direct self-employment, construction, urbanization and modernization and Banking services and local credit. For the first axis, the expert believes that the Ivorian Human Capital Formation is a prerequisite for industrialization because it is to defeat all forms of ignorance that block development through literacy, tutoring, managing the household economy, labor education, trades training, retraining ... the aim of forming human capital in this type of project is to allow it to carry trades and collective entrepreneurship participatory. The industrial take-industrialization and industrialization Agro for Anikpo Daniel, in turn, require the creation of 150 industrial captaincy for the manufacture of capital goods, and machinery, which will be needed

Cities business. For this type of project, the banking plays an important role. The expert announcement at this level, creating 10,000 local banks credit intended democratization of money and finance in favor of a million small businesses and industries of the city's business and local economies, but also of all households. A local bank credit is a set of 10 boxes supported by financial firms, households and organizations in the community. Local banks will credit available to the one million small businesses and industries and households, respectively two financial instruments, credit cards and commercial discount cards consumer credit. Clearly, the overall national development Anikpo Daniel is an anti-unemployment program and anti-poverty.

The Malian authorities Woo PPDGA Project PPDGA (First global program African Development) project interests at the highest level, the Malian authorities. This sent since Thursday, December 11, 2008, a delegation in "Côte d'Ivoire". In prospecting mission, it was during his stay, imbued with the reality on the ground for the evolution of the project PPDGA Ivorian Daniel Anikpo. Considering this project as a hope to get out of underdevelopment throughout Africa, Col. Suleiman Cisse, head of the Malian delegation, said that the industrialization of Africa depends on Africans. 'Nobody will come to Africa for us. It is up to us as Africans to do ', he has said during an awareness meeting at the City Hall of Abobo, the most populous town in Côte d'Ivoire. He railed against the fact that we go far for values elsewhere, while he has several 'next to us'. 'If the Ivory Coast is reluctant to take over the draft Anikpo Daniel, we will recover' said Mr. Daouda Ballo, a member of his delegation. Clearly, for the Republic of Mali, the theory of industrialization, Anikpo Daniel consistent with the vision of the authorities of that country, for the fight against poverty.

For the Malian delegation, 'we must create the conditions for a real take-off of the industrialization of Africa. Everything, she says, will prevent the youth to go on an adventure where she sometimes perished at sea.

Accelerate the industrialization of Africa

The African continent accounts for only 1.2% of world manufacturing value added, which is very low compared to its challenges. Hence the need to focus on African economies domestic requirements could raise the development of value chains. And it seems crucial for the continent to structure and industrial policies to raise capital to build modern and competitive industries. But how? And even go further?

There really urgent as Roland Portella, President of CADE and Developer business "The most urgent to do rather than building assembly plants and had the testimony of an engineer who said that we all skills to carry out this part, the problem now, the most urgent thing is to know organize production chains in order to have visibility like that when an investor is interested in an industry, it must be able to have more or less reliable data on all value chains, so the role of institutions is to give those looking to why these companies should refer while making corrections themselves by market research ... "

As emphasized throughout the course of the day in Africa, the industry is first to meet domestic food needs, pharmacy, consumer or building materials, it is in this context that industrialization is pledge of wealth creation and major sources of employment. Indeed, the simple production of raw materials and lettings are reaching their limits in terms of productivity. Service sectors will generate only very few jobs in relation to population growth, increasing urbanization and the influx of young people into the labor markets. Consumption needs and equipment will accelerate in the next 20 years. Tunisia, Morocco, Egypt, South Africa are the industrialized countries. Egypt, for example, exports of fertilizers, cables, textiles, electronic components, etc. Some countries such as Cameroon took the challenge to catch up by working on industrial growth sectors.

Jean-Marie Tallet is the delegate France GICAM and accountant of FISCOFIN he regularly works on these issues "the agro-industrial sector. This is the main growth area today as part of Cameroon we even spent second generation agriculture by launching the operation boss equals a plantation in encouraging entrepreneurs to turn to agriculture, it is agriculture which is also defended the concept of social responsibility, because it wants to develop Africa but do not forget the social values In business. If industrialization must be inclusive yet to identify industry leaders and financial and technical to put their "provisions just was well posed the question means that should the industrial development of Africa? This is clearly the private sector, with good leadership which means also with strategists people, but on the other hand it also needs strategists States, States that can provide a framework for industrial strategy for all components can integrate. "

For now, the rules of world trade still appear as obstacles to industrialization in Africa even though it is not yet in a phase where he was asked to be globally competitive. The real issue now is to find answers to a growing company. In these circumstances, it seems that regional integration must play its full role.

Considered one of the engines of economic development, industrialization in Africa is still lagging behind. According to a report released July 11, 2011 by UNCTAD, the continent accounts for more than a hundred of the world's manufacturing output and cannot objectively hope to reduce poverty if governments do not take effective measures to develop the sector economic.

The 2011 report on economic development in Africa, report prepared jointly by the United Nations Conference on Trade and Development (UNCTAD) and the United Nations Industrial Development Organization (UNIDO) entitled Fostering industrial development Africa in the new global environment (107 pages) advocates the adoption of a practical approach and well thought of industrialization. It must be adapted to the situation of each country and rely on numerous exchanges of views and information with the private sector and business leaders.

Africa has lost ground in manufacturing intensive labor activities that are usually the first stage of industrial development. These are essential in terms of job creation in the rapidly growing cities. The share of these activities in manufacturing value added (MVA) fell from 23% in 2000 to 20% in 2008, however, the continent is able to better stimulate manufacturing technology-intensive, especially in the field of chemistry. The share of medium-tech activities in MVA and high increased from 25-29% in the same period.

The report highlights that the level of industrialization and recent developments in the manufacturing sector are very different in the 53 African countries became 54 with the accession to independence of South Sudan. To stimulate development, the report continues, strategies "custom" must be adopted by each of the governments concerned. These would include support for entrepreneurs, using the state is needed to guide investments and business activities into areas considered essential for the long-term economic growth and job creation.

But aid should not be unlimited. It should even be suspended if the results - for example, the production of export goods competitive - not to go on time. Industrial policy should also be geared "to encourage the research process by the private sector so that it can find out what can be produced competitively."

Establish synergies with agriculture

Other recommended measures, consultation with local businesses, entrepreneurs and potential foreign investors, consultation may highlight the measures to stimulate industrial progress. Improved infrastructure - road, rail, electricity distribution - can be an important condition for growth especially in the manufacturing sector intensive labor. According to the report, a mechanism for monitoring, evaluation and accountability is also necessary to see what projects are walking, should be modified or abandoned.

UNCTAD warns, however: the development of the manufacturing sector should not be at the expense of the agricultural sector is an important source of revenue, employment and foreign exchange in the short to medium term. The UN organization therefore calls on African countries to establish synergistic links between agricultural and non-agricultural sectors of their economies.

The expansion of economic relations with neighboring countries

The report calls for measures to promote scientific and technological innovation and develop the capacity of governments to implement a consistent industrial policy with other macroeconomic policies to better contribute to development. In this context, it is advised African avoid overvalued exchange rate governments to make greater efforts to mobilize domestic resources to finance industrial development and adjust their monetary and fiscal policies to objective of industrial development.

Among other ingredients, according to UNCTAD, include not only the development of economic relations with neighboring countries, as regional markets can be a real customer for manufactured goods, but also political stability.

Data increasingly indicate that much industrial development offers significant opportunities in terms of sustainable growth, employment and poverty reduction. The organization points out those African governments have reiterated over the past decade, their political

Commitment to industrialization and adopted at national and regional level, several initiatives to strengthen the prospects of achieving their development goals.

Strengthen domestic savings

To go further, UNCTAD makes policy recommendations on how to promote industrial development in Africa in a global environment characterized by new international trade rules, a growing influence of industrial powers from the South, the internationalization of production and growing concerns about climate change. Including the promotion of scientific & technological innovation, training and education as well as access to credit and control of exchange rates so that they are not overstated.

African governments tend to focus on the allocation of resources rather than the mobilization of resources in the conduct of industrial policy. They should be strengthened by encouraging domestic savings, borrowing from finance institutions development, promoting foreign direct investment (FDI), taking advantage of opportunities for South-South as a source of financing for development and encouraging the traditional development partners to allocate more official development assistance (ODA) to promote industrial development in the region, the report says.

In 2009, manufactured goods accounted for about 40% of intra-African exports, while its share of Africa's exports to the rest of the world was approximately 18%. In addition, Africa is the region where the population and incomes rise fastest. Therefore, the continent is becoming a source of growing importance of export demand, which could help to initiate and maintain industrial development.

Following African news in recent years and watching closely the developments of the continent notorious contradictions of the political, economic and social situation in Africa we are obvious. Indeed, the continent seems to be moving at double speed. On the one hand, many Africans are no longer tolerate being constantly likened Africa to a land of violence, civil war, poverty, short ... all the worst evils which mankind can suffer. On the other hand, Africans continue to kill each other for reasons far from being the major concern of people.

Africa has the growth rate of GDP among the highest in the world (5% on average). But it is also in Africa that there has the highest poverty rate in the world with a population composed of a majority of poor and a wealthy minority.

In Africa the riches remain poorly distributed across the territories.

But the image of an Africa on the move, the continent that creates, innovates and this population that wants to move forward - which is true - is paid, worldwide, by young people, by great personalities and politicians , culture, sports and more. This is the case for example of the Senegalese singer Youssou Ndour who uses in its various concerts, his hit "New Africa" to denounce the classic image of a land of misery that the media give the Africa.

Unfortunately, what is happening on the continent, particularly in central Africa, this chips away completely different image of Africa trying to combat all forms of violence? It is true that it exists, that other Africa whose leaders wish to fight social inequality to put their country on the path of emergence. Meanwhile, the DRC, Joseph Kabila and his regime are weakened by bloody battles between the Republican army and rebels of M23. In CAR, the insurgents of Seleka eventually kneel this vast state whose management has got the best of the transitional president Michel Djotodia. For some time, the new state of South Sudan Salva Kiir is facing rebellion from his former Vice President Riek Machar.

Mali is meanwhile, is still fragile especially that jihadists North have not said their last word, despite the presence of the forces of Minusma. Faced with these cases, one is tempted to think that Alpha Blondy was right to say that "the enemies of Africa are the Africans."

below 6% by the end of 2014 Obviously, there With the soaring prices of mining, agriculture and energy sold to China but also to the development of a processing industry, the headwinds to global growth had little effect in 2013 of African economy and the pace of it is expected to accelerate in 2014 the growth rate is expected to 5% this year and 6% next year. More good news, the inflation rate announced is down for the third consecutive year, from are average. Like nowhere else in the world, there are great differences between convalescent Countries with spectacular growth rates like South Sudan (24.7% in 2013) and Sierra Leone (13.3%) and other dormant as the Central African Republic in the throes of civil war (-14.5%).

However, most companies have been slow to invest in Africa. Many of them assumed that this improvement was a reflection of a global boom in commodity prices, and thus had relevance primarily for oil and mining companies.

The recent political turmoil in countries such as DR Congo, Egypt, Libya, Morocco and Tunisia and the civil war in Ivory Coast leaders have dramatically reminded of the enormous uncertainty that businesses must face in Africa. With pro-democracy movements exploded in some of the fastest growing economies of Africa, multinational companies face a double bind: Some of the most promising countries present the highest risk.

This is not all. In Africa, infrastructure is almost non-existent, talent is scarce and the poverty, hunger and disease afflict and affect many countries. Most Western leaders, not sure about the size of consumer markets of Africa, prefer to invest in the economies of the dragon and the tiger of Asia rather than the lions of Africa.

"Is it really time to Africa?" They wonder.

McKinsey & Company conducted a study on the microeconomic situation of consumer markets in the continent. The objective was to identify the sources of growth of the economy, whether it is sustainable and represents opportunities size in sectors with high added value.

The results are surprising. During this decade, real GDP in Africa increased by 4.7% per year on average, twice the pace of growth in the 1980s and 1990s In 2012, the collective GDP of Africa $ 1.8 trillion was roughly equal to that of Brazil or Russia. The continent is among the economic regions in the fastest expansion today. In fact, Africa and Asia (excluding Japan) were the only continents that have developed during the recent global recession.

Although the rate of growth in Africa slowed to 2% in 2009, he rebounded by nearly 5% in 2010, and in 2011, it is likely to touch 5.2%.

While political unrest, war, natural disasters could benefit Africa down, the outlook for companies in terms of consumption which they will face are bright. Africans have spent 890 billion dollars on goods and services in 2008 to 35% more than the $ 665 billion that Indians have spent slightly more than the $ 851 billion in consumer spending in Russia. If Africa maintains its current growth trajectory, consumers will buy $ 1.4 trillion worth of goods and services in 2020, which is certainly a little less than India projected at $ 1.7 trillion, but more Russia's $ 960 billion. According to the Boston Consulting Group, companies like Nokia, Coca-Cola and Unilever are already achieving 10% of their sales in Africa, thanks to the growth of markets like Kenya, Ethiopia (80 million) and Nigeria (170 million).

DISABILITY WEIGHT OF DEBT

The trade deficits of the region are not alarming because they were funded by the inflow of foreign investments have tripled over the past decade and have enabled improved production capacity. Added to that the African debt levels remain historically low after debt relief granted by the creditor countries of the Paris Club.

Even the IMF disagrees against the idea that the strong growth in sub-Saharan Africa over the past decade is only linked to high commodity prices. Indeed many poor countries without natural resources have reached strong growth rates and sustainable over a longer period.

A report by the IMF analyzed a group of six countries in this category lack of mineral or petroleum resources champions: Burkina Faso (6.5%), Ethiopia (7%), Mozambique (+7 %), Rwanda (7.5%), Tanzania (+7%) and Uganda (5.4%). It identifies the common characteristics that explain, he said, their performance: macroeconomic policy progress, strengthened institutions, an increased development assistance and greater investment in physical and human capital.

VAST OPPORTUNITIES

Despite very different situations, related to development indices such as health (life expectancy increased by five months each year) and education (enrollment in secondary education, although still insufficient, increased 50% in ten years) open opportunities in sectors such as retail, telecommunications (one in four Africans has a mobile phone), banks, industries related to infrastructure, businesses related to the operation natural resources, and throughout the agricultural value chain.

Consider that telecommunications companies in Africa have added 378 million subscribers, more than the entire American population since 2000 is a sign of the vitality of this sector. According to UN data, Africa offers a higher price than any other emerging market return on investment. For several reasons: the competition is less intense and only a few foreign companies have a physical presence, and has long pent-up consumer is strong.

Thirteen years ago, when South Africa hosted the FIFA World Cup, a sentence Tswanian, Ke Nako "It's time," echoed through the world as the cacophony of a million vuvuzelas, announcing that the when Africa had come.

For the first time since the start of the financial crisis, global growth seems to really leave this time, the start seems more assured. World trade is accelerating since the end of the summer, both on the side of the emerging and the side of developed countries.

ASIA: LOCOMOTIVE GLOBAL GROWTH

This is the area that offers the best guarantee of economic growth. For 20 years, the continent is home to nearly two thirds of the world population began with extraordinary vigor economic catch-up. Hundreds of millions of people freed themselves from extreme poverty and although much remains to be done, Asia can boast of yet for the New Year the engine of global growth.

China clearly remains the locomotive of such a forward movement that even the 2008 crisis, which continues even today, seems to stop. With a double-digit growth for 30 years, the Middle Kingdom was the envy of the Europeans and Americans behind. Between 2005 and 2010, China alone has been the main engine of global growth by contributing up to 50%! It remains an economic leader in times of crisis but the giant has lost its luster for several semesters.

GDP grew by only 7.7% for 2013 and IMF projections for 2014 are dim barely 6.9%. Which is a real tragedy for a continent country needs a growth of 10% to maintain its precarious social balance.

Concern also its trading partners who have fewer opportunities as a result. Japan its first Asian partner suffers from this, but the ills faced by the Japanese are deeper and serious than a simple withdrawal of Chinese demand.

To revive its economy through foreign trade, the country of the Rising Sun has opted for a drastic devaluation of its currency.

With a 20% fall in the yen in six months, Japanese products are exported more easily but this policy for the time hailed by Japanese has a limit.

The cost of increasingly important, first that the country has to import materials.

Oil and gas have become mechanically more expensive due to the depreciation of the Japanese currency. However, this devaluation will be a boon for exports from countries in coping with global demand that is now leaving. According to the IMF, Asia, leading market of Japan, is expected to grow 5.7% in 2014 (a figure that is expected to be over by HSBC) .Notwithstanding a debt equivalent to 245% of its GDP. Besides, Greece pales with a "small" debt representing 157% of GDP ... the three "arrows" accommodative monetary-political, public expenditure, promises of structural reforms - to support the economy, will give their full effectiveness. And it's no coincidence that on December 26 the Tokyo Stock Exchange has registered its biggest gain in 40 years.

RESTORE AMERICA CONFIRMS

The United States faces the same challenge of debt. With 17,000 billion of debt, even printing money does not seem effective enough to ensure the back of Uncle Sam. To return beneath less than 100% of GDP debt, the united States out the ultimate weapon: a new system for calculating the much better growth. In other words, a thermometer indicating fever another by less sensitive to heat is replaced. This farce should give the paper a breath of fresh air to the American economy with growth that will mechanically increase by 2%. The announcement two weeks ago during his farewell press conference, President Ben Bernanke announced that the central bank will reduce its purchases of assets of $ 85 billion to $ 75 billion per month, combined with the promise of the Fed to keep rates low for as long reacted positively markets.

Still, analysts are applying for a stronger outlook for 2014 what has also led the IMF to raise its growth forecast upwards .This optimism is due to the good figures of the American economy with particular latest statistics on unemployment (which fell below 7% at its lowest for five years) and good signs from the Congress and the Central Bank.

EUROPE: SIGNS OF IMPROVEMENT

The euro zone is still the weak link in rich countries. Unemployment remains dangerously high, particularly in France with 10.9% unemployment rate and 12.5% in Italy and activity continues to disappoint. But Spain and Ireland, two of the most affected by the crisis, are recovering. They have a mountain of debt to pay off, but at least they started shrinking.

Further south, the country restored through drastic cuts their current accounts and finally seem to come out of their long slump, including Greece the worst student at the origin of the crisis, which has come back to the bond markets in 2014 if it succeeds in its primary budget surplus make (excluding debt service), and if renewed growth.

The banking union project he concludes there's one week, with a compromise on the device management failures combined bank's announcement of the European Central Bank reaffirmed its option for low interest rates allow the old continent to catch his breath.

But the big challenge for the bloc of euro countries is to clean up their banking system. This is what poses the biggest threats to global finance and the economy

AFRICA: A CONTINENT GROWING ECONOMIC

The continent is still marked by the stigma of poverty and vulnerability. Even if growth is to be sustained for even more dynamic start firstly a virtuous circle which enable the continent out of underdevelopment and to transform the structure of its economy on the other. The deal includes the changing rapidly and radically as to become a market and a key partner for the economies of the South.

The median income of African households increased by 19% in 2011 and the African middle class is expected to grow 25% by 2020 according to research from Credit Suisse, which states that only India and Latin America have achieved higher performance during the same period. The reasons for this have recently been detailed in a report by the World Bank.

According to this study, the economic takeoff of Africa has four main causes: first, the continent is currently operating its demographic transition with a young population, with life expectancy increases. Then the ongoing urbanization of the continent is one of the conditions in the long-term, industrialization of the continent.

Third, access to new technologies is exploding in Africa much higher than elsewhere (in ten years, Africa has for example from 0.7% to 70% of mobile phone users) pace. Finally, governance has improved significantly in recent years as evidenced by the growing attraction of international capital markets for African sovereign debt.

All of which indicates that if Africa continues on this path, most African countries will be a middle income country by 2030 a reality that the West has difficulty perceiving, but emerging grasp the full significance: the structure the African economy in 2013 looks a lot like that of China and India in the 1980s and 1990s.

It is no coincidence that foreign direct investment to the continent have increased 50% since 2005 (especially from Brics) and if JP Morgan has recently integrate Nigerian Treasury Bills in its index of emerging markets. The sluggishness in Europe and the United States, the markets have confidence in the take-off of Africa.

A fact all the more obvious as rising living standards Brics opening up huge possibilities for Africa's industrial development.

For the Brics are still developing, they need the emergence of Africa and its billion consumers.

Africa does not develop

Does a truism make Africa is a rich continent, as it is rich in natural resources. Even if they are not inexhaustible, Africa is still rich in arable land and much of its human resources. And yet, she is struggling to develop -it the least we can say.

Rather than learn from the successes and failures of development models that have been tested around the world, it continues to be mired in its sterile policies. Several key factors are the cause of this situation.

Bankruptcy Policy

Since the end of colonialism, nearly all African countries were led by elite without political vision for the medium to long term. These elite, which has replaced the former colonizers, was incapable of ambition and is more concerned about her than she claims to defend people's interests. Result: the colonial system was simply perpetuated in another form in the political, economic and cultural fields over the years. To this must be added the uncertainty of the economic environment that is not conducive to investment, and the reign of the informal sector.

Independence has become an addiction vis-à-vis foreign power, especially former colonial powers. Lack of endogenous or forward thinking and political will to initiate change by a synergy of actions, current policies are a visual navigation. States are managed by the week by the leaders, just long enough to accomplish the high charges they face.

The consumer market

There is no better consumer market as Africa. This is what we call, with some humor, in many African countries "universal recipients." How can we develop when we eat anything that comes from the outside without distinction and that produces nothing, or not much?

The irony is that many Africans have the quaint complex of foreign preference. Even when what is produced locally is much better than what is imported. Extraversion is not only an economic phenomenon, but also cultural. This trend must be reversed by the creation and quality research, so that African products can compete internationally.

Africa must not only be a consumer market -although the contrary, it has every incentive to engage in all-out production. Indeed, Africans have yet to prove, as it were, they did not play that banjo.

The neglect of agriculture

Agriculture has always been ranked at the bottom of human activities in Africa. The farmer is considered a second-class citizen. It is less than nothing. Most Africans want to be committed to the state. Paradoxical as it may seem, all African countries make agriculture the basis of development. But yet they do nothing to develop this agriculture. And that's not a euphemism.

It must be said, from the time of the stone, Africa has replaced the agricultural tool by iron. Nothing more. It is not with the hoe and hoe that Africa can make nutritionally self-sufficient before speaking to expand its agriculture for the purpose of marketing or processing. As the results of investments in this sector are obtained in the medium to long term, this is of little interest to foreign investors and the states themselves.

However, this applies almost all of the continent's population. With rapid population growth and climate change which is increasing year by year, traditional farming means can no longer feed the many mouths of the continent until they evolve. And a hungry man is a man who does not think, and therefore does not give itself the means of its development.

The inadequacy of the education system

More than fifty years after independence of most African countries, the education system has still not adapted to the realities of today's world and the evolution of African societies. Elementary education is still a luxury for most. And higher education is shaped largely as unemployed graduates, unable to undertake or to be integrated into the workforce as soon as they leave their training.

Unfortunately, in this context, technical and vocational education should be given priority remains the poor relation of the African education system. This is a critical development issues in Africa which should absolutely provide a suitable solution.

The socio-political instability

You can count on the fingers of one hand the African countries that can boast of having had a long political stability. Now this is a sine qua non of development. Africa suffers from the weakness of its social and political organization. So much so that the combination of internal and external conflicts voracious appetites of some of its wealth is not to insure against crises of varying severity.

One reason for this chronic, recurrent instability is difficult to learn the principles of democracy. They come to power, at worst by a coup, dynastic succession or at best by quite democratic elections, the African heads of state usually end up succumbing to the temptation of dictatorship. With the lack of republican armies, corruption, illiteracy of much of the people, clienteles, the cult of personality, and many others. All things that generate socio-political conflicts. Unconsciously or not, African peoples are themselves factories dictators.

Corruption

Corruption is a scourge in Africa, particularly affecting elites. In the absence of individual or collective initiatives of production of wealth, the state remains the only cash cow. Politics is thus the largest provider of jobs and the only way to get rich is lawful or unlawful without working. This situation inhibits any initiative and transforms some state employees, but especially those who are in power or close, in real leeches. Economies are suddenly gangrene.

If money goes up in smoke by corruption was actually invested for populations, Africa would have made a great leap forward on the path of development. But refuses to make money without working? They are not numerous, these servants and politicians in Africa. Today, they are unfortunately like human species endangered.

Good governance is not the strongest of the African leaders. Rather, it is what keeps them in power by holding elections rigged in advance by purchasing awareness not only of voters mostly illiterate, but also those who organize the elections. When

They are not altogether, worthy representatives of foreign economic and political groups that is firing on all cylinders for this purpose.

The outbreak of war in Mali and earlier events in CAR and Congo recall that Africa made the news in case of war. This feeds the stereotypes on the African continent, filled with hungry stomach bloated and face covered in flies, wild-eyed ragged soldiers who only think of rape, women raped and children circumcised: an entire continent living in grinding poverty and hunger, ethnic and religious conflict, and despair, sweetened by aid groups, but maintained by multinational corporations and international financial institutions.

To balance the picture, it will be assumed that there may be periods of economic growth (as in recent years) but they are short lived and do not benefit the majority of the population, as it depends only of an increase in the price of raw materials exported by African countries; When prices will collapse, poverty will return. GDP statistics confirm this stagnation of Africa over the long term, with strong fluctuations associated with the value of exports.

Statistical illusion

There is only one problem with this story: it is probably wrong, because it is based on false data. Any action has a margin of error, and the calculation of GDP is no exception. But in many African countries, the establishment of national economic statistics suffers from a range of significant bias, especially analyzed by economist Morten Jerven whose forthcoming book illustrates this post soon.

National accounts in Africa do not have the same quality information for all sectors. Industry, energy production, provide reliable data about; similarly, export activities are fairly well measured, in part because they are often controlled by a single national public company, and the compilation of statistics is facilitated by the fact that foreign trade passes through some Points well identified: ports, airports and border posts.

By cons, information is lacking for a variety of activities: agricultural production consumed in the country (many countries do not have to register, making it impossible for the accurate identification of agricultural land), much of the sector services, the informal economy. For all these areas, information is expensive, requires a staff that is not available the statistical bureaus of individual countries. The evaluation is not done very often.

Result, to estimate the GDP and its evolution, statisticians rely on a base year, during which they prepared better data (for example, because a more comprehensive study was conducted that year). Then we will apply the changes measured with very patchy in the economic structure of the base year to estimate the growth data.

This generates systematic biases: the export sector, better assessed, is overweight to the extent of the national GDP; especially, economic growth is systematically undervalued because that based on the economic structure of the country for a base year, all new industries are neglected. The most striking example is that of Ghana. The base year for its statistical purposes was 1993; gold, since, for example, the telecom sector has exploded from 50,000 lines throughout the country with a mobile phone penetration rate in 75% in a country of 20 million people. Now as telecom hardly represents anything in 1993, the growth of this sector is totally missed out on national statistics. Result, when Ghana made a new comprehensive assessment of GDP in 2010, this resulted in raising the per capita GDP of the country by 60%, passing in a day status of middle-income countries.

Further revisions of GDP are underway, including Nigeria and Kenya. The magnitude of the corrections to come will probably similar to these countries: 60 to 100%. The GDP of African countries is highly underestimated. Added to this the fact that the calculation of GDP per capital also depends on knowledge of demographic trends, and that the census itself suffers serious bias. Result: the per capita GDP of African countries is so biased that it is practically meaningless.

What we think? We know is wrong

 In short, all the speeches on Africa are at least partly based on totally false statistics. For decades, there is no shortage of analysis about why the African continent economically stagnant: institutions, weight of colonialism, corruption, conflict societies because borders do not respect the ethnic, dependence on raw materials, etc, etc. All these explanations of African stagnation, based on the statistical comparison between the growths of different countries have only one problem: the African stagnation of recent decades is a statistical illusion.

This illusion persists because it suits many people. Development economists, who have spent their careers analyzing the path differences and explain the African underdevelopment, did not really want to recognize that all their work has been in the commentary that statistical noise. Recipient governments of international aid did not really want to acknowledge that their country is more prosperous than previously believed, as this may reduce the flow of significant help to the state budget; Donors did not really want to admit that their allocation of international aid decisions were based on completely false statistics; and few people really want to change their ideas about Africa. The revision of the GDP of Ghana in 2010, his accession to the status of middle-income countries, is totally unnoticed: it does not fit the image of a continent ravaged by war and misery continent. While the French army is engaged in a new conflict in Africa, it does not necessarily need to remember the extent of our ignorance.And if, for African economies, after the crisis was time to recovery?

After a difficult year in 2009, the continent is expected to grow by around 4.3% in 2010, three times better than last year. These are the projections of UN economists contained in their recent report entitled "Status and Prospects of the global economy in 2010." "The prevailing sentiment on the continent is that the worst of the economic and financial crisis is behind us and signs of recovery are beginning to appear," note the authors.

At a time when there are credible signs of recovery in the global economy - the result of the tax measures implemented worldwide and to stimulate economies - Africa should be among the areas forecast to have the highest rates growth in 2010 only the region of South Asia and East at 6.4%, should outpace the continent. By comparison, growth in the euro zone will fall to 0.4% and will be 3.4% in Latin America. According to the UN economists, South Africa - the first African economic power - will perform better than Brazil, while Nigeria - the continent's second largest economy - will outperform Mexico.

Overall, the economic recovery in Africa depends primarily on the global recovery. The continent will benefit from stimulus packages that have contributed to the recovery of world consumption. In turn, the latter is expected to grow the demand for oil and minerals, favoring African exporters of these products. In addition, the continent should benefit from gradual recovery inflows of foreign direct investment (FDI).

However, beyond the forecast for the near future, the report - produced jointly by the Division of Economic and Social Affairs of the United Nations (DESA), the UN Conference on Trade and

Development (UNCTAD) and the five commission's regional Economic UN - suggests that the global economic crisis will have long-term effects. Unemployment and underemployment remain at levels of concern, affecting especially women and youth. The food prices are expected to further rise in East Africa.

Moreover, the report notes that the large and persistent dependence of most African economies export commodity represents a major structural risk to economic growth. This, they point out; they are vulnerable to fluctuations in demand and prices of commodities.

"2009" A lost year

The UN report also points out that, despite the recovery, the continent's economies do not fully realize their potential in 2010, although he notes that the past year was particularly difficult. By registering a growth rate of around 1.6% in 2009, the continent has dropped significantly. Between 2002 and 2008, in fact, annual growth was 5.7% on average.

The African region of the East - which recorded the highest growth rate in 2009 - reached only 3.8%. Southern Africa fell to 1.7%, realizing the worst regional performance. The West Africa and North Africa are more resilient, with respective growth rates of 2.4% and 3.5%.

The year was even more difficult for major African oil exporters. Growth in Angola and Equatorial Guinea has risen from an average of 16% between 2004 and 2008, to 0.2% and -3.4% respectively. Exporters of agricultural products have experienced a less pronounced slowdown. Liberia, Malawi and Uganda have recorded growth rates being above average. Taking advantage of a balance between the decline in oil revenues and in particular the increase in agricultural exports, Nigeria's economy grew by 1.9%.

In 2009, foreign direct investment flows (FDI) into Africa were also down. Rwanda has only exception to this trend.

With the exception of Ghana and some other African countries that have managed to maintain fiscal balance, the crisis has had a negative impact on the budgets of most African countries.

Echoing the complaints of several African governments on the disastrous consequences of the global crisis on their countries, the UN report notes that 2009 marks a challenge unwelcome social and economic advances made hard to reduce poverty and achieve the Millennium development goals (MDGs).

Limited impact

Even though the crisis has hit the African continent, its relatively limited integration in the global financial system saved him suffers more. Only richest and most connected to global markets in the image of South Africa have experienced a sharp decline in per capita income. A situation that is not experienced the low-income countries. Like other parts of the developing world, Africa has been hit by the global recession through trade. This was the case especially for energy exporters, minerals and manufactured goods.

Finally, let'snote that while the continent has been able to cope with the crisis, it is also due to the conservative options were preferred economic policy long before the outbreak of the crisis. So, they conclude, Africa was in crisis in a more favorable tax position than before.

Africa: the heist of the century

This is the "heist of the century." Every year, poor countries would be deprived of "at least one trillion dollars (750 billion Euros)," because of money laundering, corruption and other fraud. In a report released Wednesday, the British ONE organization founded by Bono condemns these illegal activities and opaque, which "rob" developing countries.

In terms of revenue, these losses represent at least 38 to 62,000,000,000 dollars. A sum that governments should, according to the director of ONE France Friederike Röder, to invest in the "health care, food security and critical infrastructure," which would "avoid the deaths of 3.6 million people in the poorest countries every year. "

In sub-Saharan Africa, ONE ensures that the eradication of these diversions of money could fund the education of 10 million more children per year, 500,000 additional teachers, antiretroviral drugs (ARVs) to more than 11 million people affected by HIV, and nearly 165 million vaccines.

On the eve of the meeting of G20 finance ministers under the objective of global growth, which will be held on 20 and 21 September in Australia, ONE asks the group of world powers react. "Simple and inexpensive measures" are expected. They will, according to the organization, "reclaim revenue from authors of tax fraud and creating new economic opportunities."

Specifically, the organization is calling on world leaders to act on four specific points. A "struggle against the opacity of front companies," opening amount of data, including the real owners of corporations and trusts should be established. There is also demand respect for "global standards for transparency in the exploitation of natural resources," requiring companies to disclose all information about their payments to governments. To fight against tax evasion, ONE also calls for automatic exchange of tax information mandatory for all businesses and accessible everywhere. Finally, the organization wants better access to information and data for citizens, allowing them to control the use of public resources.

These measures should also benefit developed countries. September 02, 2014, Spain declared indeed have recovered € 28 billion from financing in 2012 of a plan against tax evasion, described as "evil" slowing economic recovery.

Global Competitiveness: Africa can do better

For the fifth consecutive year, the overall Competitiveness Index (Global Competitiveness Index -GCI) puts Switzerland in the lead. Singapore and Finland continue to appear respectively in second and third position. In the African camp, significant efforts are still needed to improve competitiveness in the area of economic diversification. However, the index GCI distributes special mentions in Mauritius,

Kenya and welcomes the progress of Algeria and Tunisia. (See below for the top 10 most competitive African countries in 2014)

In sub-Saharan Africa, Mauritius (45th) than South Africa (53) and becomes the most competitive economy in the region. Only eight countries in sub-Saharan Africa are among the first hundred. Considerable efforts in all areas are needed to improve the competitiveness of Africa. Among low-income countries, Kenya (96th) shows the largest increase, gaining 10 positions. Nigeria (120th) remains at the bottom of ranking, illustrating the urgent need for the country to diversify its economy.

Middle East and North Africa, Qatar (13th) ranks first in the region, while the United Arab Emirates (19th) for the first time between the top 20 Saudi Arabia (20th) fell two places but is still among the top twenty. Israel moves to 27th position. Egypt (118th) continues its decline and lost 11 seats compared to the index last year. Bahrain (43), Jordan (68th) and Morocco (77th) also retreated. In the region, Algeria advance to the 100th place and Tunisia reinstates the rankings at the 83rd spot.

Some of the major emerging countries should also encourage their private and public and civil society to implement the necessary reforms sectors. Of the five BRICS countries, the People's Republic of China (29th) remains well ahead, followed by South Africa, Brazil (56th), India (60th) and Russia (64th). Only Russia manages to advance, winning three seats. Conversely, Brazil lost eight seats. Among Asian economies, Indonesia jumped twelve places to reach 38th place, making it the country that experienced the largest increase among the G20 economies since 2006, while South Korea (25th) fell by six places. Singapore, Hong Kong, Japan and Taiwan (China) (12th) all rank among the top twenty nations. Asian developing countries have very mixed results and diverging trends: Malaysia Ranked 24th, while countries such as Nepal (117th), Pakistan (133rd) and Timor-Leste (138th) are among the last of ranking. Bhutan (109th), Laos (81) and Myanmar (139th) are first in the standings.

Despite strong economic growth in recent years, Latin America continues to have low productivity. Thus, a general stagnation in performance is observed in terms of competitiveness. Chile (34th) continues to lead the region to Panama (40th), Costa Rica (54th) and Mexico (55th). Their positions remain almost unchanged. "Innovation is becoming increasingly critical in determining the ability of a country to ensure its future prosperity," said Klaus Schwab, Founder and Executive Chairman of the World Economic Forum. "I anticipate that the traditional distinction between 'developed' and 'less developed' will gradually subside. In future we will talk about their innovation - rich and poor countries in terms of innovation. Therefore, it is essential for leaders in business, politics and civil society to collaborate and develop training systems and the conditions for innovation. "And Xavier Sala-i-Martin, Professor of Economics at Columbia University in the United States has added:" The report highlights the changing priorities over there for another year, when s was stopgap. Now the urgency is to implement structural reforms.

Finally, the United States remains a global leader in innovation of products and services. Their progress in the ranking is due to a perceived improvement in financial markets and greater confidence vis-à-vis public institutions. However, concerns remain about their stability Macroeconomic, ranked 117th out of 148 in Europe's efforts to fight against public debt and the breakup of the euro have diverted attention from the more fundamental and structural problems associated with competitiveness. Southern countries, including Spain (35th) and Italy (49th), Portugal (51) and especially Greece (91st) will remedy the inefficiencies and flexibility of their markets, promoting innovation and improve access to finance in order to improve the competitiveness of the whole region.

Africa to conquer the Vietnamese market

Africa has waited 50 years to reach its economic puberty. Today, his guards have African roots, German thoroughness, the soft US citizen power and working power of Chinese workers. They only treat the emergency. For the rest, see a GP.

Half-dozen years of intensive sensitization, backed interesting growth figures, helped to turn the radar of global economic decision-makers to Africa. It was not easy as perceptions die hard. The last annual conference of Bank of America-Merrill Lynch, January 28, 2014 in Paris, did not mention once Africa ... But analysts will not mark down time to digest these first results as a phenomenon is emerging: the arrival of new "experts in African markets."

Strategists raptors, to broken arms, and those who have failed in Asia, America and Europe ... many are rushing to Africa, "the continent of all possible", "new frontier of global growth "," virgin market ", etc. These new "experts of Africa" you on the mainland, since their smart phone, thanks to the genius of Google News, to the dismay of their customers. But for how long? "Lying gives flowers but no fruit," warns African wisdom.

Africa has waited fifty years to reach its economic puberty. It does not pass through several decades of slavery to be swallowed by small-time opportunists. It is mainly for this reason that some Africa will remain dangerous for individuals and legal entities that the time to draw in Africa because the rope is well ... The harsh reality on the ground, or rather the creative destruction of Schumpeter, the Malawian sauce, always remind them that "he who wishes the rain must also accept the mud."

Today, the keepers of the African economy exist. 7/7, they respond to requests for short-term economic, market research, due diligence, research partnerships or international lobbying. What are they recognized? They have African roots, German thoroughness, the soft US citizen power and working power of Chinese workers. They only treat the emergency. They have worked to ensure that Africa is now the center of world attention.

"If you see a turtle resting on a wall, is that we put it there," they say.

Their ability to deal effectively with African issues, which do not attract serious customers. It also arouses the lust of the new "experts" mentioned above. But "If you lick the language of the lion, he devours you," warned the Maasai. Easy French, we paraphrase the warning Professor Ababacar Mbengue, former HEC Paris and Associate in Management, in his remarks March 1 2014: "Do not just entertain. Despite the humility, there is sharp here and recognized experts in their fields. It does not tell us. "

China to develop the Telecoms

In 2004, it took several dollars for a one-minute call to Ghana. Today, simply pay 0.1 dollars. The development of the telecommunications market in Ghana, how elsewhere in Africa, is not comparable to the past, thanks to the benefits of Chinese companies.

The telecommunications industry has developed rapidly in Africa in recent years, with a growing number of users and a drop in Internet costs. Behind this, one can see the tremendous work of Chinese enterprises. "China allows better development of this industry in Africa," revealed Dr. Hamadoun Toure, Secretary General of the International Telecommunications Association. In 2012, the number of mobile telephone subscribers reached 761 million in 2012, which made Africa the market with the fastest growing in the world. A number that is expected to reach more than one billion in 2015, while in 2020 80% of Africans have access to the Internet, according to the forecasts of the Conference of information and telecommunication technologies in Africa, was held last year.

What are the reasons for this rapid growth? In addition to the rapid development of the African economy and supports and subsidies granted by foreign countries, reforming the Telecommunications conducted in several countries, the opening of the market and the entry of international giants in this sector are the factors most important to remember. According to the newspaper "East African", world leaders, including Nokia, Simens and Vodafone have installed all research centers and subsidiaries across Africa. The continent is also become the target of telecom companies in India, Japan and Brazil. For example, Etisalat (Emirates Telecommunications Corporation) plans to invest $ 400 million in 2013 in Nigeria to advance the Internet in the country.

"We need the development of telecommunications in Africa, in partnership with Chinese companies in recent owns half share of the African market as a supplier. In some African countries, the rate is as high as 70%, "said Zhao Houlin, Deputy Secretary General of the International Telecommunications Association. It is through collaboration with China as telecommunications in Africa have undergone great changes, recognizes M.Mwendanga, professor at the University of the Democratic Republic of Congo. A government official in South Africa told that China has helped to promote not only the telecommunications industry, but also to help developed the economic and social environment of the continent. Chinese companies have played a major role in Africa in poverty reduction, agriculture, promotion of equality ENTERED sex, and the fight against climate change.

According to a report released in 2011 by an American body, Chinese groups have broken the monopoly held in Africa for ages, by the giants of Western telecoms. They helped to bring down the cost of communications, where great contributions to the industry. Investment from China has really helped real development, which directly benefited the African people. According to Zhu Ma, professor at Harvard University, Chinese companies have provided expertise in Africa, offering advanced technology, which has gradually raised the added value of African products.

Africa and its competitiveness

If the public and private sectors in Africa do not provide proactive goods and services advanced in the world market, the continent will be converted into a net supplier of raw materials and services essential good market for the production of goods and services value-added provided by others in return.

To do this, African universities must invest in research to enable them to contribute significantly to global leadership, technology transfer and participate beneficially in world affairs. If the public and private sectors in Africa do not provide proactive goods and services advanced in the world market, the continent will be converted into a net supplier of raw materials and services essential good market for the production of goods and services to added value provided by others in return.

Despite being one of the best endowed in natural resources continent, the average GDP per capita (nominal) for the period 1990-2010 was very thin, against USD 1,560 USD 16,837 global average, according to the World Bank . Power consumption of the continent is extremely low, at 3.1% of global energy consumption.

The world rankings Times of Universities 2012-2013 show that among the 400 best universities in the world, only four are African (all located in South Africa). 131 are in North America, three are

South American, 57 are Asian, 180 are European and 25 in Oceania. Outside of South Africa, no African university is among the 400 best in the world. This means that most African countries do not issue global leadership competency or technology or expertise to maximize the positive participation of Africa in the global knowledge economy.

It is important that the continent draws from regional cooperation to increase the capital base for the establishment of world-class universities on the African continent, collectively owned and operated by African countries. They attract the best trainers worldwide and / or class researchers and lead to the listing of the best talent from all African countries and the world eventually reaching a higher level of competitiveness at the hemispheric and global scales.

The deterioration of the competitiveness of many African universities was also due to the retirement of trainers and researchers who have studied undergraduate universities world class. Their places are taken by their freshly come from local universities who are not world-class counterparts. The preference of human resources for trainers and researchers cheap but inferior to their more expensive counterparts, but world-class should also be reversed. African higher education institutions need to think long term and stop compromising their competitiveness.

The continued expansion of existing universities and the establishment of new institutions at the expense of providing a quality education must also be reversed. Not doing so would be to encourage the increase of graduates who cannot get a job related to their studies in the world market because they are not sufficiently qualified.

Create mechanisms to identify the best young African talent in high schools and allow them to do their undergraduate work in world-class universities by helping them get admissions and scholarships needed boost tendency for learners competitive. Parents who can afford it should also be encouraged to sponsor talented African students to enable them to do their undergraduate studies in the top universities in the world. African governments and universities should also work with key private sector in Africa to define how they could work together to develop into world-class universities.

THE HIGHLIGHTS:

- The growth enjoyed by Africa has not yet had an impact on widespread poverty.

- A new report on the competitiveness of Africa because of the collaboration between public and private sector one of the key factors for shared prosperity.

-This Means improving access to finance for businesses and infrastructure building.

African economies experiencing a growth rate well above 5%. All observers seem to agree on the continued growth amid global recession, although the 2013 report on African competitiveness tempers this optimism and warns against a number of persistent challenges.

A new challenge

Overall, the sustained growth on the continent has not led to any significant increase in the living standards of Africans. The World Bank estimates that 48.5% of the population of sub-Saharan Africa is still condemned to survive on less than $ 1.25 a day. Job creation fails to keep pace with the population explosion: the continent has surpassed the 1 billion people (15% of the world population) and the population is expected to increase by 20% to horizon of 2030 with the decline in labor productivity and stagnation of virtually all manufacturing industries since the 1970s, many African countries are lagging behind in international competitiveness.

The path of public-private collaboration for inclusive and sustainable growth:

The Competitiveness Report launched on May 9 at the World Economic Forum in Cape Town (South Africa) reveals that 14 of the 20 least competitive economies in the world are African. To embark on the path of sustainable growth and shared prosperity, African countries need to improve their institutions and infrastructure, deepen regional integration and ensure a quality education for their citizens. Collaboration between public and private sector represents a vital engine.

By establishing the legal, regulatory and economic frameworks right, governments can lay the foundations for an enabling environment for businesses, allowing them to flourish and paving the way for regional integration. For young African acquire skills and knowledge that will enable them to become competitive in the global economy, increase investment in science and innovation and give greater priority to skills development and training. It is a more pressing as the number of 15-24 year olds now stands at 200 million across the continent obligation accordingly.

Investing in infrastructure

Of better roads, more efficient ports or a more reliable electric grid are among the many infrastructure improvements needed to make the country more attractive to investors which depends creating jobs. In addition, Africa has lagged behind in terms of technology. However, information technology and communication (ICT) have become an indispensable tool to increase efficiency and foster innovation. African economies must eventually not only invest in ICT infrastructure but also make their independent citizens through training in best use of these technologies for productive purposes.

The private sector is no exception: companies can support reform and advocate for measures that strengthen competitiveness at the national level while providing support for initiatives to facilitate cross-border trade. Public-private partnerships can also generate new approaches to competitiveness.

"African countries are now seeking to improve their competitiveness and test new approaches - such as growth poles - to stimulate investment and sustainable growth," says GAIV Tata, head of the Finance sector and private sector development in of the Africa Region of the World Bank. "Expanding access and entry into the African regional markets can support the creation of jobs."

Currently, the World Bank is working on the establishment of centers of economic activities in Burkina Faso, Mauritius and Niger: these "growth poles" are intended to attract investment in specific sectors.

The banks in turn can expand their services to provide entrepreneurs with the capital they need to grow their business. According to the report, access to credit is the primary concern of entrepreneurs in sub-Saharan Africa, also deplored the inadequate infrastructure.

Keys to success:

The decade of growth that benefited the African continent has instilled a sense of optimism about the future. But as shown in the 2013 report on the competitiveness of Africa if the continent is to keep its promises, public and private sector must bear all the reforms that will strengthen its international competitiveness and make prosperity a reality for Africans.

Mauritius (39th in the world) the most competitive countries in Africa, according to the Global Competitiveness Rankings, prepared annually by the World Economic Forum (WEF) and published Wednesday, September 3 in Geneva.

At the African level, Mauritius is followed by South Africa (56th in the world), Rwanda (62nd), Morocco (72nd), Botswana (74th), Algeria (79th) Tunisia (87th) and Namibia (88th). Kenya (90th) and Zambia (96th) completed the Top 10 African. African economies have developed in different ways. Some grew as Mauritius (45th in the rankings from 2013 to 2014) and Rwanda (66th in the rankings from 2013 to 2014) and others have declined, such as South Africa (53rd in 2013-2014) and Nigeria (120 in 2013-2014).

The WEF report was conducted among 15,000 business leaders in 144 countries and provides a global ranking of the most competitive countries, from hundreds of economic indicators.

For the sixth consecutive time this year Switzerland is the global leader in this ranking. Singapore remains in second place and the United States is now the third most popular, gaining two places from 2013.

The 10 most competitive countries have not changed from one year to another, but they have nevertheless developed differently. Four of them (Switzerland, Singapore, Hong Kong and the Netherlands) have kept their rank, 3 rose (USA, Japan and the United Kingdom) and 3 decreased (Finland, Germany and Sweden).

However, there is still much work to do in terms of structural reforms, which are essential for growth in the long term.

The progress of African economies to achieve economic growth must be accompanied by multiple efforts to boost their competitiveness in the long term, if we want to reach the continent one day lasting improvements. This is the conclusion of the 2013 report recently published on the competitiveness of Africa.

Connect African markets in a sustainable manner, the World Bank and the World Economic Forum. According to the main conclusion of this report, regional integration is a key instrument to help Africa improve its competitiveness, diversify its economic base and create enough jobs for its young population and rapidly urbanizing. "Growth in Africa must be seen in the broader international context, where the encouraging gains in economic growth contradict the underlying weakness of its long-term competitiveness. Regional integration is the key that overcomes this weakness by providing wider economic and social benefits; it should be considered a priority by African leaders seeking to ensure that Africa keeps its promises, "said in this context, Jennifer Blanke, chief economist at the World Economic Forum. The report also outlines the major political problems for the realization, more concretely, this so-called regional integration. The report includes detailed competitiveness profiles of 38 African economies. These profiles provide a comprehensive summary of the drivers of competitiveness in each of the countries covered by the report, and are useful for policy makers, business strategists, other key stakeholders and all those interested in the region. With the support of the South African government, more than 865 participants from over 70 countries participated in the World Economic Forum held from May 8 to 10 in Cape Town, South Africa. Under the theme "Delivering the Promise of Africa," the agenda of the meeting has incorporated three main pillars, namely how to accelerate economic diversification, stimulate strategic infrastructure and unlock the talents of Africa.

Axes to boost competitiveness

Competitiveness of Africa as a whole is lagging behind other emerging regions, particularly with regard to the quality of institutions, infrastructure, macro-economic policies, education and adoption technology. Large gaps remain between its top-ranked economies and those that come last. The report assesses how Africa manages to create social and environmental factors needed to fill these gaps or to mitigate them. African exports are too heavily focused on commodities and the continent's share of global trade remains low, despite the existence of many regional economic communities and the liberalization of national markets. Intra-African trade is particularly limited. The report identifies a heavy and opaque border administration, particularly for export-import procedures, the limited use of information technology and communication (ICT) and persistent deficits in infrastructure as the main obstacles to levels more advanced regional integration. It also shows that these challenges are particularly acute for landlocked African economies. The deficit in Africa's infrastructure is a serious impediment to regional integration, and this problem is further accentuated by the growth of consumer markets and urbanization. The establishment of adequate and efficient infrastructure help African economies to increase productivity in the manufacture of goods and provision of services help improve health and education and help ensure a more equitable distribution of national wealth. The report examines how the growth centers are nowadays important vehicles to strengthen the productive capacity and boost regional integration by attracting investment. As the World Bank is investing in growth areas for several years, the report "Connecting African markets in a sustainable manner," the month of May 2013 examines, in detail, how to deploy good business practices to provide more widespread benefits to the entire continent.

Africa must develop regional integration

African countries trade very little with each other, compared with Asian and European countries. One reason for this finding is partly due to the weakness of regional integration. So, how to promote intra-African investment to improve the competitiveness of the continent? What are the challenges of regional integration?

It is on these issues that experts brainstormed on May 29 at the Annual Meetings of the African Development Bank (AFDB) in Marrakech, Morocco. The theme of the forum was: "Promotion of intra-regional investments in Africa."

Regional integration is the key to the future competitiveness of the continent. Therefore, Africa must develop inter-African investment, according to panelists who have studied the issue. But the inter-African trade is only 15% on the continent. Which is a very low rate compared to other countries. Why that is the inter-regional exchange rate is so low in Africa?

The reasons are many, according to Dr. Abbi Mamo Kedir, an economic consultant in the School of Management organization University of Lelcester. "African countries are faced with the lack of capital, infrastructure and poor governance. Besides customs duties which are very expensive, "he has said. These logistical problems prevent inter-African trade to develop. The lack of expertise in human resources is also a serious hindrance to the flow of trade, he has noted. According to him, "The world of business needs a skilled workforce. Yet support policies exist in the continent to promote intra-regional investments. But they do not materialize highlighted stakeholders. So what works? According to the panelists, we must first reform the investment policies to promote trade.

Morocco, which has become an investment hub in the region in recent years, has made efforts in this direction, according to Youssef Rouissi, Deputy Director General of Attijariwafa bank. He said Morocco is very interested in the African market. "We have five banks in several countries in Africa. In addition, millions of African consumers have made us realize that we could recover the market for distribution of the food industry, "he said.

Commodity, it needs to diversify However, even if Morocco is making investments in African countries, 60% of its economy is still dependent on Europe, notably France and Spain.

Given this situation, it is imperative that Africa be united if it is to improve its competitiveness in the world market, for its part considers the Ugandan Minister of Justice, Kahinda Otafiire.

"Until now, Africa has always exported its market and will build for example, he defended his own cars.

He stated that the South has experienced a major economic boom in recent years Africa can achieve a higher level of development. But it was not enough imposed on the African market as it has the potential to do so. "This is proof that we cannot talk about growth in Africa as we have not developed regional integration,".

On the eve of the opening of the political summit between Africa and Europe, the weekend meetings of the EU-Africa-business forum that brings together nearly 500 representatives of the European international private sector, and Africa, as well as organizations international and regional. The aim is to give flesh to the main theme of the Summit, which will place its 3rd edition, from the perspective of "Investment, economic growth and job creation." seems important indeed to change perceptions around Africa, often described in terms of conflict or extreme poverty. This continent is facing obvious challenges, many, but it is also that of a dynamic economy should be welcomed and encouraged. Africa, like all developing countries, has been met hard by the economic crisis - which it has not yet CONTRIBUTE. But these are also the countries that have rebounded quickly to record growth rates that many Europeans would envy. It is this trend, recognized by most economists, it is appropriate to confirm and deepen. And there is the subject of our meetings during the coming days. Political will give the agenda, but it must be accompanied by the mobilization of the economy and civil society.

Resources and actions needed discussed to remove obstacles to trade development, the creation of small and medium enterprises, access to the energy or optimal and transparent management of scarce resources. In a word, it should work in partnership between the public and private resources to convert assets and deposits of Africa in prosperity and improved living standards. The European Union will continue to support in particular the establishment of a regulatory, fiscal and social that attracts investment and the emergence of economic activity that everyone can enjoy.

In 2025, the continent will be over 1.5 billion. Nigeria, Congo and Ethiopia are among the ten most populous nations in the world. Although African soil contains 80% platinum, 40% of diamonds, more than a fifth of the gold and the world's cobalt, although the African forests are full of resources and unexplored tourist attractions, although China India and other powers, from there to fetch their raw materials, will help to accommodate low-cost infrastructure, Africa will still not be an economic player of global significance. "This is the second finding. The ideologues of the first singers and other geological scandal that would Africa materials are attached to the destiny of the continent. The future is not written in the wealth of the basement, but in the heads. In short, the release of energy through a revolution Intelligence is training and education. Not the contemplation of the world and so-called natural resources. In the world of the next fifty years, the world of tomorrow, if not earlier, the only true wealth is the gray matter. Notice the deaf and blind states.

In 2025, the continent will have a GDP less than a quarter of the world average; half of Africans will continue to try to survive on incomes below the poverty line ... Only manage to get by some countries such as South Africa (with a per capital, GDP that exceeds that of Russia), Egypt Botswana and perhaps Ghana. Other countries are in danger of bursting; divided, they may become non-states. "Faced with this" Catastrophe ", the African elites continue to emigrate as in the past. New immigrants finance increasingly their country.

The causes of this "chaos," according to the author, are: the weight of history (human aspiration scale that was the slave trade), pandemics such as AIDS, future climate change ... But it is a major cause that Jacques Attali states filigree is the absence of a "creative class". Concept at the heart of his book. Creative class is financiers, artists, entrepreneurs, inventors and holders of technological, institutional and aesthetic innovations that are the creators of the Merchant Order since the emergence of capitalism in Bruges between 1200 and 1350, Venise1350-1500, Antwerp, 1500-1560, 1560-1620 Genoa, Amsterdam 1620-1678, London 1788-1890, 1890-1929 Boston, New York 1929-1980). And Tomorrow, Los Angeles...

Paradoxically, in the coming decades, there is the "end of the American Empire," says the author. 2050 born a disturbing world in more ways than one "super-empire" that deconstructed utilities, states and nations. And this is the first wave of the future. The unified global market and will prevail over democracy. And a "polycentric" order will emerge ... "Society tamper" or everyone will be its own prison guard may be required. What role for the Continent in this Order cannibal? Jacques Attali wrote, "While Africa will strive in vain to build the rest of the world will begin to deconstruct within the scope of globalization. Tomorrow's Africa therefore does not look like the West today; it is rather the West hand that looks like Africa today. "

By the end of the American Empire, there is a development of microcredit. In 2025, they reach more than 500 million family heads against today more than 100 million of the poorest people on the planet entrepreneurs. During "super-empire" microcredit networks become more important than the traditional banking system. The victory of market democracy open time "hyper conflict" time of pirates and privateers, mercenaries and other companies such as already exists in Africa. Kofi Annan, Secretary-General Kofi Annan spoke of "privatization of war".

The third wave engulfing the future in the next fifty years is "hyper democracy." With the emergence of a new "creative class" carries a new ethic made free and altruism, technological innovations, artistic, political. One can even say a huge institutional upheaval with the appearance of "relational business" related to fair trade, micro-credit and foundations created by the likes of billionaire Bill Gates, the founder of Microsoft and his foundation against AIDS in Africa, Warren Buffet against nuclear proliferation ... the hyper democracy will be the era of free. It will also be time for a new "creative class" composed of what Jacques Atali called "transhumant". A new time: "Women are more easily transhumant than men find pleasure in pleasing is characteristic of motherhood."

Africa ahead: reasons to believe

Ten years after the launch of the New Partnership for Africa's Development that agency of the African Union is playing an increasingly important role on the African continent.

"Of the five economies with the fastest growth in the world today, ten are in Africa" The observation was made at the Conference of Ministers of Economy and Finance of the African Union, Addis Ababa in late March of this year. And the same sources made clear that "if Africa keeps its average of 5.6% from 2000 annual growth rate - 2008, and the world's rate of 2.9%, the African contribution to global GDP from 2.4% in 2012 to 5.1% in 2034 "A wave of optimism so blowing through Africa, which also notes that foreign direct investment has increased from $ 9 billion in 2000 to $ 62 billion in 2009 While the challenges are immense: access to electricity and roads, agricultural production, education and skills development including youth, innovation and new technologies, ... there is so much to do. For example, "you would have to bridge the infrastructure deficit in Africa, nearly $ 93 billion annually over the next decade." The big question is: what is being done to the economy and African countries develop?

Originally...

First awareness: "Africa is aware that it cannot count on those first internal resources to finance its own development" says Dr. Ibrahim Mayaki, Executive Director of NEPAD. First affected resource, and by far the largest in terms of direct impact on the lives of Africans land. 4 million more hectares into production each year until 2030 just Latin America and especially sub-Saharan Africa, where the potential for agricultural land is the largest since untapped: only 2% of drinking water is used by countries in sub-Saharan Africa.

The lands are bought and therefore buy in Africa, mainly for productions that do not benefit the local people, in addition to private farmland, "China, Japan and South Korea seeking land mainly in Africa and Asia. They are interested to produce food crops, animal feed and bio-energy crops. "

Africa against Aids "90% of drugs against HIV / AIDS, first generation, that is to say, the most toxic, come from India," says Michel Sidibe, Director of UNAIDS. What places in reliance millions of Africans (communities too) and over long periods, as the treatment of a patient with AIDS is spread over 20, 30 years ... To remedy this situation, NEPAD and UNAIDS signed on March 27 an agreement to jointly develop a graduated response and an agenda for creating an African pharmaceutical industry.

Moreover, "if women had better access to education, electricity and roads, this would result in an increase in agricultural production because they are between 70 and 80% of the labor-agricultural work.

To meet these challenges, NEPAD has implemented the Comprehensive Program for the Development of Agriculture in

Africa (CAADP). Among other actions, $ 1 billion so far mobilized for sustainable management of land and water on the continent through the "Terr-Africa" initiative. Furthermore, thousands of African women (Sierra Leone, Rwanda, etc) are supported with a fund of 20 million Euros focused on micro-finance for agricultural projects, AIDS prevention and education (leadership, entrepreneurship, etc.).

Strengthen Economic Communities

Common Market for Eastern and Southern Africa (COMESA), Economic Community of African States (ECOWAS), the Arab Maghreb Union (UMA), etc ... There are many initiatives and present Africa to develop an integrated manner. Both areas of socio-economic growth and management / prevention of political conflict, these communities of countries receiving support NEPAD policies including development of regional infrastructure. And could be started work to launch the construction of the pipeline that supplies gas to energy currently Nigeria, Ghana, Benin and Togo. Credit NEPAD also support the establishment of a road network linking the countries of East Africa (Kenya, Uganda, Tanzania, Burundi and Rwanda).

Two flagship projects are under consideration, within NEPAD "Uhurunet" a submarine cable at very high speed, which will connect Europe to South Africa, through the West African coast and connecting all the countries of West Africa. There is also the "Umojanet", a cross-border terrestrial network which would leave North Africa to southern Africa...

Educate, communicate

The other major component of African development, it is obviously education. The challenge is access to information, including through the new means of communication (Internet, access to digital networks for information sharing, etc). Whole program has been developed on this: over 300 students received specialized training with the African Institute of Science mathematic- ales supported by the Universities of Cambridge and Oxford.

In addition, more than 550 researchers and regulators of national policies in biotechnology have been trained across the African continent. Particular emphasis has been placed on Information Technology and Communication (ICT), through which nearly 100 primary and secondary schools in Uganda, Lesotho, Ghana, Senegal, Rwanda, Nigeria and Kenya have been equipped in computers, networked and trained in the use of ICT.

It is with all this Mrs. Habiba Mejri-Cheikh, Director of Information and Communication within the African Union affirms that "The African media, more than others, have a particular responsibility to promote true image of Africa ... Things are not completely black or pink. Success stories do exist in Africa and they deserve to beings reported, as failures or conflicts. "

SAVE

With its poverty, its total dependence on the developed world that does not exclude its exclusion few economic sectors where it is still possible to exploit its manifesto to create leadership within it could out of its misery impotence, the SSA does not really allow today hope.

No hope for those who are or are no hope either for those who wish her well. We went from sympathetic to condescending, condescension to pity then, little by little; even this pity gave way to a deep depression and some irritation.

With the proliferation of poverty in a population that multiplies at an alarming rate, the future of Africa seems even sadder than its present. Why a whole segment of the Third World does not he is progressing, but regressing?

We often look for the causes of this disaster in the settlement. This could be an explanation that his evidence would rather futile, since no difference to the current situation. It serves, in fact, only heightening among the population in developed countries, a feeling of guilt, which we are not sure if it allows us to do a better grace gifts to Africa or if it does not become rather an incentive to close your eyes, not to see the heartbreaking consequences of the actions that have been taken.

This denunciation of colonialism is not only futile, however, but harmful, because it distorts the diagnosis of underdevelopment in sub-

Saharan Africa, biased reading of the syndrome and leads to inappropriate prescribing treatment.

YES, the "colonization" in the narrow sense in which we understand here the conquest of the world by the West, during the period from about 1825 to 1950, has certainly contributed to the genesis of underdevelopment we see in Africa today. In some areas, the gap thus introduced interrupted the natural development of the local culture, particularly the societal culture that never came to fruition.

Those who normally could avail himself of this culture have been deprived and had to rely on other models imported from elsewhere, so renouncing really shape the development of their destiny. Lucidly accept that breaking ties of continuity with their history and traditions, which would have enabled what are born and develop there any of the original models of development has had on the colonized societies adversely influence. That said, however, it has not explained everything.

From a historical perspective, 1825-1950 colonization was a flash in the pan. In sub-Saharan Africa, the average occupation lasted only two to three generations. Timbuktu was occupied in 1893, released with the rest of Mali in 1958 I met in 1974; an old "marabout" who claimed to remember the area BEFORE the French presence.

During this period 1825-1950, however, it would be more accurate to say that the world was "slave" rather than settled, since colonization, in the strict sense means to occupy a territory to install its own people, does was not usually the first goal of the company called colonization. The real settlement procedures, as in Algeria, were the exception.

India has been really administrated, the British presence there remains a thin film on the large local population; China, Hong Kong or Macau aside, was at that time neither settled nor administered, and operated only subject; Japan even immune, only made a little more power friendly Western expansion in the nineteenth and twentieth century, unlike the previous centuries, was an achievement almost without colonization. He went to the USA, during the period where there was this pseudo colonization, 20 times more emigrants that has put settlers in the colonies. Why this latest wave of "colonization" seems so superficial she have left a legacy so negative? Would not it precisely because it did not happen?

Colonize is a daunting undertaking. The Hebrews began the colonization of the land of Canaan; there are about 3500 years, with the capture of Jericho. There were lulls, but the colonization of the land of Canaan is still ongoing and the city of Jericho is not yet pacified.

Humans colonize blithely each other relentlessly. Colonization is a facet of the clash of cultures. Except as it presupposes the extermination of indigenous settlers to make room, which was Hitler's plan for Ukraine, colonization is not the most brutal manifestation of the clash of cultures.

A culture is a set of values and historical landmarks that serve as identifiers. Between people who perceive the same culture, comes a sense of belonging, a solidarity that goes beyond the immediate interest. This solidarity can form a group to build a clan society. It is between cultures that are colonized.

When we have to work with people from other cultures, if there is interest not to exterminate them, like they do every single part of the way and work, so that we can share with them that was too against what they have and we do not have, you learn to endure them.

Cultures coexist in fairs and markets, water points where they make the truce, time to drink in goods and ideas. Contact can be quick, furtive literally, but you can also have an interest in it is permanent. Multicultural cities are growing at the intersection where cultures live together and seem to tolerate.

Illusion.

People can tolerate is the index that civilization is not just a philosophical concept, but the cultures never tolerate. A culture wants to occupy all the space. It does not always win, but subconsciously she still wants to learn. She sees its relationship with other cultures if they are on their knees, and having harmless entertainment value, nothing more. If a culture does not have that arrogance, she learns from others and evolves without losing its identity until she has developed or she resigns and disappears.

When cultures coexist, each according to its strength wants to impose on others. There are mutual benefits to cohabitation, however; habits and behaviors of each other as will therefore change to enable this cohabitation. Accommodations and sacrifices are made to maintain what is becoming a new company.

The company creates its own sense of its own holding "CULTURE" cultures of origin of participants, but each is superimposed on his.

The contribution of each source to the new culture crop varies, depending on what each might have to offer or have the strength to impose. Some will identify with the new culture feeling radically transformed else does making even know they have changed.

They are nevertheless gradually changed, and the day is coming when their fellow true are no longer their original counterparts, but those with whom they live together in this new society, whose culture is superimposed over, but replace their starter culture.

"They develop solidarity. Thus English became Americans".

This consensual genesis of a society and a new culture is however not the only scenario. The interest that may not exterminate "them" does not mean that we want to always make friends. When you have the strength for yourself, you can open the door, sit in the living room, turn on the TV for the position is preferred and send the original occupants mowing the lawn. It can colonize.

Colonization means another sharing decisions and tasks, but does not remove all the effects of cohabitation. The others are there.

The circumstances are different, sometimes much better, because the others are there. It therefore creates a colonial, very different from those of the original colonizer as the colonized identity. Two separate identities, because the balance of power between them initially creates this obvious distinction, but external circumstances are the same and interests converge.

Over time, colonizers and colonized can only become, for each other, allies safer. Colonial society develops its own culture, which is unevenly inspired by cultures of origin, but in the new society, sooner or later, to supplant. This leads, in two centuries, to the situation where they are pure Spaniards, only helped a few mestizos and Indians, who will take the initiative to seek just and Spain the independence of America Hispanic.

Colonization following its normal course is a marriage that can start with a kidnapping, but where affection and love can appear. Successful, if it ends with the independence of the colonized territory and the birth of a new hybrid culture. Sometimes, the colonizer to transmit his genes almost entirely to this new culture, like the Arabs did in the Middle East. Sometimes the result is more mixed, as in Mexico, Peru, and Bolivia. Sometimes it is the culture of the colonized prevails, as the Greeks on the Romans, or the Chinese on the Mongols.

If a new hybrid culture is not born of a settlement, the settlement was a failure. When the period of intercultural coexistence is too short or that the ingredients are not there in acceptable proportions, mayonnaise does not. The invader withdrew without fertilized culture of the colonized, nor be rallied. He did for his trouble the booty he has learned. The colonized, meanwhile, finds him at the starting point, without being really inseminated, leaving only fragments of the culture of the colonizers, which he can take advantage if its own culture is strong enough to accept the graft.

The latest wave of colonization of the West has been a failure, because this "colonization" has not really happened, nor fertilization should have been with him. The West has swept the world enjoying a military advantage, not to colonize it, except a few places, but to enslave and exploit it. When he found a better way to continue this operation, he retired.

The occupation by Europe Sub-Saharan Africa has been a chapter of this pseudo colonization, a rather sordid interlude, which was not only the brutality of rape, but the sterility of coitus interrupts.

The aborted culture the 1825 settlement came in 1950 then stopped. The countries of old cultures like China, India, Korea, and Vietnam, retained in memory of the colonial adventure some technologies and socio-political theories, then resumed without much difficulty the course of their history, in the sense of their previous evolution: they are "developing". Sub-Saharan Africa, no. Black Africa is not developing.

After the incursions of the West, black Africa, like other colonized countries, returned to the status quo. Unlike others, it has not found itself in a culture that would have allowed him to pursue a satisfactory development, because such a culture was not there when the last wave of Western colonization began.

In Africa, in the mid nineteenth century, when the power began intensive tutelage of Africa who received his consecration to the Treaty of Berlin, there was no common "African" culture, but a myriad of small crops in sedimentation process by conquering each other, none of which seemed to be able to unite with Western culture to produce a hybrid culture in which Africa could identify.

Noting the absence of a partner African culture, the colonizer has implemented the acculturation tools including schooling are the most powerful, by excluding the local reality so completely that no trans-fertilisation could result, only a passage passed or failed in the dominant culture. The alternative of a hybrid culture was simply discarded.

Normally in such an unequal relationship, Africa would put completely to Western culture. She did not have time. No time, because the effective occupation of Africa was well short, but mostly because the western population settlers have never been numerous enough that they really are, outside the cities, a significant element population.

Culture shock was thus reduced to its simplest expression, avoiding friction, but also spontaneous acculturation that comes from a simple familiarity. For all the so-called colonized territories, the European presence was almost mythical, whole embodied in the official intervening only official position.

African rural populations have never had contact with Europeans other than functional; the inevitable contacts must be conquered with an occupying force population. The West Africa inadvertently violated, he would not even touch it. Consequence of this de facto apartheid, it is only in the cities, specifically in capitals, that the contact was sufficient to ensure that the resulting transition to Western civilization a significant number of Africans.

At the very end of colonization and in the years that followed, you could see in the streets of Dakar and Abidjan Brazza, African middle class and even modest, identifying himself as Senegalese, Congolese or Ivoirians, but quite westernized. It is these Africans apparently totally westernized that, over time, gradually introducing the specificity imported from an adaptation to circumstances and local conditions culture would have made a country-specific hybrid culture and its people.

For they succeed quickly, they would have to be many. For there to be had enough, he would have had the effect of hundreds of thousands of Western settlers in Africa .. but we did not really colonized Africa. We could have had the same result with few settlers, since culture is not as diffuse as the same genes - the conquistadors were not so many! - But it would have taken time Centuries.

It is the cumulative impact of too few settlers and too short a period of occupation that is the embryo of what could have become Finally, after centuries of interregnum, functional African culture will be found in the aftermath of decolonization, in a situation of great weakness and unable to rely on the love of person.

The morning after pill

Initially the colonizer, nobody in Africa felt affection for a hybrid culture. In the absence of such a hybrid culture that is acceptable and accepted, every African, the sudden departure of the colonial power, has had to make the choice to identify with Africa and the West. Rich chose the West. They chose to others that they are Africans. They imposed their choice through a cut more or less subtle with the sources of Western cultures, sometimes even by a regression to an education in the vernacular. When it is not passed, it uses the break and confirms the native bourgeois class, rich, educated and westernized in its role as an intermediary between the West and forced "the others" that has cut off from the West. We wanted to give Africa the morning after pill that does NOT bear a hybrid culture.

In each state in sub-Saharan Africa, the population has been divided into two groups of unequal size. On one side, a small elite defector who only wants to wash a few bits that still would stick to the skin of an African culture to totally identify with Western civilization. On the other hand, a mob, that cannot achieve this assimilation and whose options are a constant emigration or impoverishment.

When talking about underdeveloped, this is the mob that we speak. At the time of decolonization, this Africa ordinary world found itself on the margins of Western civilization and without the real option to return to its previous cultures, since none of them had the scope to appear in succession Western culture to become the dominant culture. The rich and the poor segment decolonized countries in Africa have taken distinct paths.

For elite already westernized, choice seemed to arise between supporting an intelligentsia that would develop a truly indigenous culture and accelerated acculturation to Western civilization. Biased choice because when his immediate survival requires a thorough familiarity with culture, customs and techniques of Western civilization, how to think a local intelligentsia will not focus more on the Masters and development of original Aboriginal culture?

The first option would have involved sacrifice and solidarity that did not exist. It has been claimed sometimes make this choice, but it's always the second option prevailed. Everywhere in sub-Saharan Africa, the desire of acculturation to Western elites is now as clear as possible, the break with the plebs as sharp as possible. Elites seek integration into Western culture, without any local input.

Only a small minority, however, realizes that dream and usually this minority expatriates. For the rest of the elites, often condemned to remain in Africa to extract wealth and exert the power that makes them "elite", the local Western culture in which they are immersed cannot meet this ideal. In the absence of a "settlement" in the strict sense, which would bring back to Africa a strong contingent of Westerners, this local Western culture cannot be fed daily by Aboriginal without further contact with the reality of the real West that through the media. Taking the television as a model, the culture they developed there can therefore only be a copy or a caricature of that projected by the small screen picture.

This culture is not consciously hybrid, because no one wants to heredity. Having to adapt to local conditions, however, it must accept accommodations, these are first considered many imperfections, but gradually, they mark it and leave traces, making a gradually hybrid culture in which these "imperfections" become the only specificity.

Inevitably, it is therefore created across Africa, local mini-cultures, hybrid without admitting that change only by their imperfections and thus subtly mediocrity, confirming the status of permanent second class of their inhabitants. Each member of the elite of a country underdeveloped fed this type of ersatz culture finds himself facing the

Western world, in the situation of a young provincial nineteenth century amount career in Paris. It's not a lost game, but it's not an easy game.

If the elites go abroad or mediocrity, the situation is much worse for the second segment of the African population. The African lower class, not westernized, found himself starting from the colonizer, without any reference culture and therefore without identity. With nothing to arouse in him a desire to belong to Africa, let alone one or other of the artificial states we have drawn on Africa.

Under the guise of creating a sense of belonging to artificial national entities - which themselves do not identify any, unless they have assimilated these national entities to their personal business .The elite of African countries have made it more difficult for their population's access to Western civilization. Which means African cultural model can he join in these societies which called national African elites are defectors?

The average African was thus placed in a position of inferiority which it is difficult to pull off, since there is not feasible for him to retreat to an earlier indigenous culture that no longer exists, the transition to the real Western culture it is closed and the road is barred to him to create a hybrid culture that would be the solution, but to create that indigenous elites do not want to work.

The average African is left without cultural identity. But without cultural identity between you and a group of your peers (peer group), it is out-growing everywhere. It is in exile even at home. Africans, in exile in their own country, they did not identify.

Tragically, because you cannot really go after one in the context of a culture in which one is unconditionally like?

Without belonging to a cultural identity, the individual is constantly inferior position since then has no choice but to perform in imported models. When access to imported models it is open while it is presumed to be known, but not well; it is for him to learn and apply. Any initiative or creativity that manifests the recipient becomes a distraction, a delay element while the sole purpose that he proposes is to tame the model life of the West and to control usage.

If, however, creativity is manifested and produced undeniable results, these results are collected and stuck as minor and marginal activities. They receive their credentials to the extent that they granted them by the "mainstream" of Western culture, which to judge the merit in its own terms and its own weight. If Picasso had been black, all periods, pink, blue or whatever, would be defined simply as facets of Negro Art.

Despite all the efforts that Africans can do to adapt to Western culture that serves as a superstreet, they came late in the race, while the rules have already been established without any reference to their specific needs, ensures that they can never acquire a position of strength or even equality. They can never take the lead, since they do not know the route of the race and that if they get detached, the pack would turn at the first junction and forget. This certainty of not being able to win no incentive to run faster.

A recent survey of bachelor graduates in a country of West Africa, indicated that, for the MAJORITY of them, the best career path they wanted began with a departure to Europe . Not only African countries are sinking ships, which can survive only those that escape, but African cultural references are themselves become traps. Individual success is scrubbing all these allusions to an African cultural inheritance that cannot be treated as a source of folklore.

Unless there is a sport or an outstanding performer - or that is in a position to symbolize Africa, becoming the African service and removing preferential treatment, you cannot succeed as an individual that if you leave you leave Africa and Africa itself.

Solidarity, in sub-Saharan Africa, is no longer a factor for individual survival, but a deadly disease. The lack of solidarity with the African society does not have to be made up, it goes without saying and is gaining even be ostentatious.

Without solidarity, however, there is no possibility of society. Without a cultural identity that allows solidarity, a society in gestation can develop. In a society in the making, the need for a joint effort is constant and this effort is not provided, the company is never born.

Without cultural identities, African countries are not really companies. This is the current situation of Africa and it is clear that this situation can only go from bad to worse. Everything is in place for when things worse sabotage. At this early disadvantage to systematically poor parents of a culture that is not theirs, colonization added another handicap, economic, that one, that Africa shares with other underdeveloped countries, by exploiting the structure of production of the colonized countries in favor of the colonizing countries.

This manipulation has not ceased with the withdrawal of the colonizers; it is therefore rather aggravated the pace of globalization. Once the formal colonization ended, the developed world, not focusing on a more stable long-term operating relationship, adopted the policy of cutting, accelerated exploitation decolonized countries and irreparably sabotaged their economies He did it by making "donations" to underdeveloped countries, particularly in the food sector. By giving its products, rather than selling the developed world could easily substitute its trade surpluses to food, local produce and naturally caused the failure of subsistence farming. The land no longer needed profitability for small farmers, were then acquired by transnational companies and assigned to monocultures for export, coffee, cocoa, etc.

The peasants were ruined, within the limits of need that were, without more, processed agricultural workers and used in these monocultures, the lowest possible wage. Others have had to migrate to the slums on the outskirts of new megacities, there to clump together into a lumped proletariat which could one day out or those that will be our nemesis.

This sabotage of smallholder agriculture in underdeveloped countries came to perfect the grip of foreign interests on the primary sector, the mining industries, petroleum, forestry were already under the control of the latter. This not only eliminated the possibility that these countries can maintain food self-sufficiency, but also had the effect of preventing that is never a local capital that would have allowed the creation of companies in the manufacturing sector.

In the secondary sector, the underdeveloped countries, already latest arrivals on the global industrial scene, had the additional handicap to depend entirely for the capitalization of their industries, the willingness of developed countries that is to say the good will of their incumbents. The industrial development of underdeveloped country could therefore obey the rationality of those who provided funding, diametrically opposed to the interests of these countries themselves rationality ,Or without secondary profitable for their own economies primary, no creation of material wealth. The underdeveloped countries have been reduced to begging systemic structural: the basic premise of the functioning of their economies is that they will lose money and that the adjustment will be made by writing books, saying that a "gift" has been obtained or that a debt was incurred that it is implied that she will not be refunded.

Funds generated for consumption cannot support a structure of modern services, which it has been set up for this purpose in the underdeveloped countries has taken the form of small islands of services, for the exclusive use of expatriates and a small local bourgeoisie. In this summary grid was superimposed a civil service that is not used to provide services, but to create jobs, largely unnecessary, almost solely to justify the distribution in the form of wages, the minimum contribution required for the country does not disintegrate, the revenue generated from this systemic begging.

No primary, secondary or tertiary adequate, there is, as a real possibility of enrichment in underdeveloped countries, as activities of extortion. First, a more or less organized crime, greatly expanding at the rate that the poorer classes understand the rules of the neoliberal game and the role of the crime in its operation. Moreover, a structure of institutionalized corruption that is present at all levels, culminating in the sale by the government shamelessly foreigners to anything that could be used to lift these countries out of their slump.

This corruption in stages, direct and indirect, is the primary source of income in sub-Saharan Africa. The economic divide is sharp between, on the one hand, a fringe mafia and enriched a tiny bourgeoisie operating and diverts public funds and, on the other hand, the rest of the population in the process of impoverishment.

The same phenomenon occurred previously in other civilizations in Europe in the Middle Ages, for example, which allowed while develops an elite that eventually became the source of all development. Why SSA underdeveloped countries he may not follow the same path?

Because the economic divide perfectly intersects the cultural divide that we have seen and therefore there is no solidarity, no sense of belonging. The tiny bourgeoisie enriched identifies completely with the West and sees the rest of the population than any other company that tolerates only because it earns in profit.

For this reason, all income, earned or stolen in sub-Saharan Africa, as they go beyond the most basic level of subsistence, are not invested in the development of the country but are immediately re-exported to foreign countries, where the there are sometimes more profitable investments but also still very much safer than what the country can offer.

Without solidarity, no development. Without solidarity, in fact, no society.

Membership, interest and solidarity

No companies in Africa? Warning! There are societies in Africa; sometimes they even raise an exemplary solidarity. But these companies are in the extended family, clan, and ethnic, traditional membership "Tons" groups within civil society, not so different from those we have recommended the constitution in a New Society. (712b). In terms of composite states of decolonization, this solidarity is NEVER.

To have functional societies in Africa should be formed to tier states where solidarity exists. This is not an immediately accessible option as states turn into the real natural groups of belonging; it would be a return to Africa before colonization. That would eliminate the current states, which could only be done with arms in, but since there is not an African State that does is set up a herd of cows of its minorities and the shamelessly exploits.

Returning power to groups that elicit genuine membership will be possible without bloodshed, sub-Saharan Africa, as part of an overall streamlining of governance. This rationalization is needed in Africa, perhaps more than anywhere else, but there try this would be premature today Can we bring about a solidarity in Africa, the level of existing states? Whether in Africa or elsewhere, there are only two ways that lead to solidarity. The first leads to solidarity of belonging, that is visceral expression of a common identity; the second leads to a solidarity of interest and, in its finished form, is a rationalization of altruism.

The first track that expresses a common identity is now barred in Africa, since this consciousness of identity simply does not exist in artificial states that it has created. We can try to encourage it, but it would have to be born naturally. It would take generations. There should be a common thought, symbols, places of memory Some wars, too, such as those which occurred in Latin America during his turbulent gestation To die together, you end up enjoying, but let us remember that in one of these wars without rhyme or reason and there had a lot, Paraguay has lost two thirds of its population. Is this the preferred model?

Not only is the sense of these artificial states in Africa does not exist, but the commitment to withdraw is often evident. There are at least a hundred ethnic groups in Africa who do not want to identify with the state where they were parked. Can we replace what seems like an impossible solidarity of belonging, solidarity associated with common interests?

The criteria here are known. In comfort, yes. In misery, no.

In a rich country already developed, a company can keep the support of its members for a long time, even if there is more a sense of belonging facade, because it is the arena of their struggles and therefore the place where they feed. It is the attachment of the charnel scavenger. Everyone gets something out of the company and therefore maintain the state worth compromises or sacrifices.

We know, however, that a common concern is the precarious foundations for lasting solidarity. For it to be stable, such solidarity implies that wealth is there to enable that participation in society is a good deal. This solidarity can exist among disadvantaged African classes, since they do not derive their participation NOTHING to society.

Something akin to solidarity may well manifest sometimes between poverty, but it is the solidarity of Jacques to plunder the castle and share the spoils. This solidarity is punctual. It is precarious, because nothing is easier than to sow dissension within a group whose motivation is purely economic. Each member of the group can be easily separated simply by meeting its own financial expectations at the expense of others.

This is a serious weakness of solidarity with interest. Even if it is initially that of "plunder the castle," anyone who wants to maintain cohesion within a group is therefore hasten to add, Equipment Company goals, motivation that is superior to immune from attempts would be made to cause the breakup. In reaching solidarity, we need only the interest is added to a cocktail of principles and intangible values: God, freedom, homeland, justice, fraternity, etc.

When you do that, true solidarity may well of the total membership of an idea, a principle, a cause, a message. This solidarity can be just as emotional as that which arises from a sense of cultural identity and, indeed, over time, tends to absorb more and more solidarity of belonging to the group bearing the idea, message, etc. It is the spirit body of Christians in the Circus, and the Legionaries in Camarón, Buddhist monks in Vietnam Can I link solidarity in the service of a cause for solidarity in the membership in a state that would make it functional last? An insurmountable challenge, because if you try, adding that higher motivation in the interest of participating in a state, get a genuine and effective solidarity, we find that, paradoxically, it removes a more solidarity honest we do not want effective.

Solidarity becomes true only to the extent where one does not expect anything. She could by itself its own justification, become unconditional, even feeding each attack which it is subject. Solidarity is born if the goal is not to withdraw but to take. Whenever there is a material benefit to be derived from solidarity, however, one quickly discovers the corruption lurking in the shadows and get back to the original scenario of solidarity of interest that requires that wealth is present or promised.

Promise credibly that in Africa today is not possible. That credibility would require that wealth exists initially that solidarity would not, which brings us back to square one.

If solidarity tier of states is impossible to create in SSA, even interest, we understand that there can not develop this solidarity in the service of a cause which we have spoken, **without a national,** free and without reference to interest. It is possible, even probable, that this kind of solidarity born in Africa. But it is not without peril.

When those who show solidarity around an idea or a message is in a weak position which is that of modest African classes, solidarity requires total commitment, but must be internalized. External structures they would put in place to guide and show such solidarity, indeed, would be unable to withstand attacks from the outside in a hostile environment.

The action engendered solidarity cannot be rotated at great risk to an external action, for those who are well connected are weak and cannot hope to help them. Outside, there is the enemy force must be in itself. This solidarity can be initially a compensatory and become a development tool when it is manipulated. This solidarity is discrete, often linked to strong xenophobia.

Solidarities that meet these conditions for free, total commitment and internalization usually born of religious movements. This is a tautology, since we could define the religious movement as one that does not bring immediate material rewards, but rather a spiritual gratification. Gratuity internalized, because even if you can see a "paradise" on the outside, it is still a projection of yourself. A religious movement based on an ultimate authority is fully internalized; otherwise it is not really a religious movement.

In the vacuum of solidarity known as sub-Saharan Africa, it can hardly create solidarity as around a religious movement. A solidarity that can be identified with a process of development without passing out, if the gratification that associates is delayed beyond the horizon. It will require sacrifices that will be required solidarity - there's always - are not made to get this bonus, which should remain out of reach, but for love of the cause itself.

Pie in the sky

Solidarity in sub-Saharan Africa cannot be born of a religious movement that around. A real religion. Atheistic Marxism played for a while in Africa the role of religion, but Marxism offered too much too soon; he could not generate solidarity with the prospect of indefinite deprivation of Africans needed. Ironically, the fact is that Marxism, which denounced the illusory promise of "pie in heaven," is finally dead not to be left today, in most of Africa, it is the Islamic fundamentalism that took over Marxism. Because it requires everything and offers nothing material. When we think of religion, it is believed Islam. Still indecisive there fifty years in Egypt and Morocco, experimental in favorable conditions in Libya, there are a few decades, currently implemented in a pilot project by Hezbollah in southern Lebanon, perhaps the solidarity of Islam can eventually become a vehicle for development. Maybe. She will truly be operational tomorrow, Iran, Pakistan and sub-Saharan Africa?

The question is not whether we like or if you do not like Islamic fundamentalism, but found that it is a force that could play a leading role in the emergence of an original model of development in many African countries. Let's say this is the most likely scenario.

While the emergence of Islam is seen as bad news for the West, however, there is an alternative that is charismatic Christian movements.

Islam is often presented as if he was the only candidate to religious hegemony in Africa. Too often we forget the influence of charismatic Christian movements and their potential for mobilization is not as strong as that of Islam. Stronger, in fact, since it can refer to mute its historical ties with Western culture from which it came.

This relationship, at one level seems a disadvantage, since the relationship is established with the colonizer, but it is a huge advantage in the unconscious, as the charismatic movements can convey the image of progress and success that is that of the West.

In Africa, the charismatic movement is no more a stranger than Islam: they are like each other, import products, introduced not invaders. A Christian alternative to Islamism is not excluded in Africa. This alternative might even be fomented by the neoliberal system, in response to what is perceived as the "danger" of Islam. The royal way to introduce this alternative would be through Brazilian charismatic movements, so two or three already have more than 10 million members, have well-established structures and know how to manage huge funds.

These Brazilian structures have the added benefit of already being "black" structures and carry in their genes any pre-colonial African tradition, yet enriched links with the folk music of America "revival". Rites of "Candomblé" and "Macumba", which abound in Brazil and all have their origin in Africa, are not part of the natural process of charismatic churches, but they live on the same territory.

Fine example of syncretism is the great Brazilian specificity terrier's "Candomble" and Evangelical and Pentecostal churches do not spit on the exchange of some guarantors of friendship, an exchange that simply shows what is really happening in the deep soul of their customers, which sometimes are also the same and merge.

Intuitively, I feel that being faced with the need to make an identification choice - all other things being equal - the average African and lower class would be challenged by a combination of "soul music" in Evangelical church and the occasional trances terreiro that by Friday at the mosque five daily prayers and the forehead in the dust.

Intrinsic value apart from one or other of these religions, the African does not seem culturally more in tune with Christian syncretism of inspiration, not far animist customs, with a hardline Islamism? The concept of Yemanja and Yoruba orixas who "go home" seems to be a concept at least as carrier in sub-Saharan Africa that the message of Muhammad and the Koran.

That said, Christian syncretism or Islamism, if a solidarity movement arises from the depths of Africa, it will be a religious movement, with all that this can bring violence, obscurantism and hatred of others.

There is not Africa that might appeal to a religious culture to raise solidarity. Experience is now attempted in Latin America, creating a uniqueness that comes justify a sense of belonging. Well explicit efforts we are doing now Bolivia to recover an identity around pre-Columbian traditions are well down that road. It is not said that this approach will be successful, but it is not proven that it will fail.

This path will certainly be used in Africa. Those who would put this religious solidarity in the service of national and social solidarity should remember, however, that often attempts to exploit a sincere to make an "effective" solidarity religious force resulted, instead, through the imposition this religious strength of those who thought they could handle it.

Beliefs and dictatorships

What to expect if SSA creates solidarity based on a religion? Expect one or the other of two bad scenarios. The first is that solidarity is, per person, remains at Level religion is infamous those who would guide action. History has a unique development and a conclusion for these situations.

"Believers", first in a weak position, develop, are perceived as a threat by those in power, are persecuted, are increasing in self-denial, and finally come to power they show a perfect intolerance. Encouraged by this success, they go by their proselytizing obnoxious to their neighbors, they convert until they have no more rivals are themselves crushed or accept an unstable peace coupled with hostile attitude with the "infidels" Solidarity that Africans just waiting to emerge in the current African societies find belonging as Christians or Islamists, it is difficult to see how he comes out a shortcut to development solidarity if they are the protagonists of the first scenario.

It is quite likely that he will no longer be fighting against poverty and inequality, only to learn to love them.

Worse, if these two religious forces are generated simultaneously, there is a real possibility, God or the devil is in it, they will oppose with fanaticism and their emulation - an understatement! - Not only will not solve anything, but could even extend indefinitely the doldrums in Africa. Africa could experience the equivalent of the Middle Ages, our religious wars ... Would not it be that boys will be boys?

There is a second scenario. Instrumental this new solidarity brings religious fervor and wanting to reap the benefits, Osagyefo (Redeemer) wants to tackle the development. He wants to do through consistent planning and intensive conditioning. A true democracy is quite impossible even before this development has taken place, so he imposed his dictatorship.

This is brutal dictatorship or, conversely, altruistic and informed, even if it is the perfect Plato's Republic, it will be immediately exposed to the open and covert attacks in the developed world. Officially, it is out of respect for democracy that the world will deny the legitimacy of this dictatorship. The real reason for this opposition, however, is that this development is simply contrary to the selfish interests of Western civilization and developed countries.

Countries which, at the time of independence or later thought capitalize on the enthusiasm - the religious fervor that is the most likely event in Africa today that enthusiasm - quickly had to come into line. See examples of Guinea, Ghana, etc. In fact, around the world, with the notable exception of Cuba, there are few who have managed to go that route long and efforts, always thwarted wherever possible by the capitalist system, have never have given the meager results.

In the current situation, the origins in Africa with an identification solidarity and belonging can only be achieved by a religious movement; or the consequences of this approach do not seem beneficial. Will he has another solution for Africa?

Re-colonize Africa?

There is another solution. Would have to be able to develop a culture of African solidarity interest, based on a rationalization of altruism. When everyone makes the effort not to capsize the boat. It is solidarity that we in the developed world. It is solidarity that installs itself appears when a certain ease and it always leads to some democracy.

This solidarity is nothing spectacular and it does not inspire poems or epics. It is, as we have said above, the attachment styles experienced by the scavenger for his grave. It is still a hundred cubits above what can be found today in Africa and is the only the only reasonable goal that can be set to a country, say, like Nigeria. Solidarity with interest, based on a rationalization of altruism is a good solution. The problem is that it is not possible that this solidarity born spontaneously of Africa itself. In no country in sub-Saharan Africa.

The development of this model requires relative ease. No puffy for some wealth, this only provide them an exit visa out of their culture, leaving others a little poorer, but ease widespread in a middle class. Minimal ease that makes it is not heroic and incongruous not to take for you and only for you, absolutely EVERYTHING we can take the core curriculum.

This minimal fluency is only possible if Africa begins in sharing the wealth. However, social economic split in SSA prevents consensus on any redistribution of wealth. This creates an insoluble dilemma. A minimum wealth and a form of redistribution of this wealth are necessary for the emergence of a solidarity of interests while a solidarity of interests must come BEFORE the development producing wealth.

No governance from a sub-Saharan African society cannot solve this dilemma. In the absence of effective consensus for at least a rudimentary form of sharing, it is impossible for governance after an African country has a chance to try and improve the condition of its inhabitants. Governance for the good of the people is possible in Africa, if it is above issues and local power games. To be carried out in Africa which has to be done, it is necessary that African governance is outsourced.

This leads to the politically incorrect conclusion, but true, that Africa cannot find the path of development if, for a time, it is governed without Africans. The time that it put in place structures to create wealth and minimally equitable distribution of the wealth created distribution.

This also leads to the conclusion, just as politically incorrect, but just as true, it would take Africa to the point where we left it.

We must give Africa that colonization should have to make, whether colonization was the civilizing mission that claimed she was instead of the operating business and sometimes it simple robbery was.

Does this mean that we should re-colonize Africa? No, the time of the rape is over. But we must find the solution to the current situation on the basis of the colonial model. When we look at the reality rather than intentions, how the colonial model presented in everyday reality? A military and police presence was in response to a pressing need to maintain order and security in support of an administrative presence to handle honestly, where corruption and nepotism had always prevailed. This is what Africa needs, there is 100 years old and that's exactly what she still needed today.

The colonial model was effective; there is no country in sub-Saharan Africa where administrative structures are not only deteriorated since independence. The great wrongs of the colonial model were, firstly, that it had been imposed and not voluntary and, secondly, it was not working for the good of the colonized countries but for the colonizers. Is it possible to recreate an outsourced governance structure that has the benefits of colonization without its faults?

Protectorate; It is quite possible and has already tried. This is the model of the "protectorate". The concept of the protectorate is a country with the administrative skills required, administers a country that does not have that power, for the good of the country and not administered the administrator country.

In its first form, the protectorate assumed that administered the country was willing to be protected, in fact, claimed that protection.

France, for example, was called to "protect" the Morocco. It soon became clear, however, that the protectorate often had an agenda other than the protection and the protective countries, led by France, were not always a perfect altruism.

To restore some self-denial, the term protectorate has evolved in a second step, a mandate to power by the League of Nations, to take him under his wing a country helpless and destitute. At the same time, we gave up the fiction that the protected countries had consented. He was a minor, incompetent, we would think about it. Act for his own good.

It soon became equally clear, unfortunately, that for countries mandated was not always pure and that if, in the best case, a benign tutelage applied without killing or scandals is that the country mandated really offer any interest and that the person to whom he had entrusted only gave little attention to his "protection".

After World War II, arrived strategy, innovative for Europe, but already tested successfully in Latin America by the USA. Remove all settlements which served them so dearly cost, giving them independence and relying on local satraps to manage the operation. The criteria and changed the pattern of the protectorate apparently fell into disuse.

Only in appearance.

In fact, he continued under another name. What France has offered to African countries at the time of independence was a form of protectorate, Marianne reserving foreign affairs, including defense and control of finances including the currency of his colonies. Some officials sprinkled over the administration of the young nations would be sufficient to avoid the nonsense and to ensure that good things follow their normal course, all valuable resources such as juicy contracts always finding their way to Paris.

It is a protectorate of fact, one might call a "power independence" and that works for almost 50 years. He saved France from the many critical and life moult legionnaires and some missionaries. In the debit side, however, it must be remembered that he gave nothing more to Africa than what a protectorate of conventional design would have brought them, avoiding only their leaders, as in France the boredom of a reporting occasional accounts.

The "assisted independence" did not yield anything more than a traditional protectorate decolonized countries. Most importantly, it has brought them much less than what they brought the colonial regime, the difference is a net gain for the former colonizer. It took a very astute management of propaganda, coordinated between all colonial countries for the Independence Day, is not celebrated in every sub-Saharan country, as a day of mourning and burning some vestiges of it old days.

Today, everything happens as if the countries of the French African Community were departments that elect their prefects calling presidents, but who are not represented in the National Assembly and that we therefore have to s occupy that if you have something to be learned. Are we could not do better for Africa and assisted independence?

When you look at it in all lucidity, we understand that the underdeveloped countries, especially the former colonies of Africa, now need to be protected. They need a protectorate. They need to outsource their governance, because in a situation where they were left, no endogenous governance cannot settle there that has a chance to improve the lives of their inhabitants.

The underdeveloped countries have undoubtedly needed to be protected, particularly against those who claim their guards. If the developed world does not agree to give them some protection equitable status protectorates true, we will all be guilty of increasing misery and endless injustices that are the daily lot of underdeveloped countries in Africa. Tomorrow and forever.

The terms of the partnership

How to reconcile the idea of a protectorate to that of freedom and human dignity of those we want to protect? Returning first to the original principle of the Protectorate, a voluntary administrator between a state and a given society, but making sure it does not act now simply those of a principle, but of relationship a reality. He does not need the consent of the citizen was extracted under threat of a gunboat, batteries pointed at the presidential palace.

Therefore speak over protectorate, but the "full partnership". The full partnership is completely administered society under the leadership of the state administrator. Two things distinguish a protectorate. The first is that it is not imposed by force, but wanted by the company administered; the second is that it is subject to strict rules of law. The citizen is not left to the thank you of any director becomes its occupant.

Submit a partnership with rules of law is possible if two conditions are met. First, if the international community, the United Nations level, acquires control bodies necessary to verify that the partnership agreements are respected and, then, if a balance of power is established on the planet, allowing that be put at the disposal needed UN force credible response.

If a control structure is created, the propensity of any officer to want to be helpful, or at least interesting, vigilant visit. If a balance of power established in the world, respect it rightfully become the best compromise and the United Nations become a respected source for arbitration. We speak also of the move towards a "world of law."

Within this framework of international law, the full partnership can be an effective solution. It can be if these partnerships are not mere subterfuges to better exploit the Third World, but if they are not deemed concluded only to help the needy. Generosity is not a strong assumption in international relations. The idealism has no future. Those who help protect and want to get paid to help and protect. They want to draw a profit too. This requires that interventions partnership to be mutually beneficial for both the one who protects and for those who are protected. We can carry out pilot experiments supported entirely altruistic tiny country, to make examples and lapping partnership mechanisms, but we cannot institutionalize large-scale type of relationship that serves only the party.

Whoever administers must make a reasonable gain, according to criteria that international standards could set the parameters.

The state administration should take the assurance of a well-planned development in order and peace. The whole world will also find interest in solving the problem of underdevelopment otherwise appears insoluble.

Logistics partnership

The full partnership begins with an agreement between two states. A State "director" who offer to take over the governance and administration full of another company and the state of the company to administer, which accepts substitute for governance and administration of those countries administrator.

It's a totally consensual substitution, which support both parties specify in what they expect and what they will bring. This agreement shall be for a defined term of 20 years which can be extended or renewed at maturity. There must be a binding contract, as submitted by the parties to the jurisdiction of a third body in an international organization like the UN or the Court of Justice in The Hague, for example, guaranteeing the validity of the contract itself and the validity of each and every one of its clauses.

This contract is enforceable and binding, because both parties agree to the intervention, military need, an international UN force to enforce that contract. Acceptance in both of this condition should go hand in hand with a commitment of the UN to bring the necessary force that gives its binding contract.

When the state of a country director and the state to administer a country have accepted the principle of such a full partnership, we must determine the terms, conditions, stipulations, penalty clauses. It is especially important to determine the quantitative parameters, as it is not a matter of pious vows.

The performance achieved by the administrator of the State Development administered countries will be evaluated by an impartial third party that the parties have designated. In most cases this will be an international organization such as UNESCO, is not excluded that the UN create an ad hoc body whose monitoring and evaluation of these partnerships would be the only functions.

In any case, all relevant data for the performance of a full partnership agreement will be completely transparent and thus subject to value judgment of the international community. He will not fail others, potential competitor's administrator country to scrutinize and if necessary terminate its action.

Typically, the administrator country commits first, over a period of 20 years, to bring the country administered, which he will assume full control, an increase in its standard of living of a percentage as administrator and administered will generally agreed . Say 10% per year, for example, which is absurd, since China has already achieved this performance and continues to grow around this size.

The country director is also committed to achieve certain specific objectives and implement, in accordance with a specific timetable, some infrastructure perfectly identified. He agrees, for example, in the health sector, subject to control by WHO concrete results; achieve verifiable and quantifiable goals according to the standards of epidemiology. As for life expectancy, infant mortality and the eradication of infectious and endemic diseases, for example.

It is also committed to the establishment of an education system whose programs meet the criteria established at the outset who will have consensus, and take effective measures to ensure the dissemination of this education in of the population, according to the timetable and standards that have been defined and agreed at the outset.

The agreement will provide for the development and rationalization of the country's agriculture administration and the establishment of an industrial structure, indicating the objectives and import-export policies that will be applied. The establishment, also a structure of services, taking into account the standard of living achieved. If exceptional circumstances require that partnership during an unexpected time assistance is provided to the country given this aid will be treated as a loan and repaid, but international organizations control of the partnership will be vigilant that this fortuitous event does not bias more than is required by the development agreement must.

The country director, finally, must of course be committed to provide the state of the country administered at the end of the scheduled term of the contract, all the power he has assumed responsibility. If certain clauses in the partnership agreement have not been met, compensation, the amount of which has been initially set for each of them will then be paid to the country administered as immediate compensation (lump sum) or periodic payments that will last long after the end of the contract.

If the contract is accepted, its entry into force shall be conditional on ratification by a referendum, held under United Nations supervision in the country administered. It can be expected that 50, 55, 60, 66% of the population will have to be agreed that the agreement is ratified.

Following the referendum and the formal signing of the agreement in full partnership, administrator countries to date, completely taking charge of the country to administer. He landed with his troops, police, and administrators.

The course of the partnership

The country director arrives with bag and baggage. Especially, with experts who will occupy all key positions in the administration. The problem of African countries is not, in fact, that the African Minister formed Sorbonne less talented than its European counterpart; it is often more! The problem is that the impact of its ideas and its guidelines do not go much further than the door of his office.

The infrastructure of middle managers and skilled professionals that allows the state to be a real machine to administer and control does not exist in the underdeveloped countries. The mass of those who claim to be the workings of today's secretary who types the letters to site supervisor in the bush - have neither the competence nor particularly motivated to perform this function.

Governance from outside which can be effective if it is based on an administrative structure itself imported. Imported complete without a hiatus which could up and increase the disorder and corruption. The country director arrives with all the necessary resources. The laws of the country director, with some exceptions that have been able to agree, also entirely replace national laws administered, which for the duration of the agreement no longer has legal value.

The borders are completely open in both directions, trade between the country and the country directors administered. Wherever possible, the administrator will see countries that administered the country can enjoy the same benefits import-export enjoyed by the country director in all its business arrangements with third parties.

If partners do not agree to this extension in this area and only in this area, given the country's products are subject to different conditions, but the administrator country will make the necessary adjustments to its economic policies so that these impediments be removed as soon as possible, or it will compensate the country administered.

The government in the country administered at the time of the signing of the agreement in full partnership, is an advisory board; all who are part of the government are part of the new advisory board and receive salary and other benefits significantly increased to compensate for loss of earnings they may suffer because they do not govern the country more administered.

There is not to be mean about this, because there are not so onerous conditions than it will be less than what would have cost corruption.

Any conditions that are transparent are acceptable and, lest we forget, will be ratified by popular referendum.

All local authorities are also transformed into advisory boards, each in the territory and in the areas covered his skill before the arrival of the state administrator. In parallel to these advisory boards that are already in place, will create other industry advisory boards at the convenience the state administrator, who will assist it as necessary to take the pulse of the people.

The state administrator, for example, has every reason to consult teachers on the development of education, health care professionals on the evolution of medicine, traders on the overall economic development as well, of course, union structures in place that will be maintained and available on working conditions.

None of these advisory bodies, however, must have some decision-making power, nor be allowed to use some leverage whatsoever to influence the policy of the state administrator. It is unacceptable that these consultative structures assume the right to discuss afterwards the conditions of partnership that the state administered initially agreed and which the people endorsed by referendum.

It would be unthinkable, for example, the representative organization of workers come to discuss the evolution of the wage structure and therefore interfere in the politics of redistribution of wealth, since such redistribution policy has been inserted fully transparent in the original agreement. If we talk about a 10% increase in the standard of living per year, we must think of a salary increase that is consistent with this objective, but this does not exclude the possibility that wages be increased more than others.

It is possible that the lowest salaries be raised further, for example, and that higher wages would be to a lesser extent. These differences are justified. They will, however, fall within the range that will be defined in the original contract has been concluded and ratified by referendum.

5 years in 5 years, local, regional and national elections in the country administered appoint new representatives to the various advisory boards. These representatives will be elected according to the principles of contractual democracy, each selected independent representatives by those he will represent and not under the banner of bringing together parties into factions who have different views of the evolution of society. These different views should be put on hold for the duration of full partnership, in which policies are the sole responsibility of the administrator state.

The government that was in place in the country initially administered the thus remains as an advisory board for five years and can be replaced by another, and so repeatedly until the end of the eighteenth year of the mandate of the country administrator. A campaign of political awareness and then engages a year before the end of the term of administrator country, elections were held involving this time of parties, each of which must present its vision of society.

These elections were held under the supervision of the United Nations and other international representatives, to ensure unquestionable legitimacy. It was at one of those parties that have been elected as the country director transmits powers at the end of his term. The government is elected May, if it wishes, to negotiate with the country director for an extension of the partnership, but if such an agreement is reached, it will also be subjected to a referendum.

During the last year of the term, future elected rulers gradually being integrated as interns in government and administrative structure of the country administered, before completely taking control as scheduled at the beginning.

Among the changes that the country could lay administrator, it is one that he will not assume liability under any circumstances: Streamlining governance between subsets constituting the country and given the division of powers between these subsets.

When internal dissent in a set are such that it is impossible to establish a credible justice process much less efficient development model that makes consensus, the first solution is to split the patchwork and more homogeneous components . This is the fragmentation of governance that will occur around the world at the pace of rationalization that will lead us to the global state, as we discussed, following this global trend, we could split Africa in more homogeneous components, ethnic scale, even tribal, and it may be time to do even more in Africa than elsewhere. This action, however, being full partnership, would be premature.

Fragmentation of governance is beneficial to avoid strife, if a consensus can be reached as to the powers that are being given to higher authorities; those that meet the common needs and style are the others. It would be unrealistic to expect such a consensus in Africa, while the common needs are basic needs that, overall, are not even minimally satisfied.

This fragmentation of governance presupposes also an abundance of qualified administrative resources, allowing bearings intermediate decisions are created, not always because the objective effectiveness requires, but because it is adding a subjective dimension of satisfaction. This satisfaction is a critical component of optimal functioning of a society, but it is premature to be interested and seek optimization by this refinement, before the essential administrative mechanisms have not even begun to run correctly.

Before one can respond to the cultural diversity of Africa through distributed governance, we must first ensure that Africa is simply governed and administered, it is not and that only partnerships kind described here may provide. The country director will not redistribute the country's governance administered. No insurance, moreover, no guarantee that he does without a second thought.

If this was clear at the outset, no country would agree to let administer. IT'S A State that gave A company to administer and this is ONE company that must make the country director in State A at the end of his term partnership.

The supply and demand, a full partnership

How will negotiate agreements full partnership? At first, just as the concept is widely published and disseminated. Secondly, countries that want to act as director's country, or who would be administered as part of such a comprehensive partnership must occur.

When came forward all who have an interest in this type of agreement, negotiations can only take place between the parties.

Simultaneously, the principle must be agreed at the United Nations, since they may have to accept jurisdiction over the agreements that may occur with the consequences, including that of having maybe one day intervene militarily for enforce.

Which countries may benefit from acting as directors States? First, all countries now have significant technical assistance to underdeveloped countries and not only get no benefit programs, but are well aware that it does not even result of their interventions a concrete result which would justify to their own people, that assistance which it paid the price. Presumably in Canada, Sweden, Norway, the Netherlands, Switzerland.

Then, once the model has been tested, other countries will follow the same path, because it will appear more correct in the eyes of their own people, to have this kind of agreements under international control, rather than managing occult protectorates that serve only the interests of a company. Thus, in France Gabon would best picture, if it does not seem to serve only the interests of which countries will want to be administered? Initially, countries whose leaders will see a good deal, this type of agreement guaranteeing them good pay for a while, while passing the towel on their past transgressions which could eventually create problems for them. They will be certain that the full partnership agreements they have passed will be respected and they will thank you in more of a revolution that sometimes may come sooner than we think.

Aging dictators who made their corn may find attractive this graceful exit which also ensures their place in history by the visionary that progress began.

Secondly, will be in the running countries where the situation is so desperate that it is expected that it will train political parties whose agenda is to sign such agreements. As soon as a democratic outcome is thus given to the people so that they are expressed on the subject, much of the Third World will choose this voice with enthusiasm.

In many countries, the party will offer to negotiate such an agreement will be brought to power with enthusiasm against those who simply offer to do the best with the skills themselves have, traditional approach is already everywhere discredited.

The parties that want to offer this approach can find fairly easily obtain financing from countries wishing to become future managers. It is clear that those who propose this approach will be treated as traitors and quislings by their political opponents, but in the end, it's a popular referendum under control cut that approach much more democratic than most of the United Nations current elections.

What is the practical result of a full partnership? Administered for the country, a real increase in their standard of living, a genuine development that the vast majority of countries formerly colonized third world have not experienced since the departure of the colonial power. An increase in GDP of 10% per year is not illusory; we reiterate that China succeeds. This growth rate five times in 20 years the standard of living of the population. Everyone can calculate the effect of this leap forward on one or other of sub-Saharan Africa, most of the past 20 years, have instead continued to get poorer.

This result is possible because the investment required and the country, given its political instability and lack of proper infrastructure, no one would give him without taking effective control of the country occult which is costly and dangerous will become accessible as if they were made in the country itself administrator.

The country director, for his part, has found an outlet for many experts whose salaries will be paid by the country administered cohorts. It makes a sale of services under very favorable conditions. It is also a captive market of the country administered only to the requirement not to think only for his own benefit, but the real long-term interests of the country administered.

It is a market that will remain captive, moreover, long after the partnership agreement, because of his own or complementary techniques to his own country as the administrator will be introduced and the huge market for spare parts and consumer products will continue to be necessary for the equipment it installed there. These benefits are the same as having a colony; it is not necessary to repeat here all the details.

I cannot think of a better way to solve the problem of underdevelopment. I see no other way to save Africa. This is how we will proceed once we have thought about it. Thus conduct a New Society.

Develop Africa out of traditional patterns

Africa is paralyzed and diplomas do not stop abound moldy. I mean paralyzed for here half a century it is free and it is trying somehow to illuminate. But Africa that has not been as wars of mass destruction or natural calamities that Asia takes off economically or politically.

Seen there, the tone is different. A parent will show you a bridge that connects the village to that of his wife. Another will tell you that his son was able to enter the business school and eventually his life as prefect or governor. For this, we had to pay a pretty penny to the school principal. They will tell you so many things that do not rhyme with the development and well-being. In short, we will always tell you that New York was not built in a day ...

Nobody will tell you that Dakar is a city whose urban planning and development were fifty years ahead of Seoul. All unaware that Kinshasa had roads and gardens that was not in Manila in 1960 how many know that Asian countries do not drowning in raw materials and their only wealth is the gray matter and the political will to develop their country?

It would be hard to explain to a childhood friend, college graduate, that emerging countries owe their development to themselves.

They love their country to invest and build a future for their children. Corruption there also exists as inequalities, frustration and other evils of the countries where democracy timidly his way.

In these emerging markets, politics and democracy are increasingly different ways. Citizens are not only interested in the Masonic lobbying, clan or ethnic. They disassociate themselves increasingly recurrent political speeches or engaging in single parties. Their focus is now their daily problems. These problems are concrete, visible, accessible and shared.

Following the example of My-Society, a British organization that develops websites for improving democratic life, many projects have been realized in the neighborhoods. This mode of communication has allowed citizens to express, very simply, local problems in their street, in their neighborhood. Problems they would like to resolve their elected (abandoned vehicles, cleaning the floor, bad light bulb ...). All reports are documented, are aggregated and sent by mail to the services of the corresponding municipality. They are free to respond here or not. Here is a model of democracy that is of relevance to Africa. This democracy is far virulent speech, interest-free for the citizen expects the concrete. This model takes into account the citizen rather than waiting for everything comes from above.

The challenge of agriculture in Africa

Agriculture is the backbone of African economies. According to data from the World Bank, the sector employs nearly 60% of the workforce but only participates in 12% of the annual wealth created on the continent. Given this poor performance, policy measures have been taken at both national and regional levels to make the best performing sector. In a recent article, Patrick had the PPAAO designed for ECOWAS countries and funded by the World Bank in this connection. With the support of international institutions or NGOs that consider all that agriculture is the main line of development in Africa, many such programs have been designed for African countries, to improve productivity or to improve production. Despite all this, the results provided by the sector remain inadequate. Many African countries that have uses outside to dispose of food. This encourages them to ask questions about the factors that hinder the development of this sector.

This article seeks to identify obstacles to the development of agriculture in Africa and propose some solutions to enable the sector to show its real capabilities.

Enormous potential, just waiting to be exploited

Africa has abundant natural resources: agricultural land, minerals, oil, forests, rivers, fauna, gas, etc. The continent is crossed by numerous rivers and towering, which originate in large lakes. The earth is not uncommon. According to data from WDI (2012), only 43.8% of arable land (about 800 million ha) are used. Topographically, the continent consists of broad plains crossed by rivers that feed the plants mineral lands; some mountainous bands and some not very high plateaus. Thus, the lands are in their Africa's largest favorable for growing plants but also to the practice of farming majority.

The climate is relatively mild, although seasonal and very intense. While the Dry Areas (Sahara and Kalahari) receive slightly rainy, tropical areas (west, central, east) records up to two rainy seasons. The wettest region of the continent is a coastal strip west of Mount Cameroon with 9991 mm of rainfall per year. This rainfall, which dictates the pace of the performance of African agriculture, promotes the development of a fairly diverse flora. On coastal areas, there is a marsh and mangroves with aerial or floating trees. Away from the coast, we found rather inauspicious forest areas to agriculture, followed by savanna areas in some regions (northern Guinea and Sudan). Regarding water resources, the World Bank estimates that only 2% of renewable water resources are used, should be compared with the 5% worldwide. Furthermore, the ecosystem of Africa is an important production base for agriculture and animal husbandry.

Faced with this huge potential, it is hard to think that all projects and programs funded by bilateral and multilateral funding partners (in the form of grants or loans) are unable to launch this key sector.

A politico-administrative situation unfavorable ...

If it is certain that the performance of the agricultural sector is highly dependent on rainfall, the history of African countries shows that the political turmoil they experience cannot really promote agricultural development.

For example, the Ivorian conflict has greatly impacted the "cocoa" sector of this country. The Rwandan case is also speaking.

More generally, conflict affect the practice of agriculture, people are more driven by their survival instinct, abandon their farms.

In the same vein, political change in Africa (which seems to not some promotion of good governance) rather takes the air of a political war that leaves no room for continuation of the programs undertaken by the pension precedents. Instead of defining development programs based on a shared vision and led by an accepted and recognized by all stakeholders in the political debate institution, these programs come mostly from the politician vision of a party or an individual s 'hasten once in control, suspend or remove existing programs and revive those who according to his vision would be the best, at a time when the term of office to the executive becomes increasingly tight (14 years max). This discontinuity in the management undermines an area that needs investment followed. This lack of monitoring should also be noted in programs that have reached their term ... And socio-cultural factors that hinder the emergence of a sector, inefficient Farms in Africa are structured around the family (nuclear or extended depending on the region). Consequently, there are only a very small areas sizes varying between 0.5 and 2 hectares of farm assets with very limited for subsistence and rely on rudimentary methods of work. The family labor there is the main contribution. In such operations, investment cannot be valued, particularly in human capital. Moreover incomes are quite low and therefore cannot allow expansion of farms. While large farms exist, they belong to industrial agribusiness, whose only interest is to safeguard the raw materials needed for their activities. According to FAO, the small size of farms is a major constraint to production in Africa.

This lower performance of the sector is linked to many factors that programs have attempted to curb, including those related to improving productivity through mechanization of agriculture. However, this transformation envisaged seems drag. It is estimated the productivity of land in Africa to 42% (CEA, 2009) with a force of production of 58%. Statistics, that reveal the "under-exploitation"of Africa's agricultural potential.

The inclusion of technology in African agricultural practice is actually limited by the low level of farm household income but also by the lack of a credit system supports the acquisition of modern tools Farmer. They might as well not have the funds necessary to acquire the necessary tools, or obtain sufficient to invest in the expansion of their business loans. A situation made more difficult by the lack of education.

Moreover, households do not always have the correct information regarding the programs and projects to improve the performance of the sector, to assimilate training and field visits by the parent bodies. Moreover, these programs and / or projects conducted by utilities in external financing have specific goals and target only minority holdings. Regarding the latter, the support systems used by farmer's utilities are sometimes inappropriate due to insufficient training of agents. That said, not conducive to "economically" profitable farming ancestral practices, remain the key technology of agriculture in Africa.

Added to these socio-cultural issues, that inhibits some actions to advance agriculture. In Central Africa, for example, the most dynamic farmers are reluctant to take risks or innovate for fear that their "success" does not cause hair loss. In this country, farmers with good performance are suspected by their peers to use occult practices. Such attitudes, which can be found in some socio-cultural groups in Africa are a real development of agriculture blocking, insofar as individuals prefer to remain in a position accepted by his society to emerge to be rejected.

Solutions are they possible?

Given the difficulties that hinder the development of Africa's agricultural sector, it would determine the possible ways to exploit rationally the continent's potential, improve the performance of the sector so that it can provide to households that use a significant and sustainable income.

Above all, it is necessary to establish a framework of good governance in the agricultural sector, and to support decisions on available information on the sector. It would, moreover, rethink systems of credit to farmers. Many countries have a "Credit Agricola" but these banks also" risquophile" than conventional banks, very often offer only seasonal loans (short term) and rarely fund structuring investments in the sector. We should put it to use, in addition to micro-finance institutions, while defining more flexible mechanisms to allow farmers to exploit the opportunities in the financial market.

Beyond these actions within the economic environment and could be answers on the politico-administrative, other points require special outreach and care to enable programs to improve the production or productivity to have the expected impact. In view of the difficulties which require the sector should be based on models of development of farms that integrate the operating mode of these, while improving the quality of technical support and easing requirements for access to rural credit.

Given the integration of technology into difficulty the agricultural sector should move towards integration of livestock and culture to induce a gradual shift from manual cultivation to animal traction, which a gateway is safe for the introduction of more sophisticated technique.

In addition, it must take advantage of sociological research to address the social and cultural considerations that inhibit entrepreneurship farmers.

African agriculture is just emerging, despite efforts by governments in this direction with the support of financial and technical partners. This situation has its roots in fairly complex administrative systems and socio-cultural considerations, which create bottlenecks public actions undertaken to improve the sector's performance. In this context, it should while seeking to raise the level of public services in Africa, taking into account the socio-cultural characteristics of the target populations, all in a stepwise process, in order to bring them to s' appropriating the tools that are available to them and incorporate good practices they consider themselves favorable to their activities.

The threats are not so far away

Although poverty is declining across the world, nearly 800 million people still fall back into poverty if threats such as financial crises, fluctuations in food prices, natural disasters and violent conflicts are not supported, because these threats seriously impede progress. "The global economic impact of the violence amounted to 9.800 billion in 2013 This colossal figure represents twice the total African GDP, or 11% of the gross world product," also said Nardos Bekele -Thomas.

The Government voluntarism guarantee for future success

"Kenya is determined to eliminate inequality and to provide opportunities for all, including through decentralized governance system", said the Secretary of State for Planning Kenyan and Decentralization, Stephen Wainaina. For many observers, particularly for UNDP, "the report calls for institutions and more responsive laws to make societies more equitable and inclusive, especially for groups of people identified as" structurally vulnerable "often for reasons of discrimination and exclusion related to their gender, ethnicity, occupational or socio-economic situational optimistic generation, ambitious and high demand for education: it is the conclusion that emerges from the large study by the New York Forum Africa which runs from May 23 to 25 in Libreville (Gabon). More than 5,000 Africans aged 15-26 years from 42 countries on the continent 54 responded to the online survey. Respondents - 85% between 18 and

26 years; 55% male, 45% female; from Gabon (16%), Cameroon (9.8%), Ghana (9.7%), Nigeria, Senegal, Rwanda, Kenya, Ivory Coast (between 5 and 8%) , South Africa, Ethiopia, Morocco (between 3 and 5%); 60% of students (high school or university), 30% had a job, 10% unemployed) - see the rather blue horizon and value the effort and work.

For 90% of them, their standard of living will be better than their parents, their career prospects better than their elders (82%) and 76% are convinced that the capacity and voluntarism at work make the difference . Educationally, 92% involve a university degree and 86% a master's or doctoral degree. 70% find a match between their training and work. Compared to the state, 40% admit to support him, but 66% found it insufficient. Paradoxically, this application of state is accompanied by a strong desire to study abroad (62%). This raises the issue of brain drain.

Unemployment as concerns

Given the need for economic development in the agricultural sector, the fact that only 16% of young people interested in the industry is a problem. 50% prefer indeed science, 25% business, marketing and economics, 66% business curriculum and technology. The public sector is not spared with less than 20% interest; it is the poor relation of aspirations, where 60% of young people seek private overwhelming support services to companies (40%). Question: how Africa will she grows with a public sector neglected?

Who said private non-job security?

We now understand that for 30% of respondents, unemployment is the top concern. 50% of them had difficulty finding work, when they found it. So there is a gap to reduce: that formed between the young and the job market. Next, there is the market for entrepreneurship. But money and capital shortage. 56% of young people had a hard time finding. And only 12% of those who have become entrepreneurs benefited from the support of the state. The major problem is access to seed capital. Remains the first circle: almost 75% of young people have used the family, friends. It is therefore up to the political and economic decision makers to restructure areas they are responsible for combining the best of local requirements of economic development and globalized aspirations of African youth.

"A laboratory of ideas for development of Africa." Thus Richard Attias, the promoter of the New York Forum Africa (NYFA), describes this meeting of leading policy-makers, economic and international investors interested in Africa. At the heart of trade, May 23 to 25 in Libreville (more on lepointafrique.fr), "the transformation of the continent." The NYFA 2014 intends to focus on ways and means to free the competitiveness of African economies by adding value to natural resources and human as much, and in the service of an integrated vision of the continent.

Hence the Citizens Summit, the big news of the NYFA. A people's manifesto will be established, the result of the meeting between senior political and economic authorities and sixty Africans under 30 years. This manifesto will be sent to the ten largest companies in each country of the Economic and Monetary Community of Central Africa, the main educational institutions and vocational training funds Train

My Generation. Goal, according to Attias: "Ensure that training and skills match the real needs on the ground."

Africa has made significant progress on human development: poverty is declining, incomes rise and performance in education and health care. The Human Development Index (HDI) of the United Nations Development Program (UNDP) shows an annual increase of 1.5%, 15 countries at now in the top rankings (average development to very high). African countries with a high level of development or progression are well integrated into world markets through a range of diversified exports and create jobs.

Room for improvement, however, remains in terms of inclusion, gender equality and environmental sustainability. The exclusion and unequal access to economic and social opportunities are still an obstacle to human rights, the improvement of livelihood and skills training. Environmental challenges - climate change, depletion of natural resources and access to energy - are also an obstacle to sustainable human development. That is why the development agenda post-2015 fixed for Africa focused on equitable economic and inclusive growth objectives, structural changes, with key words empowerment, governance, social change and equality between the sexes.

Increased integration in the value chain can enhance human development in Africa. New technologies and innovative capabilities are two key factors to derive maximum benefits, whether strings local, regional or global value, and manage the risks to the poor and marginalized. The establishment of value chains in order to increase agricultural productivity can create jobs and greater social cohesion, especially in countries emerging from conflict. Small producers, the poor and women have everything to gain from more efficient value chains. Governments, the private sector and cooperatives should protect their rights by promoting resilience, streamlining and competitiveness.

The world is getting better and better. This is the first finding of the Report on Human Development 2013, presented on March 14 in Mexico City by the United Nations Program for Development (UNDP). "No country among those with complete data are available today has an HDI [Human Development Index, Ed] lower than he had in 2000," notes the organization.

But if, in the light indicators "education, health and income," the standard of living has improved globally over the last decade, the trend is even more noticeable in the South, which experiencing rapid progress. As its title indicates, "The Rise of the South", the report confirms that the dynamics have changed sides to be in this large block of geographic borders undefined, primarily driven by three major developing countries that are Brazil, China and India. "By 2020, their combined production [three of them] will exceed the combined production of Canada, France, Germany, Italy, the United Kingdom and the United States," said Helen Clark , Administrator of UNDP. The report adds that in 2050 these three countries account for 40% of world production.

But what part does African countries in this great set? According to the report in 2013, only a few such as South Africa, Ghana, Uganda, Rwanda and Tunisia stand out. Between 1990 and 2012, these countries recorded increases in HDI much greater than what was envisaged.

Landlocked

"Developing countries do not yet fully participate in the development of the South, grade report. Thus, the change is slower in most of the 49 least developed countries, especially those that are landlocked or geographically distant from world markets. "In this category, 33 African countries, all located south of the Sahara, are slightly on the sidelines of the general movement.

Identifying winning strategies, the UNDP report also attempts to identify the mechanisms of development based on decades of observations. Equity, democracy, environment and demography are the four pillars on which the pinned latecomers are strongly encouraged to build.

Human development is one of the main challenges that face today is sub-Saharan Africa. Human capital is indeed a significant factor in its fight to reduce poverty and achieve the Millennium

Development Goals (MDGs).

The assistance provided by the Bank in this region overriding objective of enabling them to achieve high sustainable economic growth by ensuring that growth is distributed in a manner favorable to the poor and accompanied by an improvement social services. The experience that made industrial countries such as the newly industrialized countries has shown that the success of such strategy was through the development of human resources. No country has succeeded with human development levels as low as those observed today in most SSA countries.

The Office of Human Development in the African region is responsible for helping sub-Saharan Africa to accelerate the development of their human resources. The human development strategy established for these countries is to improve the lives of their people by giving them access to education and quality health services, as well as interventions in social protection. Three sub-sectors make up the services of Human Development: Education (EDU) Health, Nutrition and Population (HNP); and Social Protection (SP).

Education.

The Bank supports the development of quality education in most African programs. Our aid is to: focus on quality primary education for all by 2015; improve secondary, tertiary, technical and vocational, and provide education to orphans; address shortages of teachers and textbooks, and address the question of the links between HIV / AIDS and education.

Health, nutrition and population. Support in this area seeks priority: reducing communicable diseases - HIV / AIDS, malaria, "onchocerciasis" (river blindness), tuberculosis and childhood diseases - in groups of poor people; improving nutrition; increase attention to issues of population and reproductive health; and improve health systems through a reform of staffing, pharmaceutical policy and the establishment of a sustainable and equitable financing. The aid strategy followed in this regard by the Bank seeks above all to establish an enabling environment for interventions to be cost-effective which is best left to the implementation of development partners.

Social protection.

Priority areas for support in this area are as follows: development of social protection strategies; risk assessments; pension reform; and implementation of safety net programs for vulnerable groups. This action is primarily intended to protect the elderly and the poor, and support for orphans and the disabled; to provide income support to households affected by economic shocks; and prevent critical shortages consumption among poor households. The strategy in this regard is to target assistance to individuals, especially children and vulnerable young people, while strengthening the support provided to poor households and communities level to enable them to better manage the risk of income.

The current portfolio disservices Human Development Area Africa compared 94 projects with commitments of more than $ 4 billion. In addition to lending, these services carry out analytical work on the country, provide policy advice to implement and work with development partners to harmonize the assistance provided to client countries region.

Macroeconomic Outlook

Africa retained in 2013 an average growth rate of about 4% a performance superior to that of the global economy (3%) and highlights the resilience of the continent face new regional and international turmoil. But the results are very mixed group of countries and one region to another. In sub-Saharan Africa, growth stood at 5% in 2013 and expected to reach 5.8% in 2014 Excluding South Africa this group, predictions are respectively 6.1 and 6.8%. The two most dynamic regions in 2013 are the East Africa and West Africa, where growth a met or exceeded 6%. In addition, low-income countries are doing better than the MICs of the upper North Africa and Southern Africa slice, growth standing at over 6% in the first case, against less than 3 % in the second. The medium-term outlook for the continent are positive: the average growth is expected to accelerate, brushing the top 5% in 2014 and between 5 and 6% in 2015 and it will renew with levels before the start of the global recession in 2009 These forecasts indicate a gradual recovery of the global economy but aussisur stabilization of the political and social situation in African countries currently affected by conflict. But in the event of a prolonged downturn in the international economy - or a less than expected net social and political tensions on the continent appeasement - this forecast could be revised downwards.

Inflationary pressures have eased in many countries, with the stabilization of energy prices and declining food prices. Combined with prudent fiscal policies, these developments have given a little room for maneuver for monetary authorities, which have lower interest rates. But in countries that lack of fiscal discipline and whose currencies have depreciated, a tightening of monetary policy was necessary to curb rising inflation.

External financial flows and tax revenues in Africa

The external financial flows and tax revenues exert a growing influence on the prospects for development and economic growth in Africa. Financial inflows from abroad have quadrupled since 2000 and are expected to exceed 200 billion (USD) in 2014 their composition has gradually evolved, foreign investment and the transfer of migrants from non-OECD sub behind this positive trend. The recovery of foreign investment - direct and portfolio - since the economic crisis of 2009 has now been completed and is expected to a record $ 80 billion in 2014, which would make these flows the primary source of financial contributions to Africa. If resource-rich countries continue to be the preferred destination for foreign direct investment in Africa, manufacturing and services are gaining ground, with more than 750 operations in new projects. In line with a trend that began in 2009, official remittances continued to rise and are expected to reach 67.1

billion USD in 2014 Conversely, the share of official development assistance (ODA) in total external inputs is down from 38% in 2000 to 27% in 2014 (for an estimated USD à55.2 billion). Nevertheless, ODA is still the largest source of external finance for African low-income countries. Tax revenue, steadily rising, should not be considered as an alternative to foreign aid but as a component of government revenues increase as countries develop. They reached USD 527.3 billion in 2012.

Trade Policies and Regional Integration

Taking advantage of the good prices of raw materials, African exports are growing faster than anywhere else in the world in 2012, with a rate of 6.1%. But they account for barely 3.5% of total world exports in that year - a portion that fails to take off. The intercontinental manufacturing trade value added grew faster than exports to the rest of the world. in eliminating bottlenecks and accelerating industrialization, Africa could strengthen exchanges and more firmly into the global value chains. The economic rise of East Asia shows that, to attract foreign direct investment in value chains, countries must adopt reforms and targeted trade policies, implement efficient infrastructure for trade and offer incentives for the adoption of value-added technologies. All these initiatives must be undertaken simultaneously with the regional and national level. The African suppliers are losing ground in the continent imports relative to competitors outside of Africa. If imports grew twice as fast as exports, at an average of 13.8% per year between 2000 and 2010, African countries have not fully participated in this growth. Similarly,

African suppliers need an environment conducive to trade if they want to take a greater share in the value chain of services. Regional organizations have launched major initiatives to accelerate the industrialization and investment in regional infrastructure, but they still need coin be reinforced.

Political and economic governance

Political governance in Africa has improved since 2000 elections become increasingly peaceful and participation of women in politics is increasing. Governments have increased their capacity for collecting and administering taxes. They are determined to fight corruption and illicit capital outflows facing huge liquidity needs - even though both are far from over. It remains many challenges.

In recent years and especially in countries undergoing democratic transition, the population does not hesitate to take to the streets to demand jobs and better wages. It also follows more closely the actions of its leaders, including through digital media. Violence by non-state actors fell in 2012 but remain important for report levels between 1996 and 2010 According to recent surveys, more than a dozen African countries are in the 65 countries of the world with a high risk of unrest civilians. Since 2000, conflicts between African states are fewer and less lethal - but new threats are emerging. The conflicts between factions now mostly the same country, but they re-spring increasingly on neighboring countries. Faced with these risks, the international community is beginning to adapt its responses. Evidenced by the collaboration between the African Union (AU), European Union (EU) and the United Nations (UN) to organize operations in cases of insurrection or hardening of mission mandates of peacekeeping. Better governance and social peace are two key conditions for growth and development. Several promising initiatives aim to end the capital evasion and improve revenue management, particularly in industries extractive by the 2013 edition of Doing Business Report of the World Bank, 15 of the 20 countries where doing business is the most difficult are on the African continent.

The global chains-value

The global values chains (GVC) are made by firms optimize their sourcing strategies by separating the stages of production. If it is accompanied by an up market, integration into the CVM could accelerate structural transformation in Africa. Trade in value used to measure global value chains. To date, Africa only captures a small part, but growing. Productivity gains resulting value chains are easier to reach than the employment growth.

Globalization has changed the mode of production of goods and services. The vision of trade is limited to the level of a country no longer reflects reality. It is replaced by networks of production, even for a simple product covers many countries, and often the entire globe. We call these networks the global value chains (GVC) (Box 6.1). They are made by firms that use advanced communications and regulation to optimize their sourcing strategies through a geographic reorganization and separation of production stages. The global value chains offer new opportunities for structural transformation in Africa. Countries can be integrated into global value chains at some point, usually the assembly in manufacturing and production of commodities in agriculture. Ideally, this strategy offers opportunities for upgrading through the transfer of knowledge, product differentiation and achieving new milestones, adjacent in the value chain. Measures trade in value (as opposed to traditional gross measures of trade) can give an idea of the degree of integration into global value chains and the advantages conferred. So far, Africa accounts for only a small share in world trade measured in value, but the total level of integration in the CVM is high compared to other regions. However, this is mainly due to the downstream integration of African raw materials exported to other parts of the world to be transformed: the share of value added in Africa is very low. On the gains from the global value chains, they are more easily induced export growth and productivity than employment. Success depends on the ability of a country to respond to external demand and the nature of the value chain and business leader.

The main drivers of participation in global value chains (GVC) and progression within them are specific to each country and each value chain. A review of country-specific parameters shows that Africa benefits from endowments attractive, but that productive capacities and inland infrastructure hampering Africa. With regard to specific factors of value chains, the balance of power between business leaders and providers as well as the commitment of leading companies to develop local interactions are critical. This section looks at the factors influencing participation in CVM and progress in the agricultural, industrial and services sectors. In all sectors, although most of the value added is created outside Africa, participation in CVM provides opportunities for employment and learning, and there, in Africa, a significant margin increase value. The main factors for upgrading are meeting standards, the promotion of local entrepreneurship and improving internal technical capabilities. Additional opportunities may arise from targeting devalue regional chains and emerging markets.

The global value chains (GVC) make it even more essential structural transformation in Africa. The shortcomings of Africa on the business environment, infrastructure, productive capacity and skills are the main barriers to structural change (egg AFDB et al, 2013 and 2012. CTEA, 2013; GEF, 2012, World Bank 2013, OECD, 2013a and 2013b;" Ramachandran" et al, 2009).. The accelerated development of global value chains exacerbates these problems, African countries suffering a competitive disadvantage when it comes to attracting investment CVM, especially in the manufacturing sector. Any policy to take advantage of global value chains must effectively address these shortcomings, especially in terms of infrastructure and skills, environment enjoyed by entrepreneurs and openness to trade, including with 'other African countries. This chapter addresses these needs synthetically. For countries that do not move forward to these problems, integration into global value chains remains marginal and the growing range highly unlikely. The only option left for them then is to attract CVM through low binding social and environmental conditions.

The youth challenge

The African population, the youngest in the world, is experiencing rapid population growth: the number of older people aged 15 to 24, currently exceeding 200 million, will double by 2045 The coming decades will arrive on the labor market of hundreds millions of young people of all qualifications.

According to the International Labor Organization, only 16 of the 73 million jobs created in Africa between 2000 and 2008 were held by young people aged 15-24 years. Youth employment is hampered mainly a problem of quality jobs and candidates in low-income countries, and a problem of quantity in middle-income countries. In the first, young people mostly occupy precarious jobs (egg in the extraction of rare earth metals) or are the working poor, while in middle-income countries in the top, they are rather unemployment, partial unemployment or inactive. Aggravating factor for youth employment in Africa: they are more affected by depression than by unemployment. The consequences in terms of poverty are notable, since about 72% of young Africans live on less than $ 2 a day.

But what are the sources of jobs? Neither the public nor the private formal sector, which is growing yet, cannot absorb this influx of young job seekers. Main source of jobs with a living wage, private companies, however, need support to grow, become more competitive and ultimately create jobs.

The informal sector and the agricultural sector will remain by far the biggest job creators. It is for the government to initiate measures to remove the obstacles that many small informal businesses face, so that they grow and create jobs.

Take the example of mobile vendors, significant share of new urban jobs in sub-Saharan Africa. In the informal sector, workers seldom have a dedicated location, and are hounded by the police, municipalities and wholesalers. These often take advantage of their position of power to force street vendors to borrow money at very high rates.

Faced with these difficulties, street vendors in some countries have organized or are involved in urban development.

In Dar es Salaam and Durban, associations of street vendors have established good relationships with municipal authorities; work permits issued to them, and infrastructure have been reserved for them in central locations.

Another major problem is the inability of schools and training centers to provide young Africans the skills and knowledge sought by employers. However, the main hurdle remains generally weak demand for labor.

Governments need to be more active in this regard. While there are public programs on youth employment, but the results are inconclusive. Concerned, a misunderstanding of what works and what does not work, because of a profound lack of available data on employment in Africa, and a frequent lack of coordination between government agencies.

If the short-term outlook is bleak, the long-term horizon seems to clear up, as long as African governments really address the difficulties faced by young people.

Boosting economic sectors booming and creating jobs go through the levers of opportunities that are optimizing education, new technologies and rapid urbanization.

Paradoxically, it is in the informal and agricultural sectors, long considered the brakes, found most often this entrepreneurial spirit without which the employment prospects of young people cannot grow. The government must now seek to exploit this resource.

A declaration of intent was signed at the headquarters of the African Union (AU) in Addis Ababa, Ethiopia, at the beginning of September, between economic UN Commission for Africa (UNECA), the Commission African Union Commission (AUC), the International Labor Organization (ILO) and the African development Bank (ADB).

In an article published on September 14, 2013 BizTechAfrica, a social network specializing in African affairs, especially in the ICT sector, the signing ceremony began with a word from the AU Commissioner for Social Affairs Dr. Mustapha S . Kaloko, which emphasized the importance of this agreement to provide a unified through which youth employment in Africa can be promoted platform.

The statement attributed to each of the above international organizations responsible for creating job opportunities for stimulating development and youth empowerment in Africa. According Biz-Tech-Africa, this joint initiative for youth employment in Africa requires that the four aforementioned international organizations are focusing on the production of knowledge about the intervention in policy and direct intervention.

According to the statement, the African Union is forced to "defend, promote and monitor the implementation of the Declaration on the promotion of employment and the fight against poverty, which was adopted at the Special Summit of Heads of State and African government in Burkina Faso in September 2004.

Here again is yet another unconvincing statement in addition to many other statements signed by international organizations, and that failed. Instead of stimulating markets and small and medium enterprises on the mainland, international organizations such as the ADB and the United Nations have decided to continue signing empty statements. These statements do not make sense if the central African governments do not adhere to it. In fact, these meetings and signature of such statements is a waste of time and taxpayers' money.

Africa needs more than declarations. The foundation of human capital Africans, especially young people, should be directed towards the production - not consumption, especially Western products. African youth need to be rubbed in entrepreneurial initiatives that fit more in South-South cooperation. Entrepreneurship skills must be taught to African youth.

The private sector in Africa remains porous. Instead of signing such agreements and provide financial assistance to African countries, aid ends up in bank accounts abroad, organizations like the ADB, ILO and the UN should rethink their strategy ensuring that African youth is an integral part of the renaissance of Africa.

Entrepreneurship and business partnerships between African youth and those in the "diaspora" could be a way forward. Encourage young people to participate in local government is another avenue that has not been exploited.

This raises questions about the role of state cooperation in Africa is to ensure that such statements focused on youth employment bear fruit. African states should finally see their youth as the future and work with it to ensure that Africa achieves its full potential.

It should also get rid of the old obsolete education system inherited from the former colonial masters, and adopt an education system based on business development and growth.

That means that, if properly designed and implemented, can be beneficial to African youth.

There is no single determinant to the challenge of youth employment in the African region. It is rather a combination of factors contributing to aggravate a situation that has become, therefore, a political priority for the region.

In sub-Saharan Africa, unemployment rates remain relatively low because the vast majority of young workers in the workplace cannot afford not to work. However, these young people regularly suffer from underemployment and lack of decent working conditions. Of the 38.1 percent of the total working poor in sub-Saharan Africa, young people make up 23.5 percent. Young women tend to be more disadvantaged than young men in access to work and face worse working conditions than their male counterparts. Employment in the informal economy and informal employment is the norm.

In North Africa, the unemployment rate (from a general workforce more educated) are very high (23.8 percent in 2012, with an increase of 3 percentage points between 2010 and 2011 and a steady increase since 2007) and expected to remain high over the next five years. Unemployment can probably be considered the source of the Arab Spring uprisings. At the same time, the participation rate in the labor force for women are the second lowest in the world (33.4 percent in 2012, just after the Middle East). Informality is less marked than in sub-Saharan Africa, but still persistent.

The ILO cooperation on youth employment in Africa

ILO work on youth employment has focused on three main areas: technical assistance to the tripartite constituents, advocacy and knowledge development and dissemination.

In terms of technical assistance to the tripartite constituents on youth employment, support is mainly but not exclusively achieved through technical cooperation projects. Currently, the ILO is implementing technical cooperation projects in 27 countries in the African region. This portfolio has a budget of over 80 million USD.

The areas are identified with constituents and vary but include, among others, the following:

Counseling in employment policy. These services cover a wide range of activities, integrate decent work into national and regional development strategies for legal advice on core labor standards, advice on specific topics of interest in the country (for example, the development of national action plans on or access to finance youth employment legislation of the Democratic Republic of Congo, Egypt, Malawi, Mali, Morocco, Senegal, Togo and Uganda);

The employment services, skills development and training to the labor market, focusing in particular on technical and vocational education, apprenticeship programs, and services tailored for the professional integration of young people disadvantaged (eg, Benin, Burkina Faso, Comoros, Egypt, Liberia, Zambia and Zimbabwe);

Job creation, including business and support the development of entrepreneurship, services business development and public works labor-based (eg, Kenya, Sierra Leone, Somalia, Africa South, South Sudan, Sudan, Tanzania and Uganda);

Other areas where actions are taken, often in collaboration with constituents are: data collection and assistance to national statistical offices, workers' rights (eg, Lesotho), migration (eg, Mauritania and Senegal), the fight against the worst forms of child labor), prevention and management of HIV / AIDS in the workplace (eg, Kenya and Malawi) and support for young people with disabilities (eg , Malawi).

Regarding advocacy for youth employment, the ILO has launched a partnership with the African Development Bank, the Commission of the African Union and the Economic Commission of the United Nations for Africa (ECA) to 'jointly address youth employment at the regional and national levels. In addition, the partnership between the ILO and the World Bank and the United Nations in the global network of youth employment has led to a research focus on Africa and ad hoc projects (eg Relief Fund Youth Services).

The ILO is also active in promoting the creation of youth employment, labor rights and employability through dedicated events. Eleven national events of youth employment have occurred in the area between March and April 2012.

In terms of knowledge development and dissemination, the first "decent work indicators for Africa" report, which was published in 2012, contains specific indicators Youth comparing the performance of countries for which data release. In addition, the ILO is to conduct investigations of school to work transition (PAG) in nine African countries. These surveys provide the primary data that are rarely available. Regarding policies and programs, the region is developing a plan to help the global database of ILO policies for youth employment.

Africa must mobilize more domestic resources

African countries need to diversify their sources of funding including mobilizing more domestic resources, said the Executive Secretary of the Economic Commission of the United Nations for Africa (ECA), Aboulie Janneh, at the Conference of the CEA, which began Wednesday in Tunis.

The continent is expected to increase domestic resource mobilization to supplement international public aid, loans and private capital flows, said Wednesday the head of the CEA. The combined consumer spending in Africa amounted in 2008 to $ 860 billion while its combined reserves were 470 billion at the end of 2009.

Fiscal consolidation combined with austerity measures may lead to an overall reduction in demand and a double dip recession with negative consequences for African exports, has tempered the head of the CEA.

"There are interesting examples of diversification of production and trade flows on the continent. Recent Economic Performance in Africa is not only due to external demand for its goods, but also as a result of the growth in services such as banking, telecommunications, tourism and construction, "said Janneh Aboulie.

For example, Africa's exports to Asia increased from 14% in 2000 to 27% in 2010 this ratio is similar to exports between Africa and the United States and Europe, its business partners traditional.

"The role played by governments in developed during the global economic crisis countries have encouraged states to have a more strategic role, including the return to planning on the continent," said the head of the CEA.

Organized by the Economic Commission for Africa (UNECA) and the African Development Bank (AFDB), the conference's theme this year, 'An Agenda for Africa: economic recovery and growth long term.

Through the prism of official development assistance and foreign direct investment flows of export earnings of certain agricultural products

The start of partnership relations between Europe and the Caribbean and Pacific countries Africa-(ACP) in 1963, when the first agreement was signed in Yaoundé, which defined non-reciprocal tariff preferences between the two entities. The Agreement "Yaoundé II" on the conditions for financial and technical cooperation, intervened in 1969, and that of "Lomé I" in 1975 this adds to previous agreements some trade protocols, said additional, and stabilization fund. As for "Lome", it expanded in 1980, Stabex device mineral products. Finally, "Lome" confirmed these options in 1985 while "Lomé" introduced two conditionality in line with a commitment to support the development of the private sector and invited him to enter into a program of structural adjustment in the event of deteriorating macroeconomic aggregates. Despite this long tradition of partnership with Europe, the growth rate of most countries in the region remained below the ambitions and progresses to some of them, at a rate below that population. The result is a decline in GDP / capita in some countries and, consequently, an increase in the incidence of poverty in the space of ECOWAS. This is in part due to relatively low levels of investment rates in most countries of the region. Besides, this is evidenced by the low attractiveness of the region with respect to foreign direct investment (FDI), despite a strong market for nearly a quarter of a billion consumers while aid flows public development assistance (ODA) was relatively strong. The low investment rate and thus the growth of economies in the region stems Does the rule of ODA on I'IDE?

Several studies have attempted to identify the effects of aid and foreign direct investment (FDI) on growth. In the analysis of the link between FDI and growth, it denotes an opposition between two streams: one defending the idea of a positive impact of FDI on economic growth and the applicant a negative effect of FDI on the rate growth.

For advocates of the first current, FDI is an important means of technology transfer (Borenzstein, De Gregorio and Lee, 1998). Companies that install through FDI inflows increased allocations of the economy in technological and organizational knowledge transferable to the rest of the economy (Caves, 1996). As a result, FDI contributes significantly to productivity growth in the economy of host (De Mello, 1997) and can stimulate growth by facilitating the incorporation of new inputs and new technologies in the production function (Feenstra and Markusen, 1994).

If in developed economies, the positive impact of FDI on growth is evidenced in the least developed countries, however, these are variables such as enrollment rates that determine the greater the effect of FDI on growth. Indeed, the channel of technology transfer can only be operational if the host country has a minimum level of human capital (Bronstein, De Gregorio and Lee, 1998).

For other authors, capital flows, increasing the availability of savings in the economy, stimulate the accumulation of capital and help reduce its cost (Deepak M. et al. 2001). Consequently, they can enhance the total factor productivity in the economy, by improving the allocation of resources and promoting the development of domestic financial markets. In addition to their impact on technology transfer, FDI promote accumulation of human capital of the receiving country (OECD, 2002 a; Alaya, 2006). Indeed, the demand for skilled labor by multinational firms encourages states to invest more in education (Blomstrom, Kokko and Zejan 2000). The IDE also contribute to the intensification of trade with certain assets of multinational corporations such as quality and product labeling, as well as their ability to penetrate world markets (OECD, 2002).

The spillover effects from FDI inflows (in human capital accumulation, increase the rate of investment, technology transfer, increase in total factor productivity, greater penetration of foreign markets, etc.) and offer the economy, the opportunity to build competitive advantages over time (Alaya, 2004). Several studies and conclude that complementarily between multinational and domestic companies and thus FDI and domestic private investment (Rodriguez-Clare, 1996, Markusen and Venables, 1999). Indeed, FDI can drain domestic investment when their influx contributes to the transfer of technology, the introduction of new knowledge, the overall effectiveness and improvement of the business environment.

However, other studies seem to suggest that a negative impact of FDI on economic growth. Indeed, the existence of barriers to market entry that discourage the entry of new firms and cause the output of local farmers market may arise from the behavior of firms. It can also cause crowding mechanism between FDI and domestic private investment (Alaya, 2006), as observed from the rest Caves (1996) in developing countries. This negative correlation between FDI and economic growth is explained by the effect of domination exercised by foreign firms. The latter may result in a deterrence of business development of research and development of local firms (Brewer, 1991). According to Saltz (1992), the impact of FDI on growth is generally lower in developing countries that have removed any constraint on repatriation of earnings from these investments. Their negative impact on GDP growth can also occur when the receiving country is poorly endowed with human capital (Blomström et al., 1992). This negative effect can also result from the "Dutch disease" in developing countries heavily endowed with natural resources and whose exchange rate appreciates following induced adverse effects of the operation of the latter.

As for the impact of official development assistance (ODA) on growth, some studies suggest through its growth while others highlight its potential positive effects under certain conditions. For authors such as Easterly (2006), the majority of assistance to developing countries for 50 years has been ineffective due to lack of control over the people who manage this assistance. Other authors such as Feyzioglu et al. (1998) determined that most of the envelope of this aid is devoted to public consumption. For others, it is misleading to call "development aid", the flow of capital transferred from the North to the South as such. Bauer (2002), it is more of a hindrance to development aimed at maintaining the underdeveloped countries in their status.

Bauer (2002) rather puts forward the importance of private property and the rule of law on economic development.

However, some authors have mixed views on the issue of the aid-growth. Burnside and Dollar (1997), aid can not, by itself, produce positive effects. Its impact can only be measured in the context of "good policies". These authors defend this position, highlighting the significant impact on the growth of a variable combining the level of support and quality of policies. The effect of an additional dollar of aid and depends on the quality of economic policies and the aid itself. Collier and Dollar (2002) suggest the existence of decreasing returns to scale assistance. In other words, the effect of aid is positive but decreases as the volume of aid increases. However, the robustness of this assumption of decreasing returns to scale has been questioned by many authors, especially Hansen and Tarp (2001). Other authors have concluded their work in the same direction as Burnside and Dollar (1997) arguing the idea that aid was not ineffective in principle, but rather because of the use made of it.

In this paper, we trace and analyze major trends in FDI and aid in the ECOWAS and build on our profile of some determinants of

FDI flows by relying on stylized facts. The analysis is conducted by distinguishing four sub-periods: one that goes above the adjustment period (1960-1979), a second where most economies in the region were under adjustment and ranges up to consideration of the social dimension of adjustment (1980-1990), a third covering the period pre-monetary adjustment of the countries of the Franc Zone (1991-1994) and the last post covering the evaluation period (1995 -2006).

In what follows, we first describe in the first section of the socioeconomic situation in the region. The trends of aid and FDI in the ECOWAS space are analyzed and finally, the profile of some determinants of FDI flows prepared.

The growth challenges facing ECOWAS countries has led most economies develop strategies for attracting investment and a favorable investment code to increase their gross investment rate. Furthermore, over the past decades, efforts to diversify economies have resulted in a more pronounced integration of non-traditional partners, particularly in Asia, in the economic fabric of ECOWAS countries. At the same time, flows ODA (ADP) remained significant and many states in the region depend.

For some of them, the same APD determines the fiscal effort of the state to the rest of the economy. Around the AO is it an economic area using pro or pro-IDE? Generally, the countries' investment rates in the region depend on their propensity to attract more FDI or ODA.

The review of related FDI and SA certifies that the region of the AO is an economic area pro-aid. Indeed, over the different sub-periods, ODA flows were generally higher than those of FDI. However, there has been in recent years a tremor in FDI flows since their growth rate became more sustained than ODA.

Examination of the structure of flows in the region attests that the polarization of countries around the ODA flows and / or different IDE. Overall, Nigeria, Liberia and Gambia are the savings that attract relatively more FDI than ODA.

Moreover, in some countries such as Mauritania and Liberia phases divestment is noted as net FDI flows are negative.

The rule of ODA on FDI seems to affect the effort to build domestic. Indeed, an examination of the investment rate attests that it is modest in most countries in the region. Only Cape Verde, Ghana and Mali are characterized by a relatively large accumulation effort.

Investment rates are generally modest, the performance achieved by the economies of the region during these three periods are relatively meager. Consequently, although most of them are given the ambition to integrate the club called emerging countries, growth rates are still low. Furthermore, it is characterized by high instability. If the Ivory Coast, Mauritania, Togo and Nigeria stood out in the region in the aftermath of 60 years, it is now Liberia, Burkina Faso, Cape Verde and Mali, which stand out in the region as being the fastest growing companies in the post-devaluation period.

The modest growth levels also reflect a weak foreign demand for countries in the region.

A review of the export rate certifies that except Nigeria, which however has the largest domestic market, the growth of most economies in the region is driven more by domestic demand components.

This strategy is not viable in view of the small market size of the different economies, except Nigeria. However, despite the importance of the local market, Nigeria is the country that has one of the highest in the region export rates, next to The Gambia, Côte d'Ivoire and Mauritania.

The pace of wealth creation is relatively low, resulting in a steepening of the distance between the GDP / capita of the countries of the region and the developed countries and the so-called emerging countries. However, some countries in the region have levels of GDP / capita relatively significant. The GDP / head of Cape Verde and Côte d'Ivoire respectively reached 1,166 and 599 dollars2. In emerging markets like Brazil and Malaysia, it is 3745 and 3916, respectively, while for developed countries such as Germany and the USA countries, it reaches respectively 22,762 and 34,081 dollars.

Due to the low performance in terms of growth, however, unstable in the region, growth in GDP / capita is also low and sometimes negative. The best performances in terms of increasing GDP / capita in recent years are those made by Liberia, Cape Verde and Burkina Faso.

Overall, the review of historical data confirms that over a long period, the rate of population growth is more sustained than the creation of wealth for most countries in the region. In addition, during certain periods, the growth rate of GDP / capita is negative while the population continues to increase significantly in many countries.

The increasing population of sustained relative to the speed of wealth creation so, it follows high levels of poverty in the West African region.

The high levels of poverty resulting in large, unequal profiles favored by anti-poor growth observed in most countries in the region revenue.

Push factors of FDI

FDI are they polarized around "good student" or "sinners"? In general, economies with low human capital and infrastructure endowment and unfavorable business environment have little attraction for FDI. In addition, high poverty rates generally translate into pressure on public resources for redistribution and therefore levels of taxes and / or higher debt levels. Also, the rule of ODA on FDI may cause a risk of crowding out of FDI that could have perverse effects, in a context of "bad policy" to encourage an inefficient allocation of resources.

In this sub-section, we examine the level in terms of relative endowments of human capital, infrastructure and business environment of the countries in the region and ease of access to technical inputs.

Human capital

In the early 1990s, which were marked by the World Summit on the Millennium Development Best 'students' school enrollment in primary schools were Cape Verde, Togo and Nigeria showed that enrollment highest. In secondary education, it is Nigeria, Cape Verde and the Ivory Coast who had the best profile.

The review of tertiary attested that it was Senegal, Mauritania and Togo who had the highest rates. Overall, Cape Verde stood out as the country with the best performance in terms of enrollment.

However, much effort has been made by other countries in the region to reduce their deficits in human capital. Between 1991 and 2005, it is the Republic of Guinea, Mauritania and Mali that show the best growth in the primary level. Cape Verde, Benin and the Republic of Guinea is the country that has risen faster their enrollment in the secondary level. In the service cycle, Ghana, Senegal and Mali show the best performance.

From the point of view of health infrastructure endowments, Burkina Faso, Nigeria, Ghana and Togo show the best ratios in terms of availability of hospital beds. These levels are quite distant from the standards displayed by developed countries and emerging ones.

Business Environment

The business environment is very complex to measure, but is one of the most critical signals in attracting foreign direct investment. To get an overview of the state of this crucial institutional factor view, we use as a proxy index easier to undertake that could synthesize most related to the business environment in which constraints facing investors.

This index easier to undertake is captured by the number of days required to open a company. The countries in the region in which the number of days required to start a business is the lower are Ghana, Nigeria, Gambia and Cape Verde.

Infrastructure and providing technical inputs

Roads are one of the most essential in the deployment of private capital public goods. If we use as a proxy road density in order to assess the relative endowments of infrastructure in the country, "good performers" in terms of road network are respectively Cape Verde, Gambia, Ghana and Cote d'Ivoire. These countries have the highest levels of road densities.

Much more than the cost, access to technical factors of production (electricity, water) is a major obstacle to the expansion of private initiative in the West African region. In particular, many countries in the region are facing decades to severe energy crises. These problems are usually exacerbated by changes that occur in the oil market where the price of a barrel sometimes reaching levels difficult to sustain.

The review of the electricity supply capacity in the region attests that only few countries appear generate surpluses. The production potential is sometimes diminished by the age of the network creating major losses; which substantially reduces the effective supply of electricity.

Examination of trends in ODA and FDI flows show that the relative weight of the latter is relatively lower. This weakness of FDI inflows partly explains the low levels of investment rates in the region. As a result, the levels of growth of the GDP and GDP / capital remain relatively modest. Moreover, modest levels of growth do not favor an increase in the tax base and, consequently, helps to increase the dependency ratio of the states vis-à-vis ODA contributing to a vicious circle. It is therefore necessary to increase more vigorous pace of wealth creation in the region. It is true that a quarter billion people, mostly made up of poor could be a handicap. However, it also represents a quarter billion potential consumers in the region that could be a major issue for firms in competition and in perpetual search of markets at the margin in the context of globalization. Consequently, it is urgent to transform the stresses in the region of opportunity. To this end, it is important to reduce to see better tackle factors repulsion FDI and business and therefore:

The Millennium- Development Goals

The world "leader" significantly raises the enrollment rate and the level of health coverage.

- Density the region in infrastructure

- Ensuring access to technical factors at low cost

- Improve the business climate and eliminate all the weaknesses that force our economies to operate en- below their production frontier in September 2000 at the Millennium Summit in New York have adopted a series of ambitious targets to achieve tangible progress in reducing poverty and improving living conditions in the world.

They stressed on this occasion the special needs of Africa, the poorest continent on the planet, which has fallen behind in almost all development indicators. Heads of state and government will return to New York in September 2005 for eval-luer what needs to be done to achieve these goals.

The international community increasingly concerned that, despite some modest progress in a limited number of areas, Africa will not be able to get closer to achieving the Millennium Development Goals (MDGs) by the target date 2015 without mobilizing efforts and more energetic resources of African countries and the international community. We provide below an overview of trends in sub-Saharan Africa for a series of key targets from 1990 to date, and indicate the directions for the continent achieves these goals.

- 1 -Halve, between 1990 and 2015, the proportion of people whose income is less than one dollar a day.

While the rate of indigent people in all developing countries fell from 27.9% in 1990 to 21.3% in 2001, it has increased in sub-Saharan Africa. This has also increased the number of poor Africans, which rose from 227 million to 313 million during this period.

- 2 -Ensure that, by 2015, children everywhere, boys and girls around the world are able to complete their primary education.
- 3 -Promote gender equality and empower women.

In sub-Saharan Africa, the rate of primary school enrollment of girls has increased relative to that of boys, 83% to 86% between 1990-1991 and 2001-2002; the goal is to reach 100% in primary education, preferably by the end of 2005, and in secondary and higher education by 2015 the share of women in non-agricultural activities increased from 32% to 36% between 1990 and 2003, while the proportion of women members of legislative bodies of countries in the region has doubled from 7% in 1990 to 14% in 2005.

- 4 -Reduce by two thirds, between 1990 and 2015, the mortality rate of less than five years.
- 5 -Reduce by three quarters the maternal mortality ratio.

The lack of sufficient data did not accurately determine the mortality rate in 1990 in most regions. However, in 2000, the rate (expressed as the number of women who died during childbirth per 100 000 live births) was 920 in sub-Saharan Africa, more than twice the average of 450 for all developing countries.

- 6 -fight against HIV / AIDS, malaria and other diseases.

Although the number of HIV cases has stabilized in sub-Saharan Africa in recent years, there is still the highest in the world, seven out of 100 adults living with the virus. AIDS is the leading cause of premature death in the region. Malaria is also a concern general, 90% of the one million deaths from malaria each year occurring in sub-Saharan Africa.

- 7 -Ensure environmental sustainability. Reverse the loss of environmental resources. Halving the number of people without continuous access to potable water and sanitation services.
- 8 -Establish a global partnership for development.

This would involve the establishment of a close to the special needs of the least developed countries open, regulated and non-discriminatory trading and financial system, which would deal thoroughly debt issues in developing countries and make more accessible the benefits of new technologies.

The slow progress in Africa on social indicators may be related to the inability of policymakers to solve the problem of food insecurity, the theme of this report. Food insecurity in Africa predates the MDGs. Since the mid 1980s, the number of food crises in African countries has tripled, and new challenges such as climate change and agriculture underutilized only aggravated the problem. How does this phenomenon affect the other MDGs, particularly those in health? And how concerted efforts to improve agriculture, food distribution and nutrition can accelerate progress on other MDGs?

Measured by their efforts, the three countries African- Burkina Faso, Mozambique and Namibia, showing the way for accelerated progress on 16 of 22 indicators available.

Many countries in Central and Western Southern, Eastern, have significantly improved their growth rates and are among the top 20 countries. And for most of the indicators of progress has been accelerated. In North Africa, Egypt has opened the way for acceleration or maintaining its growth rate in 11 indicators, followed by Morocco and Tunisia with 9-8 indicators respectively. In the rest of Africa, by contrast, 40 of the 50 countries have maintained or accelerated the pace of progress in at least 11 indicators between periods post-2000 and pre-.

The analysis confirms the commitment and commendable efforts that African countries are towards the MDGs and the need to review the metrics of progress in this context.

Goal 1: Eradicate extreme poverty and hunger

The poverty reduction lags economic growth

Africa is the second region of the world with the fastest growth. Poverty has fallen faster there since 2005 as compared to 1990-2005, but not fast enough to achieve the goal by 2015 most workers are employed in precarious low-wage jobs and low production. High inequality in most African economies has placed poverty reduction behind economic growth. However, the accelerating growth of the continent provides a unique opportunity to reduce poverty and create jobs through proactive policy interventions. Create more decent jobs faster calls for structural transformation of African economies with bold industrial policies that promote value addition and economic diversification.

Rising food prices and recurrent in the Sahel and the Horn of Africa drought are among the factors behind the slow progress in nutrition levels

The performance of African countries in reducing hunger is variable. During the period 1990-2012, three (3) countries reduced hunger by 50 percent or more (Ghana, Democratic Republic of Congo and Mauritania), 19 have reduced hunger between 20.0 and 49.9 percent 13 and have reduced from 0.0 to 19%.

Goal 2: Achieve universal primary education

Primary school in Africa is becoming the norm, but the quality of education remains a challenge.

Most African countries have achieved universal primary education with greater than 90 percent rate. Consequently, the continent as a whole is likely to reach Objective 2 However, low achievement and improving the quality remains a challenge. Indeed, one in three people enrolled in a primary school outside the school system. Reasons include a late entrance, poverty, poor education and lack of awareness of the importance of school. About 30 percent of students in six years of schooling cannot read a sentence, and girls are more likely to drop out than boys. However, there is some good news: some school feeding and access to nursery schools have played a role in reducing the dropout rate programs.

Goal 3: Promote gender equality and empower women

Nearly half of African countries have achieved gender parity in primary school .

African women are becoming more independent: more girls attending both primary and secondary cycles and ensure more women in positions of political power. Nearly half of African countries have achieved gender parity in primary school, while the parity at the secondary and tertiary levels has improved, the lack of data makes it difficult to measure progress. At nearly 20 percent in 2012, the proportion of seats held by women in national parliaments in Africa is only surpassed in Latin America and the Caribbean. While Africa is making great progress towards Goal 3, early marriage, the power dynamics of households and small business opportunities for women, slows progress. These challenges must be addressed if Africa is to achieve all the objectives and indicators by 2015.

Goal 4: Reduce child mortality and improving maternal health

Despite progress, Africa still has the highest burden of child and maternal mortality in recent years, the mortality rate of under-five and maternal mortality rates have fallen significantly. During the period 1990-2011 the continent has reduced its mortality rate of less than five years to 47 percent. But an inexcusable children and pregnant women still die every year number of preventable causes. To accelerate progress, it is important to have integrated interventions in maternal and child health. This must be done by focusing on infant mortality and adopting comprehensive policies to address the underlying causes of maternal and infant mortality.

Goal 5: Combat HIV / AIDS, malaria and other diseases

Although tuberculosis and malaria remain serious health threats, Africa as a whole has stopped their spread; Africa has stopped and reversed the spread of HIV / AIDS, with lower prevalence rates of 5.9 percent in 2001 to 4.9 percent in 2011 and thanks to a strong political will, targeted interventions and antiretroviral treatment available for the majority of the population. Although tuberculosis and malaria remain serious health threats, Africa as a whole has stopped spreading. Infections and deaths from TB have declined sharply in recent years, like malaria cases and deaths are linked. Improving the prevention and treatment has played a major role in these declines.

Goal 6: Develop a global partnership for development

As a percentage of their combined GNI, ODA to developing countries and least developed countries in general decreased by 4 per cent in real terms in 2012 after a decline of 3 percent in 2011.

Donors still well below their commitments on official development assistance (ODA) to developing countries and least developed countries are unlikely to significantly increase funding in the short and medium term. As a percentage of their combined GNI, ODA to developing countries and least developed countries in general decreased by 4 per cent in real terms in 2012, following a decline of 3 percent in 2011 in real terms bilateral ODA to Africa has also declined in 2012 Total ODA in all developing countries in Africa that are landlocked, has increased an average of 2 percent in nominal terms over the period 2009-2010. These trends can be attributed in part to the crisis of sovereign debt. And are likely to continue in 2016 ODA reductions were observed in the countries of the euro zone crisis hit hard as Spain and Portugal.

For action

In this section, we discuss various options. Presentation follows the logic of a tax reform process such order. In the short term, policymakers should focus on ways to expand the most effective but also the most equitable tax base in the way - by removing tax advantages by addressing abuses by multinational companies on transfer pricing and taxing extractive industries impartially and transparently. The medium-term structural imbalances require strategies that target the informal sector, enhance fiscal legitimacy and administrative capacity and seek international cooperation to improve resource mobilization. The longer-term goal, which is to generate revenue based on a more balanced tax structure, can be achieved using instruments, such as urban property taxes. It is progressive taxes whose scope can be expanded to keep pace with the rapid urbanization in Africa and meet the substantial needs of urban infrastructure. Development partners can easily provide assistance in this area.

Ideally, can African countries to improve their tax systems? Recent studies have made a number of recommendations on the treatment of tax for policy makers on the continent. Volkerink (2009), IFC (2009), Keen and Mansour Bahl and Bird (2008) call to raise taxes low and relatively tightened on a broad base rate, to the extent that it facilitates the recovery and management. They also recommend eliminating exemptions and tax loopholes and avoid over-dependence vis-à-vis trade taxes. VAT has become the main indirect tax, replacing taxes on sales and even sales. The basic message is to maintain a simple and applicable to a broad base low, flat rate for all.

The most effective way to increase government revenue is to implement policies that will increase the tax base through a sustained economic growth. The collection efficiency also helps to mobilize resources without overtaxing the economy.

Ideally, any tax increases must be devoid of effects on growth and should not harm an already weak private sector in many African countries.

To raise revenues, a state can raise the level of taxation of existing taxpayers and / or increase the number of these. African countries should favor the second option. Plus the base is broad, more stable it is, since it is based on a diverse set of taxes and imposes a burden lightened on each type of contributor and economic activity. It also allows for greater involvement of citizens in the national political process.

Fiscal policy should take into account administrative constraints

Governments must first identify policy options that are theirs, and maximize revenue for each of the selected options. In most African countries, the choices are limited in the short term by the capacity of the tax administration. Stakeholders often overestimate the results that fiscal policy will reasonably achieve. Thus, the continent has at its disposal fewer redistributive industrialized countries tax policies. Upgrading the Tax Administrations is a prerequisite for reducing income inequality through progressive taxation.

Copy redistributive strategies in countries with high administrative capacity can be very productive against either unintentionally or because these policies favor the middle classes. It makes more sense to raise rates in higher education, to introduce road tolls, vehicle registration fees, which are elements key consumer of the richest Africans. However, the implementation of its measures can be complicated politically; they target the elite that have the greatest influence on legislation. Bolnick and Haughton (1998) suggest that African countries rely more on indirect taxes, even if they are raised to a high level and that their base is restricted. Property taxes may also be considered to ensure the redistribution of income. Again, the elites, who are more likely to contribute to these levies, may combat legislation that would put in place.

In 1980, African leaders met in Nigeria to adopt the Lagos Plan of Action was seen as an African plan designed not only to stem the crisis that developed in African economies but also to cope with the constant problems under development on the continent. However, the ink of the Lagos Plan of Action has barely dried as the World Bank issued its famous report of Berg who paved the way for the imposition of orthodox structural adjustment and neo-liberal agenda to African countries. During the next two decades, African countries, under penalty of conditionality's of donors have been forced to implement measures that are essentially complicated economic problems of Africa. Faced with the exhaustion of the possibilities of the Washington Consensus, which forms the basis of orthodox adjustment measures, we are once again looking for other development paradigms can transform Africa. Initiatives such as the discourse of renaissance given by President Thabo Mbeki in Cape Town, the Millennium Action Plan (MAP), jointly formulated by the President of South Africa, President Obasanjo and President Bouteflika and the Omega Plan Abdoulaye Wade were merged and initially called "New African initiative (NAI)" and be consent the New Partnership for Africa's Development (NEPAD), demonstrate that political efforts are underway to ensure that the 21st century and the new millennium beyond Africa.

Ironically, these initiatives have resulted in the adoption of NEPAD continues at a time when the World Bank announces its publication on the ways in which Africa can claim the 21st century. It seems that a new race to the definition of the parameters and the substance of the development agenda of Africa was triggered. Which way will Africa, under the direction of who and what are the mechanisms?

The Council for the Development of Social Science Research in Africa (CODESRIA) and Third World Network (TWN) Africa invite intellectuals and civil society activists from Africa to submit proposals for papers in order to allow critical review of research on alternative development framework for Africa outside of structural adjustment. This conference aims to ensure greater dissemination of the contents of these important documents among intellectuals, policy makers and African activists to initiate a debate on the merits of these publications in the hope that other perspectives of alternative development policies Africa will emerge as well as establish a network of African intellectuals who are interested in research to advocacy for the prospects of development policies that are different from those of the World Bank-sponsored networks.

Among the issues to be addressed at the conference include: the experience of twenty years of (mis) adjustment in Africa, prospects for the development of an African development strategy in the context of globalization, the points common and differences between the various initiatives that have been consolidated in NEPAD, a review of NEPAD in relation to the Lagos Plan of Action, NEPAD compared to structural adjustment and the publication of the World Bank entitled Africa can claim the 21st century?, instead of NEPAD in the context of the Pan-African Project, including the revival of the integration / sub-regional and continental cooperation, the development component of NEPAD and the strategic issues that are related to implementation.

Overview

The least developed countries (LDCs) face many challenges: extreme poverty and persistent, weak and poor economic growth, limited capacity, poor infrastructure and inadequate social services, among others.

Although the problems of LDCs have been recognized by the United Nations since the 60s and have been the subject of several action programs and international commitments, their economies are weak. In Africa, where 34 of the 53 ECA member States are LDCs, persistent economic and social problems remain.

It is to address these challenges that the Declaration and Program of Action in Brussels were adopted at the Third United Nations Conference on the Least Developed Countries, held from 14 to 21 May 2001 in Brussels and later approved by the General Assembly in its resolution 55/279 of 12 July 2001 the Program of Action provides a framework to reduce poverty and improve human development during the decade 2001-2010. To follow up, 30 targets and 63 indicators have been set.

The overarching goal of the Program of Action is to halve the proportion of people living in extreme poverty and suffering from hunger by 2015 In addition, the program includes seven commitments that outline the key issues that LDCs should be working with their partners in the development process: a) Fostering a people-oriented; b) Promoting good governance at national and international levels; c) Building human and institutional capacities; d) Establish the necessary production capacity for LDCs benefit from globalization; e) Enhancing the role of trade in development; f) Reducing vulnerability and protecting the environment; g) To mobilize financial resources.

Also discussed are several cross-cutting issues such as gender equality, HIV / AIDS and the environment.

The Brussels Program of Action emphasizes the role of the regional commissions of the United Nations in monitoring and reviewing progress towards its implementation. The regional commissions should ensure address in the normal course of their activities, needs and problems of LDCs. In this regard, the Economic Commission for Africa (CFA) produces, since 2002, an annual progress report on the implementation of the Brussels Program of Action in African LDCs, highlighting the achievements of the country and the obstacles they face.

The first half of the decade of the implementation of the Brussels Program of Action (2001-2010) having elapsed, the United Nations will convene in 2006, a mid-term review of the implementation Program with all stakeholders. This report is part of this review focuses on the progress made since 2001 in the 34 African LDCs.

The key findings

Despite progress in the implementation of the Brussels Program of Action, the situation of African LDCs is very heterogeneous. Some have achieved economic growth, particularly the oil-producing country, but it is fragile and has not yet led to job creation, poverty reduction and human development major; Improving governance in many African LDCs, but in some cases there are setbacks regarding elections, human rights, rule of law, promotion of women and economic governance. Conflict is also a major cause of poverty in many countries; In African LDCs, human development is still low, which is a source of additional barriers to economic growth.

Several African LDCs have made significant progress towards gender equality, but much remains to be done; Lack of infrastructure, particularly in landlocked LDCs, continues to seriously hamper efforts to benefit from trade and promote economic development; African LDCs are still struggling to mobilize domestic resources. The debt relief and official development assistance could help alleviate this problem. In this regard, the OECD countries have, on average, not reach the targets set by the Brussels Program of Action; as a regional institution, ECA has contributed to the implementation of the Brussels Program of Action through its general activities and technical advisory services. However, this contribution was not made explicit in the context of the implementation of the Program.

The report makes the following recommendations

Should accelerate and sustain economic growth to achieve the overarching goal of reducing poverty; Job creation is crucial in the context of poverty reduction. It is not directly addressed in the Brussels Program of Action and should grant him an important place in the second half of the decade of the Program (2006-2010); Issues of gender should be integrated into the process of policy development; African LDCs, particularly those emerging from conflict should ensure that their development programs are subject to political consensus; To accelerate human development, governments should increase investment in education and health, particularly for vulnerable groups of society. With this in mind, it will consider including expanding access to secondary education, as well as structures for prevention and treatment of HIV / AIDS and malaria; The OECD countries should ensure that African LDCs enjoy debt relief and flows of official development assistance (ODA) sufficient and sustainable to meet commitments under the Program Action in Brussels; ECA and other key regional organizations should intensify their support to African LDCs to meet the commitments made in the Program of Action Brussels.

Trends and progress in African LDCs since 2001

This section discusses the observed trends and progress towards achieving the seven commitments of the Brussels Program of Action in the 34 African LDCs, given the limitations on the availability of statistical data. For most analyzed variables in this report, data were available for the period up to 2002 unless otherwise indicated; the data come from World Development Indicators (World Bank, 2005).

Fostering a people-oriented

Commitment 1

stresses the need to create enabling national action and international general conditions to engage in the path of accelerated growth and sustainable development and poverty eradication (paragraph 22 of the Program the Brussels). This objective requires to regularly save a growth rate of gross domestic product (GDP) of at least 7%, which is the minimum necessary to reduce poverty as indicated by the CEA (1999), and wear the investment / GDP ratio to 25%.

Trends in economic growth

During the period 2001-2005, general macroeconomic conditions have improved in most African LDCs. As shown in Figure 1 (see also Table 1 in Appendix 1), the economies of these countries recorded an average growth of 6% in 2001, 4.8% in 2002, which fell to 4 6% in 2003 before rebounding to 6.5% in 2004 This surge in economic growth was largely driven by strong global recovery, higher commodity prices, greater macroeconomic stability, improved results agriculture, improved political stability, debt relief and increased ODA flows (CEA, 2005a).

Since 2001, the growth rate of African LDCs averaged 5.4%, higher than the average for sub-Saharan Africa as a whole (3.9%) and the group of all LDCs (5.1 %).

The rise in oil prices has clearly contributed to the increase in growth rate of GDP of the subgroup of African LDC oil exporters (Angola, Equatorial Guinea, Sudan and Chad), as shown in Figure 1 Average rates recorded by these countries during the four years from 2001 to 2004 overall ranged from 6.9% to 33.7% in Sudan in Equatorial Guinea, with a combined average of 16, 4% against 4% for non-African LDCs oil producers.

Of the 34 African LDCs, 10 have recorded a lower growth of 3% over the four years from 2001 to 2004, while the majority (20 countries) grew between 3 and 7%. Only four African countries exceeded the growth target of 7% set for this period. Of these four three countries are oil exporters: Angola (8.8%), Chad (16.1%) and Equatorial Guinea (33.7%); about the fourth, Mozambique (10.7%), it has enjoyed a massive increase in aid flows and foreign direct investment.

The subgroup of African landlocked LDCs faces particular challenges regarding infrastructure and access to markets. Because of these constraints, it recorded in general, with the exception of Chad, lower than other LDCs3 economic growth.

Investment

On the basis of these growth rates, there is the role of the investment. To monitor this dimension, the second objective of the Brussels Program of Action sets a target investment / GDP ratio of 25%. Although this goal was not achieved, however, the ratio has increased in African LDCs from 18.6% in 2001 to 19.3% in 2004 At that time, only Lesotho had exceeded the target of a ratio of 25%, with investments reaching 41.1% of GDP. However, several other African LDCs towards, Gambia (23.9%), Madagascar (24.4%), Chad (24.7%) and Zambia (24.6%), while seven other countries posted ratios above 20% in 2004 investment / GDP.

Poverty reduction and human development

The reduction of poverty is the overarching goal of the Program of Action in Brussels, since this phenomenon persists in many African LDCs. As shown in Figure 2, the proportion of the population of African LDCs live on less than a dollar a day varies from 15.4% to 64.7% in Senegal to Niger. The average poverty rate in African LDCs (45.6% in 2001) is similar to that of sub-Saharan Africa. While poverty persists in most African LDCs, there have been improvements in some countries since 1996, as shown in Figure 2 In addition; the current trend of economic growth suggests a reduction in poverty in coming years, if the benefits of economic growth are distributed equitably.

Human development is an important objective of the Brussels Program of Action. If one refers to the Human Development Index of the UNDP (HDI), the HDI of African LDCs averaged 0.439 in 2003, below the average of all 50 LDCs number (0, 518) and sub-Saharan Africa (0, 515). However, as evidenced by the HDI trends are encouraging insofar as 15 African LDCs (out of 21 for which data were available) showed an improvement of indicator between 2000 and 2003.

The level of human development of African landlocked countries is lower than that of neighboring coastal countries. For this sub-group of countries, the value of the indicator was on average only 0,385 in

2003 against 0,485 for coastal African LDCs. In addition, while the level of human development is improving in the latter group, it remains stationary in African landlocked LDCs.

Gender

Another important part of the commitment one is the objective of strengthening the role of women and to address inequalities in ensuring the inclusion of gender in policy frameworks; legal and institutional. Question intersectional registered in Brussels Program of Action, the integration of women is linked not only to one's commitment, but also to other commitments discussed later in this document, particularly the aspects related to education and health engagement 3 progress towards this goal is measured by the indicator 27 (Objective 9) tracks the percentage of seats held by women in national parliaments from data collected by Inter-Parliamentary Union (IPU) 4. Some African countries are making significant progress in this area.

For example, Rwanda, where women make up 52% of the population and 34% of households headed, ranks first globally, with 48.8% of women in the lower house, followed by Sweden with 45.3% (as at 30 November 2005). The percentage is on average only 15.2% in the 33 African LDCs for which data are available.

Policy frameworks

Action to promote people-oriented, African LDCs must integrate the Brussels Program of Action into their national development strategies. Strategy papers for poverty reduction (PRSP) in this regard constitute key policy frameworks. In January 2006, 20 of the 34 African LDCs have developed a full PRSP and six others had established an interim PRSP (as a step towards developing a full PRSP) 5. Although the PRSP define many policies related to commitments contained in the Program of Action Brussels, this program is explicitly mentioned in any of the PRSP adopted by LDCs listed above. However, the Millennium Development is discussed in detail in 11 PRSP (see Table 2 of Appendix 1 for details of the progress made by African LDCs towards achieving).

Commitment 2: Good governance at national and international

The importance of promoting good governance at national and international levels is highlighted in commitment 2 of the program. A recent study by the CEA entitled Africa on the path of good governance shows that governance has continued to improve in African LDCs over the past five years.

The main conclusions of the study (CEA 2005c) are: Legislation on party registration was relaxed registration procedures have been liberalized in many African LDCs.

A majority of people questioned about their political system deemed competitive in Benin, Burkina Faso, Gambia, Lesotho, Mali, Mozambique, Uganda, Senegal and Tanzania, and but not in Chad.

"Voter turnout" was particularly high in African LDCs, with a comparable rate, if not higher than that observed in other regions of the world. Since 1999, this rate is higher than average in Ethiopia, Malawi, Uganda, Senegal and Tanzania.

The status of women and their participation in public life in African LDCs have improved. Despite these successes, much remains to be done regarding the representation of women in parliaments and in particular to senior positions.

In African LDCs, there is more respect for human rights generally, even if the difference is great between perceptions and reality.

In many African LDCs, service delivery remains poor, but improved slightly in some of them. The quality of public services varies greatly from one country to another. In Burkina Faso, 62% of households surveyed felt it was good or very good.

In January 2006, 17 African LDCs have acceded to the Mechanism of peer review, voluntary process designed to improve the economic Policy governance at the firm level and in the context of socio-economic development in Member States.

Building human and institutional capacities

Commitment 3

A key element of the development program of the African LDCs is the mobilization of the population and capacity building to enable them to participate in economic life. This point was recognized in Commitment 3 Program of Action in Brussels, which aims to strengthen the human and institutional capacities in developing social infrastructure and services, by taking action on population, education and training, health and nutrition and sanitation. Some of these topics are reviewed.

Education

A basic need that LDCs must meet to be able to compete in a global economy or the knowledge and skills of playing an increasingly important role. Some African LDCs have made progress in this area, including Cape Verde, Uganda, Rwanda, Sao Tome and Principe and Togo and are on track to meet the goal of providing education primary education for all by 2015 in other African LDCs, the general level of education is low in terms of numbers and rates of success, access to secondary education, the literacy and gender parity.

The average net enrollment ratio in primary education for African LDCs was 65% in 2002 against 63.3% in 2001 should be compared to the 68.1% recorded by all LDCs and 63 7% achieved in sub-Saharan Africa (2002 figures). However, to make further progress in the field of education, LDCs must not only increase enrollment but also ensure that children remain in school.

The indicator that best reflects this aspect is the success rate in primary education (Goal 7 indicators 15-17). This rate reached 68.7% in 2001: 68.9% for girls and 67.1% for boys.

Although progress has been made in terms of access to primary education and, to some extent, the success rate in this cycle, there are still obstacles to increasing access to education secondary in African LDCs. The gross enrollment rate in secondary education was on average only 24.9% in 2002, though up 4.3% compared to 2000 recorded in 2002 by the SSA rate and all LDCs was 31.8% and 31%, respectively. In African LDCs, the enrollment rate in secondary education ranged from 7% to 69.7% in Niger and Cape Verde.

In African LDCs, the average adult literacy rate was 54.8% in 2002, slightly above the average of the 50 LDCs (54.2%) and less than that of sub-Saharan countries (59.3%). Current progress in the field of education are more clearly highlighted by the youth literacy rate, which has increased significantly in African LDCs, reaching 70% in 2002, representing an increase of 12.8 % compared to 1990.

The aim of the Brussels Program is to eliminate gender disparity in primary and secondary education by 2005 and achieving gender equality in education by 2015 Indicators for this purpose shows that there are major differences: the average ratio of girls / boys in primary and secondary education was 82.4% in 2002 (Indicators 24 and 25), while in terms of literacy, the report young women / men was the same year 80.3% (Indicator 26).

Health, nutrition and sanitation

Commitment 3 also includes a variety of measures related to health, nutrition and sanitation (and has 12 associated objectives). Infant mortality has declined somewhat in African LDCs, from 104.4 per thousand live births in 2000 to 101.7 per thousand in 2003 These percentages vary from country to country, from 26 thousand only Cape Verde to 166 per thousand in Sierra Leone. Vaccination is an important way to reduce infant mortality. The rate of vaccination against measles was only 67.5% in 2003, although on the increase of more than 5% compared to 2001, but in Cape Verde, Gambia, Sao Tome and Principe, Tanzania and Zambia, the immunization coverage rate is over 85%, which means that these countries are likely to achieve the target set in the Brussels Program of Action with respect to infant mortality.

One of the problems associated with the most difficult to solve is that health posed by the huge social and economic costs occasioned by the HIV / AIDS scourge that hinders development, particularly in several southern African LDCs. At the end of 2003, the average prevalence of 5.9% in African LDCs, which represents a decrease of only 0.1% compared to the level registered in 2001 Regarding the fight against this disease some African LDCs have managed to stop the spread, but Uganda is to date the only African LDCs on track to meet the target in the fight against HIV / AIDS, reversing the current trend rate prevalence (see also Goal 6 of the Millennium development). The HIV-related tuberculosis has also spread in African LDCs where the prevalence of HIV is high, and the disease is now a leading cause of HIV-related deaths (CEA, 2004).

Malaria continues to be a debilitating disease in African LDCs, where it kills about 20% of children fewer than five years. In addition, the disease has a pernicious effect on the economy - according to some estimates; it results in a loss of economic growth of about 1.3% per year. However, progress has been made in some African LDCs. For example, in Benin and Burkina Faso, over 25% of pregnant women sleep under insecticide-treated nets. Similarly, the proportion of children under five sleeping under a net increased to over 50% in Eritrea and The Gambia (WHO / UNICEF, 2005).

Malnutrition is a chronic problem in many African LDCs, where 36.5% of the population consumed less than the minimum caloric intake required 20028.

Access to safe water and sanitation also continues to be a serious problem for African LDCs. In 2002, 59.7 and 32.5% respectively of the population benefited. These figures are very close to the average for all LDCs (57.6 and 34.6%) and that of sub-Saharan Africa (58.2 and 36%). The levels are much lower in rural areas where the proportion of the population with access to sanitation is only 22.2% against 51.3% in urban areas. Similarly, the proportion of the rural population having access to water is only 50.9% against 78.7% in urban areas.

Set up production capacity

The Brussels Program of Action also aims to overcome the various obstacles structural or relating to the offer that impede economic growth and sustainable development. Commitment 4, in particular, the development of physical infrastructure (roads, railways, airports,

ports, information technology and communication), adoption and technology transfer, business development , agriculture and agro-industry, manufacturing and mining industries, rural development and food security, and sustainable tourism.

Physical infrastructure is essential to increase intra-African trade and promote integration in the global economy. Two-thirds of African LDCs do not have the manner to roads, ports and other transport networks access, which is not without consequences, especially for landlocked LDCs. For example, they must pay to export their goods, freight and insurance representing 32% of the trade value, against 13% for all other landlocked countries (CEA, 2005).

The availability rate of personal computers in African LDCs is still very low, with only 8.7 devices per 1 000 inhabitants in 2002, a figure that is increasing compared to 6.46 per thousand in 2000 therefore the number of Internet users is also limited, with an adoption rate of 6.52 per thousand in 2002, however, due to the proliferation of Internet cafes, the number of Internet users has more than doubled between 2002 and 2003.

Commitment 5 - Enhancing the role of trade in development

Trade is an important engine of economic growth in African LDCs. Although they represent only a tiny fraction of global trade flows, the LDC economies are highly dependent on external trade. This is evidenced by the share of exports of goods and services in GDP, which averaged over 26% in 2004 against 24.4% in 2001, compared with the share in 2004 was 22% all LDCs and 32.6% for sub-Saharan Africa.

Although exports have increased, African LDCs are dependent on one or two primaires10 products. Such dependence exposes these economies to export revenue volatility, which tends to inhibit growth. For example, export revenues from Angola and Comoros are dependent on more than 88% of a single product (UNECA, 2004).

Accession to the World Trade Organization (WTO) is also part of the objectives of the Brussels Program of Action. Of the 34 African LDCs, 25 are already members of the organization, three (Cape Verde, Ethiopia and Sudan) are poised to join and both have observer status (Equatorial Guinea and Sao Tome and Principe) . Only four African LDCs (Comoros, Eritrea, Liberia and Somalia) have not yet begun formal negotiations with the WTO.

Commitment 6 - Reducing vulnerability and protecting the environment

In African LDCs, poverty and overcrowding lead to environmental degradation and loss of resources. Deforestation, which is a waste of environmental resources has increased in most African countries. It is estimated that in the 34 African LDCs, the proportion of forested land decreased from 26.1% in 1990 to 24% in 2000 It was in Burundi that deforestation is the largest, representing 60% of total area woody. Conversely, Gambia and Swaziland forest cover increased from 10 to 39% between 1990 and 2000 Similarly, Cape Verde has increased its forest area of more than 140%.

Another indicator of environmental degradation, the percentage of the population using solid fuels, a practice that contributes to both deforestation and air pollution. In African LDCs, this rate ranges from 36% in Cape Verde 95% in Burkina Faso, Ethiopia, Malawi, Sao Tome and Principe and Chad.

Displacement caused by civil wars or natural factors, a problem faced by many African LDCs in recent decades have exacerbated environmental degradation caused by overcrowding and poverty.

Commitment 7 - Mobilize financial resources

With low savings and underdeveloped financial markets rates, African LDCs face many obstacles in their efforts to access the resources they need for their development. Mobilizing domestic financial resources is essential in this regard. On the other hand, the potential role of official development assistance (ODA) to support the achievement of the Brussels Program of Action recognized in this document. The objective 28 commits donor countries to spend 0.20% of their gross national income to official development assistance to the PMA11. However, in 2003, the share of ODA flows from OECD countries accounted for only 0.08%. It was up from 2001 (0.05%), but remained below the 1990 level (0.09%). In 2003, ODA flows have however surpassed the target of 0.20% for the following countries: Belgium, Denmark, Ireland, Luxembourg, Norway, Netherlands and Sweden.

The debt relief is also an essential part of resource mobilization because it can spend money that would otherwise be used for debt service, investments in the social sector and infrastructure. As part of the Initiative for Heavily Indebted Poor Countries, 13 countries have reached the completion point (Benin, Burkina Faso, Ethiopia, Madagascar, Mali, Mauritania, Mozambique, Niger, Rwanda, Senegal, Tanzania and Zambia). Nine have reached the decision point (Burundi, Gambia, Guinea, Guinea-Bissau, Malawi, Democratic Republic of Congo, Sao Tome and Principe, Sierra Leone and Chad), while six others have reached the point of pre-decision (Comoros, Liberia, Central African Republic, Somalia, Sudan andTogo). In addition, again as part of the Initiative, 21 African LDCs have benefited from debt relief in 2005 totaling 38.96 billion, from $ 90 million to Gambia 10 4 billion for the Democratic Republic of Congo.

Foreign direct investment contributes significantly to address the lack of resources in African LDCs and proves especially important when it comes to finance investment in physical infrastructure. In the 34 African LDCs, net inflows of foreign direct investment accounted for 5.9% of GDP in 2003 This rate is higher than that of sub-Saharan Africa as a whole (2.5%) and higher the average for all LDCs (3.6%) was mainly due to significant investments in the natural resources sector.

Tasks and obstacles

The above trends indicate that some progress has been made in implementing the Brussels Program of Action for the period 2001-2005. In particular, economic growth was higher than the average for sub-Saharan Africa. African LDCs also have accumulated improvements in political and economic governance. In addition, slow but steady progress has been made in the areas of gender equality, child mortality and enrollment in primary education. However, mid-term, African LDCs still face many challenges. The main stem from the weakness and fragility of the economic growth. Moreover, this growth has not benefited the general population, having failed to create jobs and reduce poverty (ECA, 2005a). Other problems include conflict, low levels of human development and lacked financial resources, both local and external.

Slow and not inclusive economic growth in African LDCs

A more rapid and sustainable growth is a necessary but not sufficient to improve living conditions and reduce poverty conditions. Unfortunately, in many African LDCs, economic growth is insufficient; it has averaged less than 3% between 2001 and 2004 in 10 countries. This slow growth can be attributed to an accumulation of factors (physical and human capital) insufficient and low productivity growth. Furthermore, economic growth is hampered by poor governance, instability / political conflict, lack of infrastructure, limited trade and unsustainable environmental practices. Furthermore, high population growth tends to erase part of economic growth.

The fact that growth does not benefit the entire population can be explained in part by the concentration of economic activity in the mining sector. For example, in the oil-producing African LDCs, although the growth was unusually high, its impact on poverty reduction was limited. As the oil industry is a capital intensive and operating closed circuit, there has been little job creation and spin-off benefits for the rest of the economy (2005).

African LDCs and developing countries in general are characterized by high inequality that is not directly addressed in the Brussels Program of Action and the Millennium Development. However, given the low per capita income in African LDCs, a simple redistribution is not likely to significantly reduce poverty, although a better distributed growth would have a greater impact.

Another feature of economic growth in African LDCs is its volatility due to the effects of price shocks in commodity and dependence of agricultural production rains. Since the early 1990s, volatility, represented by the standard deviation of economic growth is more pronounced in African LDCs than in sub-Saharan Africa (see Appendix 1, Table 3). This volatility is also higher in the subgroup of African LDC oil exporters.

In the long term, African LDCs need to diversify their economies and make structural changes to reorient the business, which is currently focused on primary products to the agricultural processing and manufacturing. To do this, it will also perform the tasks outlined above, namely: providing support to the private sector; develop physical infrastructure, improving public governance and business management; invest in education and health, and promoting gender equality.

High prevalence of conflicts in African LDCs

In African LDCs, conflicts are often the cause of a collapse of government which is accompanied by economic turmoil and volatility. According to estimates, conflicts reduce the rate of per capita growth of 2.2% per year during the period of confrontation and 2.1% five years after the end of hostilities (Collier and Hoeffler, 2000; Fosu and Collier, 2005). Conflicts and wars discourage investment and trade distorting

Agricultural production also diminishes during the wars and conflicts. In Angola, a country that has been at war for thirty years, she has remained at the end of the 1990s much less than it would have been if there had been no conflict.

Twelve African LDCs have recently been or are still in the grip of a conflict situation that neighboring countries are suffering, too, against the economic and political jolts. For example, the conflict in Côte d'Ivoire (country that is part of the PMA) has an impact on Burkina Faso and Mali, because the Ivory Coast is a major transit country for these landlocked LDCs. Moreover, conflicts generate flows of displaced persons and refugees, accentuating poverty due to the loss of jobs and livelihoods.

The success of strategies to reduce poverty in African LDCs through the establishment of peace and political stability. This requires efforts to achieve the aftermath of a conflict, a political consensus about programs and development policies capable of ensuring sustainable economic growth.

Low human development in African LDCs

The level of human development in African LDCs is low compared to other LDCs and African countries. In many African LDCs, it is even lower than suggested by GDP per capita (if one refers to the difference between the rankings according to GDP per capita and HDI).

As economic growth contributes to human development, progress in the formation of human capital can lead to increased economic output. In particular, it has been amply demonstrated that people healthier, better fed and better educated are more likely to be part of the assets and thereby contribute to economic growth. It has, for example, been shown that improving the health and nutrition bore directly on labor productivity, particularly among the poor.

African LDCs should continue to work to promote human development by improving access to education and health care. Furthermore, when economic growth is open, the income of the poor increases, which has the effect of driving progress in the field of human development, to the extent that households can spend more on health, nutrition and education.

Insufficient external resources and debt relief

In order to achieve higher and sustained rates of economic growth, African LDCs must mobilize both domestic resources and external resources. In this context, the overseas development assistance and debt relief can play a key role in liberating resources for priority sectors such as health, education and infrastructure.

Participants at the G-8 Gleneagles (2005) agreed to cancel the debt of 14 African countries. This should be extended to all African LDCs.

The most indebted African countries have benefited from the Initiative for Heavily Indebted Poor Countries, which has given some notable results:

Social spending has increased by 20-50% in heavily indebted poor countries that have reached the decision point.

Mozambique has launched a free vaccination program for children.

School fees were abolished in primary education in Uganda, Malawi and Tanzania; in Benin Similar action was taken in favor of rural areas.

Mali, Mozambique and Senegal are about to increase their spending on HIV / AIDS.

Barring a total cancellation of the debt, the Initiative for Heavily Indebted Poor Countries probably cannot achieve its overall objectives, which are to do away with repeated rescheduling, to achieve sustainable growth and to increase spending on social programs and poverty reduction. Countries that have benefited from the initiative are the burden of their unsustainable debt. For example, Uganda, the first country to complete the program still suffers from a level of debt too heavy to bear. Four heavily indebted poor countries (Mali, Niger, Sierra Leone and Zambia) will pay more each year to service their debt during the period 2003-2005, between 1998 and 2000 Three other African LDCs (Ethiopia, Guinea Bissau and Uganda) will have to pay nearly as much as before the initiative.

African countries emerging from conflict are in great need of funds for reconstruction. Or in the case of these countries, debt relief under the initiative for heavily indebted poor countries has been hampered by a shortage of funds, the slow pace of disbursement and lack of flexibility.

ODA is an important source of external financing. Despite the strong recovery in recent years in the form of aid, it is still insufficient to finance a significant reduction in poverty in African LDCs. Moreover, the increase in ODA flows, largely the result of contributions under the emergency and is not necessarily due to the flow of nature to sustainable poverty reduction. While ODA to areas such as health and education increased, this increase will only return to the levels reached in the early 1990s.

In addition to the low volume of ODA, there is the problem of the quality and effectiveness of aid that has not been properly treated. Coordination between donors in assembling and disbursement of aid can reduce the cost of it and improve its effectiveness, as evidenced by the joint urgent appeals, coordinated by the UN, which are launched for many LDCs African crisis.

Disbursement of aid is often unpredictable, causing difficulty budgeting and planning to recipient countries and causing them to develop spending plans over the medium term.

Much of the aid does not completely successful because it is related to the import of goods and services from the donor country. Tying lost the country that receives 25-40% of the profit it could draw (Economic Report on Africa, 2005b). Only a few donors (UK, Ireland, and Norway) give completely untied aid.

The award of grants instead of loans is particularly important for African LDCs

The aid would further implement the commitments of the Brussels Program of Action if it was targeted more precisely the regions where poverty is rampant on a large scale.

African LDCs also need to attract more private capital, particularly in the form of foreign direct investment and remittances from migrant workers. Regarding foreign direct investment, governments should encourage flow to sectors other than mining, which can create more jobs and have a ripple effect on other sectors.

Remittances from migrant workers are an important source of financial flows to African LDCs. For example, in 2003, they accounted for Lesotho and Cape Verde respectively 26.5% and 13.6% of GDP (UNECA, 2004). It is necessary to increase the impact of remittances on growth and poverty reduction. Address weaknesses in the formal banking system would facilitate this process. Financial institutions must include design specific products for this massive influx of funds and direct them to productive investments.

Role of ECA in the implementation of the Brussels Program of Action

ECA was founded in 1958 and responsible for the formulation, implementation and monitoring of development policies in Africa. In this respect, the treatment of systemic problems and issues facing African LDCs is part of the activities in the ECA program and technical companies to assist Member States advisory missions.

Program activities of ECA
Through its Division of Economic and Social Policy, ECA prepares annual reports on the progress made by African LDCs in implementing the Brussels Program of Action. In addition to this activity under its mandate, the CEA performs other activities related to the Program of Action relating in particular to the economic and social policies, gender, information and services for the development,

policy and development management, trade facilitation and regional integration and sustainable development.

At the request of the African Heads of State, ECA contributed OECD publication of the document "Mutual Review of Development Effectiveness" in a shift, whereby the relationship between donors and beneficiaries based on compliance have been replaced by relationships based on mutual responsibility, in order to ensure the effectiveness of aid. Donor countries are focusing in the context of mutual accountability on the quantity and quality of aid, recipient countries must accelerate their consideration human development, capacity building and improve their political and economic governance.

Through its African Centre for Gender and Development (CAGED), ECA has played a leading role in efforts to address persistent gender inequalities in developing new instruments, working to build capacity and based relevant African political institutions. CAGED has trained over 140 senior national policy makers from African LDCs, and experts on gender equality from regional economic communities, the African Union and the African Development Bank (AFDB). ECA also organized five sub regional meetings on the implementation of the Brussels Program of Action. In addition, through the CAGED, she contributed to the inclusion of the gender perspective, worked for the promotion of human and legal rights of women and developed skills in business management in women business in African LDCs.

Through its Division of Policy and Development Management, ECA also contributed to the evaluation and monitoring of the state of governance in Africa. In 2004, she organized the Forum for African

Development (ADF IV) on "Governance for a Progressing Africa", in collaboration with the African Development Bank and the African Union. He then had the 2005 publication of a study entitled Africa on the path of good governance, which took stock of the lessons learned from 23 countries, including 15 African LDCs. This report identified significant steps to improve governance in African LDCs, whose participation in the electoral process and strengthening the rule of law. All this bodes well for improving the governance and implementation of the Brussels Program of Action.

Equally important is the link between activities on governance and the African Peer Review Mechanism, by which African countries consider their progress towards better governance in the context of their own a peer review. Some 26 African countries have acceded to the Mechanism and the CEA provides to each of the main stages of the process through its Support Group Mechanism APRM, which is under the Department of Economic Policy and social, technical support capital to countries that submit to the scrutiny of their peers.

The Division assists largely makers in African LDCs to develop their national strategy papers for poverty reduction (PRSP), which is an effective policy tool to reduce poverty and to channel resources to the priority sectors. Since 2001, ECA brings together the country working on a document of this type, the majority of LDCs, for an exchange of experience and knowledge within an instance called African Learning Group on PRSPs. The consensus that emerged from these discussions is that the second generation PRSP should lay the groundwork for stronger growth deal with the issue of economic transformation and deepen partnerships around approaches that originate in countries same.

As recognized by the Brussels Program of Action, the HIV / AIDS is the biggest problem the leaders face in Africa today. Division of Economic and Social Policy ECA played a key role in the redevelopment of HIV / AIDS as a development issue rather than a health issue. She stressed that reclassification as part of its collaboration with the African Union, WHO and UNAIDS, which has resulted in the publication of the document "Scoring African Leadership for Better Health." In addition, a committee of HIV / AIDS and Governance in Africa (CHGA) was created ECA, under the Assistant Secretary General of the UN, to offer comprehensive and complete solutions to African LDCs and Member States, both in terms of prevention and treatment.

ECA campaigned vigorously for debt relief for African LDCs. The Department of Economic and Social Policy, for example, co-organized and supported technically a forum on debt relief in Dakar in 2003, attended by experts and policy makers, much of which came from African LDCs. The conclusions of this forum have helped support African LDCs in their negotiations on debt relief. ECA has also cooperated with the African Union to establish the African common position on the issue of external debt.

To promote the role of trade in development, the Division of Trade and regional integration of ECA assisted in the three following areas:

- Adoption of common positions and strategies by African LDCs in trade negotiations.

- Achieving the best possible results in the ongoing negotiations in the WTO.

Technical assistance to improve access to regional and international markets

It is in this context that the African Trade Policy Centre (ATPC) was established at ECA, with the support of the Canadian Government, in order to provide advisory services and technical support to African trade negotiators.

The Division also assisted African LDCs in their negotiations with the European Union on Economic Partnership Agreements (EPAs). This was done through a series of meetings at which light has been given to the potential impact of EPAs in African LDCs, regional, sub-regional (COMESA and ECOWAS) and national.

ECA product, through the Division of Trade and regional integration, a study entitled "Assessing Regional Integration in Africa" to help African LDCs and the regional economic communities to identify the problems and opportunities of regional integration.

Management of natural resources, including Africa in general is generously endowed, is closely linked to trade. To contribute to environmental sustainability in African LDCs, ECA, through its Division for Sustainable Development, contributed to the Report on the development of water resources in Africa. To finance measures in the framework for the Vision for Water in Africa, ECA has worked with partner agencies to establish the African Water Facility and the African Network on Water, which will drive its engagement with civil society. In addition, ECA has played an important role in the mobilization of leaders at all levels of society, in order to boost efforts to make water in African LDCs vital resource for development and peace regional.

Through its Division of Information Services for the development, ECA has helped 26 African LDCs develop their policies and plans relating to the national information infrastructure and communication, and the collection, management and dissemination of ICT statistics. This action responds to the recommendations of the Initiative "Information Society in Africa" and reflects the recognition of the role of information technology in the development of African LDCs. In addition, ECA coordinated the participation of Africa in the World Summit on the Information Society, recommending mechanisms through which African LDCs can use digital opportunities to achieve the Program Brussels Action.

Effective monitoring of the Program of Action Brussels is not only important but is based on credible, reliable and complete. Through the Department of Economic and Social Policy, ECA continues to work with its partners of the Advisory Board on Statistics in Africa, to facilitate the dissemination in African LDCs good practices in development of statistical systems. It also remains a key partner in the Forum on Statistical Development in Africa, which is working to establish a regional framework of 10 years for the development of statistics and capacity building in Africa.

Technical assistance

ECA organized several advisory missions in African LDCs since the Launch of the Brussels Program of Action.

Division of Economic and Social affairs sent a mission to Sudan in 2005 for participating in a seminar on the macroeconomic framework directive and the reduction of poverty. The objective of the mission was to review the findings of the draft report on the macroeconomic framework and the PRSP Sudan. The members of the mission were presented important communications and made detailed to help the national team PRSP recommendations.

At the request of the Government of Mozambique, ECA provided technical assistance devoted to the analysis of the impact of HIV / AIDS on industrial production and sustainable livelihoods in the country; In 2005, the Division and the Division of Economic and Social Policy, Policy and Development Management organized five missions in four African LDCs to help them design and implement their mechanism of peer review; CAGED provided advisory services in six African LDCs on the legal rights of women. He also created, for the Information Network of Women Entrepreneurs Development (RIFED) in East Africa and West Africa, two operational sub-regional centers, both of which have their headquarters in LDCs Africa, namely Uganda and Togo; Division of Policy and Development Management organized advisory missions in four African LDCs to facilitate political participation of civil society in development; Division of Trade and regional integration organized country missions for LDCs in Ethiopia, Mali and Rwanda on the potential economic effects of trade agreements between the EU and African LDCs. In the future, the technical assistance will be provided to at least two other African LDCs;The Division of Information Services Development has organized training courses on networking technology for African women and capacity building seminars for policy makers, parliamentarians and the media in Africa; she provided advisory services on regulatory frameworks and national mechanisms relating to ICT and the collection, management and dissemination of ICT statistics in 26 African LDCs.

The implementation of the Brussels Program of Action for African LDCs is in line with the ECA activities to support Member States. The mid-term review of 2006 is an opportunity to take stock of the progress of African LDCs in implementing the Program of Action and the role of the CEA in this regard.

The way forward to move forward

The Brussels Program of Action is part of the wire agency law of the Commission, which addresses the needs of African LDCs in the context of its activities to Member States. However, we need more integrated ECA Program of Action, is refocusing on specific activities and closely monitor the implementation of the second half of the Program during the period 2006-2010. This renewed effort can be based on three specific strategies, namely: priorities, synergies and communication.

Priorities

The ECA activities proceed directly with program requirements for the development of Africa, which was defined in 2001 as part of NEPAD. This program clearly highlights the special needs of African LDCs which are presented as the strategic objectives of comprehensive development framework of the African Union.

The Brussels Program of Action is the heart of Africa's development. As part of the overall mandate of the CEA, special emphasis should be placed on the needs of LDCs in terms of economic and social policy, which are an integral part of the mission of the Division of Economic and Social Policy. In addition, it is necessary to focus on policy analysis and action opportunities in African LDCs. An important part of this program is to help strengthen the capacity of national statistical offices of the African LDCs through Team Statistics Division.

The cross-cutting nature of the seven commitments of the Brussels Program of Action requires the involvement of all substantive divisions of ECA. However, it would need for a group like the Inter Division for Economic and Social Policy coordinates the activities and products of the substantive divisions in light of the Program of Action.

In summary, the future work program of ECA on LDCs should include:

A thorough analysis of the situation in some African LDCs, made from the analytical framework of the Brussels Program of Action. For example, a number of the Economic Report on Africa could focus on the said Program of Action, with a thorough analysis of the situation in African LDCs; An expansion of the work of ECA on strategies for poverty reduction in order to be included a section devoted to African LDCs.

Synergies

Efficiency implies that the CEA created synergies between the activities and products of all divisions. For example, the African Centre for Gender and Development CAGED should ensure that the contribution of each division actually takes account of concerns about gender. These synergies should be created not only between but also divisions between ECA headquarters and sub-regional offices. As the latter provide a crucial link between the analytical work done ECA headquarters and advocacy with decision makers at sub-regional level, it is necessary to coordinate activities for LDCs, both at headquarters and in offices sub regional.

ECA should work more effectively with regional economic communities, which are its main customers at the sub regional level. Better coordination with these institutions will improve communication and consideration of the Brussels Program of Action in the sub-regional frameworks.

The Brussels Program of Action is consistent with the mandates of UNESCO and UNICEF. Synergies can be further strengthened in some thematic areas through collaboration with specialized institutions such as UNCTAD and other strategic partners. For example, efforts to achieve education for all, in the context of the

Brussels Program of Action could be harmonized between UNESCO and ECA. Similarly, the presence of specialized UN agencies in the Member States should be utilized to provide analysis and monitoring more targeted commitments and indicators at the national level.

As the African Union which sets the overall scale of the continent political agenda, ECA should, at an early stage, ensuring its collaborative activities to achieve the objectives of the Brussels Program of Action.

Communication

It is important that the technical, advisory missions and analytical work are related to each other, especially in the context of the Brussels Program of Action. ECA should, in addition to its current practice of meeting its regulatory obligations, focus more on policy analysis and advocacy on LDCs, in accordance with its mandate.

To ensure better dissemination of the main results of the Brussels Program of Action, it should be ensured that the products are available on a multimedia support; should also strengthen the activities of monitoring the impact of the measures adopted. Force is also to focus on targeted distribution and substantive dialogue with sub-regional and national levels.

ECA could facilitate the organization for the benefit of African LDCs, a friendly forum for exchanging information based on the relevant policy documents, data and reports on the country, as well as links to other areas of relevant action. This knowledge exchange will provide more efficient and user-friendly systems for benchmarking and monitoring of the commitments contained in the Program of Action Brussels.

Resources

Commitments and indicators represent key areas of ECA activities. Therefore, the regular work program of ECA for 2008-2009 will focus on the relevance and timeliness of the Brussels Program of Action. Allocate resources to facilitate inter-group synergies and monitoring of the Program of Action in Brussels.

In July and August this year, Jerry Rawlings, former President of Ghana became the High Representative of the African Union (AU) for Somalia, visited several African capitals. Objective: to invite African Heads of State to a pan-African conference on the famine in the Horn of Africa. "I am convinced that African leaders will rise to the challenge," he repeated at every stage of his journey. However, only the presidents of four countries (Ethiopia, Equatorial Guinea, Djibouti and Somalia) traveled to Addis Ababa, Ethiopia, August 18.

The low turnout did not, however sapped the enthusiasm of Jerry Rawlings. In his opening speech, he urged Africa to prove to the world that "we are not able to take care of us." Africans have pledged 50 million dollars in aid. The African Development Bank (AFDB) has done better with 300 million.

More than 12 million people live under the threat of a severe famine in the Horn of Africa. Somalia and other countries in the region need at least $ 2.5 billion to prevent further deaths, according to the World Food Program. In August, before the donor conference organized by the AU, only 45% of this amount had been paid. With $ 350 million announced at the meeting and other contributions, pledges have reached 63% of that amount in late September, according to the United Nations Food and Agriculture Organization (FAO).

Jacques Diouf, the Director-General of FAO, said in September that the response of the international community to the famine was "late and inadequate." However, it considered positive a meeting mid-September between the governments of the Horn of Africa and representatives of the ADB and the World Bank.

During this meeting, the two banks have committed $ 500 million additional dollars in long-term development of the region.

It has even been criticized African leaders for not having responded quickly enough to face the crisis. The conference of donors in Addis Ababa has been postponed once to allow time for the country to raise funds. Various observers believe that the $ 50 million pledged by African governments are insufficient and that the majority will be paid in the form of an "in-kind", while a more flexible financial assistance would be. In addition, the way in which governments provide such assistance was not specified.

"Disappointing"

Nicanor Sabula, a member of Africans Act 4 Africa, a coalition of civil society, said that the level of participation in the donor conference was "disappointing and embarrassing." This reaction helps to "enhance the image of an African Union which would be a club president," he adds.

But this overlooks the fact that African countries (including Kenya) substantial numbers of refugees they bring facto-invaluable. Kenyan Prime Minister Raila Odinga announced in July that his government had spent so far, $ 110 million to provide food to more than one million refugees on its territory.

For his part, Jerry Rawlings is currently experiencing private sector leaders to encourage them to contribute to relief efforts. If African country pledged $ 50 million during the Addis Ababa meeting, ordinary Kenyans with the help of private companies have managed to collect more than $ 60 million in less than three months. Kanayo Nwanze, president of the International Fund for Agricultural Development of the United Nations, said that "Africa should not wait for the international community pays its problems."

Haruni Odhiambo Nyaru enlarges his house. Martin Omondi Onyango bought a cow and a goat. He pays the tuition of his younger brother and built a house for his mother. Now that his crops improve (its 0.8 acres produce 30 bags of maize to 90 pounds against 12 previously), Wilfreda Ongonda Ochieng believes that her family is eating better and even has a surplus it sells. For all three, if the newspaper has changed for the better, thanks to the creation of the Millennium Village of Sauri in western Kenya.

New seed varieties and fertilizers are responsible for increasing yields and incomes of three farmers. "I was already using fertilizer before but since the Millennium Project, fertilizer gave us a real boost," said Wilfreda, a widow of 45 years at the helm of an operation which employs 11 people, including members of his family.

Launched in 2004, the draft Sauri is the first in a series of 14 Millennium Villages for Development (VMD) in 10 countries in sub-Saharan Africa. The VMD supported a number of foundations and businesses. Among them, Sumitomo, which provides mosquito nets, and Ericsson, which donated cell phones to health?

This initiative is led by a triumvirate consisting of the United Nations Development Program (UNDP), the NGO Millennium Promise and the Earth Institute at Columbia University, both based in New York. The villages are pilot projects to be implemented on a larger scale and replicated in the context of achieving, by 2015, the Millennium Development Goals (MDGs). Adopted in 2000 by world leaders, including the MDGs aim to reduce poverty, improve access to health and women's empowerment.

Quick Wins

Eleven villages Group VMC Sauri has about 75,000 inhabitants and covers an area of 132 square kilometers. About 98% of households involved in agriculture in one form or another.

The sudden increase in maize yields of Wilfreda may seem exceptional. But it is the average among program participants. Production has tripled throughout the villages. Hence a significant reduction in child malnutrition. "The seed and fertilizer have enabled us to achieve immediate results," says Jessica Massira, team leader of the project and responsible for a group of villages.

With yields rising, the program was able to focus on diversification, bringing farmers to multiple revenue streams at different times of the year. Which protects low prices after a bountiful harvest?

"Farmers need food but they also need money, Ms. Massira analysis. Through horticulture, livestock and fisheries, they can quickly make more money. We have achieved remarkable results. "And as pointed Willy Diru, agricultural coordinator," Once the food security and safety, we have worked with various companies to produce onions, tomatoes, cabbage and peppers. There is also a cooperative for fresh produce. "

Meals and nets

Through diversification of production and improvement of crops, farmers participating in a school lunch program. Result: The attendance rate was 94%. All over the world, often children do not like going to school, but for the children of rural Africa, "go to lunch" is a reasonable compromise.

Along with the increase of agricultural production, communities have preserved more than 200 drinking water sources that feed more than 26,000 people. They built walls and installed pipes to bring water to the taps. Villagers installed fences to keep cattle away. The access to a supply of better quality water rates rose from less than 40% in 2006 to about 90% currently.

Steps are also being taken to combat certain health problems. Bednets and home testing have reduced the prevalence of malaria. It went from 45% in 2005 to 7% in 2008.

Reviews

Despite these figures, the Millennium Villages Development subject of much criticism, mainly from development actors, activists, environmental activists and intellectuals.

The use of imported fertilizers would lead to a dependence on these inputs, say some. Others add that intensive agriculture weaken water supply and soil, with the key negative side effects similar to those seen in India after the Green Revolution. Still others believe that barriers to foreign village development, including corruption, are not considered. And that there are few studies that compare the VMD villages not receiving such assistance, which makes efficiency difficult to assess the program. Finally, too much time, money and attention would be devoted to a small number of people.

Exit strategy

These charges vary by ideological or political orientation but critics often share a common theme: the dependence on external aid. The VMD may be the only program of large-scale development whose followers truly to establish an exit strategy. But does it give the desired results?

It is easier to consider a real reduction in aid dependence when source revenues are created. For example: instead of offering subsidized fertilizers to farmers, we could sell them by granting them loans that they repay after harvest. The relationship between farmers and project managers would be commercial and reduced risk of addiction. Similarly, schools would collect funds by charging those who wish to print documents after school hours.

Nonetheless, a visit to a similar to Sauri, the Millennium Cities Initiative (MCI) project in Kisumu, the capital of the province, illustrates the difficulty of self-reliance in the health sector. According to a hospital employee, the Millennium Project complete supplies - such as disposable medical gloves - that the government should provide, but it does not do so in sufficient numbers or timely. Maintenance of ambulances across the territory is provided by foreign and Israeli government sent the necessary equipment and a team to build the emergency room of the hospital. "The Israelis have all led and completed the work in 17 days," said Opiyo-Omolo Belinda, public health specialist at the IVM. "I hate to say it, but it would have taken six months to Kenyans. That said, local people were able to see that putting all his will, could happen. So much the better! "

"The challenge is sustainability," admits Ms. Massira about the health sector. "We understand that we must first demonstrate and then move out to the government and the public. If people get used to the services, it will require the government. "

Bart Knols, chairman of the advisory board of the Dutch Malaria Foundation, has extensive experience in Africa, and has visited Sauri. He calls the anti-malaria initiative "quite commendable in the sense that offering a complete set of services (medicines, vaccination, health and education) can bear fruit." But he also worries about the future. "Where I am more skeptical, it's regarding the viability of this approach, when he will step down and the Kenyan government will provide these services.

"Regain" the initiative

Beyond the capacity of governments, it is also about whether the people will take over. There is evidence that this is already partly the case. For example, farmers who want to try beekeeping are organized into groups of ten. Groups select one member to receive additional training. It will then be the guide. Martin's brother, Jared Omondi Onyango, learned to build and maintain greenhouses under the Sauri project. It now constructed to others.

More interestingly, the group of workers Manyatta B which supplies tap water 8,000 households in Kisumu who's IVM has a partner. After an initial grant from the French government, the community organized to build and operate the system. They set a lot more affordable than those charged by operators of private tankers price. Revenues allow them to maintain the system and they still have enough money for training of operators and local workers.

While the debate continues internationally on the Millennium Villages development, local people seem enthusiastic. "I think they will succeed because the program was designed to last," says

Stephen Onduu, purchasing manager at the hospital in Kisumu, "They will get there if they meet the residents to discuss an exit strategy.

Based in Paris, Bill Hinchberger is a freelance journalist and communications consultant. He traveled to Kenya as part of a project organized by the European Journalism Centre in Brussels and funded by the Dutch government.

In the peaceful mountains of Lesotho, a small landlocked kingdom in the heart of South Africa, the mood is gloomy. Long, the country has benefited from its extreme dependence vis-à-vis the larger neighbor. But things are changing.

And not for the better.

The economic difficulties facing South Africa slowing Lesotho's economy and now the government is struggling to balance its budget.

Even for the casual visitor, the South African presence is everywhere visible. Thousands of Basotho (Lesotho nationals) working in older neighbor. It is also home to the kingdom supplies water and electricity. Finally South Africa generously shares with Lesotho income of a customs union that contributes significantly to the budget of the tiny state. To this we must add the ubiquitous South African companies in other sectors, including retail, insurance and banking.

But this ultra-dependence beneficial previously, proves less profitable. Despite modest gains made in recent years, Lesotho remains one of the poorest countries in the world. The 2011-2012 budget is "the most difficult that the government has ever adopted," admitted the finance minister, Timothy Thahane. At issue: the slowing economic growth, rising unemployment and falling incomes of migrant workers who lose their jobs in South Africa. Lesotho also faces declining agricultural production and life expectancy, as well as high rates of HIV infection.

As if that were not enough, the sluggish economic situation in South Africa has forced Lesotho to rethink the management of its economy. The country has experienced a 30% decline in domestic revenues and a monstrous budget deficit of 15% during 2011-2012. Now the government is considering applying for loans from international financial institutions. It also hopes to gain support from foreign donors.

Transfers down

A drastic fall last year, its share in the Southern African Customs Union (SACU) dealt the hardest blow to the budget. SACU, the oldest customs union in the world (it recently celebrated its centenary), maintains free trade among member countries (South Africa, Botswana, Lesotho, Swaziland and Namibia) and apply a common external tariff States non-members. The revenue is controlled by South Africa under an agreed formula. Since 1969, SACU accounts for more than half of Lesotho's budget revenues.

"We were very aware that about 60% of the state budget is funded by SACU," declared the beginning of 2011 the Governor of the Central Bank of Lesotho, Retselisitsoe Matlanyane, a local magazine. With the recent global financial crisis, trade between SACU members has declined significantly, reducing by half the customs revenues of Lesotho.

The decline in remittances from migrant workers in South Africa is another blow, Lesotho is heavily dependent on external remittances. The 2011 report of the World Bank on migration and remittances indicates that about 457,500 Basotho living abroad in 2010, with a total population of 2.1 million. The Bank also estimated that remittances have contributed $ 525 million in 2010, or 30% of GDP.

Despite the rise in world prices of minerals, South Africa is going through a mild recession in recent years. This has had a major impact on Lesotho whose companies were forced to lay off, especially in the mining sector, thousands of employees, including Basotho migrants, reducing remittances that they carry with them.

The textile sector was also affected. Weak demand for apparel in the United States has reduced revenues and led to a widening budget deficit. As part of the African Growth and Opportunity Act (AGOA), an American law, Lesotho has become one of the largest textile exporters in Africa south of the Sahara. AGOA allows eligible African countries to sell their textiles to the United States taking advantage of unique privileges. But the overvaluation of the South African rand - to which the national currency, the loti, is pegged - has hurt the competitiveness of the second largest employer in Lesotho.

In addition, authorities are concerned about the fate of the textile industry if a clause in AGOA is not renewed after it expires in September 2012 This provision allows eligible AGOA countries, including Lesotho and Kenya, to source fabrics from third countries such as China without losing the benefits of AGOA.

Our main challenge will be the expiration of AGOA. The textile industry employs 45,000 people in the country, "said the governor of the Central Bank. The textile export revenues make up 20% of the GDP of Lesotho. Some company's manufacture of clothing has already closed because of weak demand.

The situation in agriculture is equally depressing, three out four "Basotho" living from subsistence agriculture. But the contribution of grain production to GDP increased from 4.8% in 2000 to 1.8% in 2010 just adds Thahane. The UN sounds the alarm. Agricultural production is declining and could be interrupted in most of the country if steps are not taken to reverse soil erosion and land degradation and reverse the decline of fertility.

White gold and diamond

Despite economic hardships, Lesotho is doing less badly than other countries in the sub-region, such as Swaziland and Zimbabwe. And hope to reverse the trend exists, if current policies to give the economy a new direction are effective. During the presentation of the budget, the Finance Minister announced new measures to revive agriculture, diversify exports and markets and attract investors by relaxing the laws on foreign investment. However, these policies can only be effective if the economies of the major partners in the country, including the United States, the European Union and South Africa, passed their recovery.

Water declares affectionately Basotho is "white gold" of Lesotho. Revenues from the sale of water under the Lesotho Highlands Water Project should increase with the construction of the dam- Metolong.

As part of the project on water, created in partnership with South Africa, Lesotho exports water to its neighboring Gauteng province through a series of dams and tunnels in the mountains. Gauteng, the hub of the South African economy has very little water and must appeal to Lesotho to quench its thirst. This multi-billion dollar also generates enough hydroelectric power to meet approximately 90% of energy needs of Lesotho.

Lesotho could also count on the profits of mining exports, in a context of rising world prices of precious metals. Revenues from diamonds, although still significant, are rising. The government plans to generate more revenue by cutting and polishing diamonds locally.

Good news, it was announced a small increase in SACU revenues in 2012, however, the extent of this improvement will depend crucially on the new revenue-sharing formula currently being studied. American lawmakers have also introduced a bill to extend AGOA. If this bill is passed, Lesotho can count on a steady flow of income from its textile exports to the United States, provided, however, that the American economy continues its recovery.

Lesotho also aims to attract foreign investors. According to the 2011 Doing Business Report of the World Bank that assesses the business climate in the country, Lesotho is ranked 138th out of 183 countries in the running. Relaxes the trade restrictions, the government could easily attract investors in the sectors of mining, textile and retail industries.

However, major challenges lie ahead. There including the likelihood of another global recession could jeopardize yet well designed Lesotho economic programs. For now, however, the tiny mountain kingdom understood the dangers of its ultra-dependency-via the general South African neighbor.

UN and Lesotho: Development Partners

Not surprisingly, in 2015, Lesotho will not achieve the Millennium Development Goals (MDGs). The eight goals set in 2000 by world leaders include reducing poverty and hunger; ensure better access to health care, water and education, to promote equality of opportunity for women and the environment.

With three years to go, the copy of Lesotho is far from satisfactory. The country is expected to reach two of the eight goals (education and women's rights), record of slow progress in three others (HIV / AIDS, environment and international partnerships) and fail on three tables (poverty reduction, maternal health and child Health).

The fight against HIV / AIDS and poverty reduction is a top priority, says the UN Resident Coordinator in Lesotho, Ahunna Eziakonwa-Onochie. "Since the group most exposed [HIV / AIDS] is also the majority of the workforce, it is very difficult to imagine a march towards development in a context where new infections persist," she notes a concerned tone. His concerns are justified. A quarter of the population lives with HIV. Lesotho has the third highest in sub-Saharan Africa infection rates.

However, Ms. Eziakonwa-Onochie cites Lesotho as a model in several key areas: higher literacy rate lumber, a strong hand and subsidies to farmers to boost production. Yet the economic dependence of Lesotho face to its rich neighbor's make it vulnerable to external shocks and prevents realizes business opportunities globally.

"The government intends to make economic reforms but lacks the means," she analyzed. The national budget is not enough to fund key sectors and donors are reluctant to loosen the purse strings.

In addition to providing financial and technical support for projects to fight against HIV / AIDS, the United Nations is also very present in the government's efforts to revive agriculture. The UN provides expertise in electoral matters. This was the case recently with the adoption of a law that reformed the electoral system. More than a dozen organizations of the United Nations are present in Lesotho. They assist the government in areas such as the promotion of good governance, reducing poverty, protecting the environment and achieving the MDGs.

The assessment of NEPAD can be illustrated in three major points: first, NEPAD is the only continental development initiative. It exists and lasts for 10 years, with proven results in areas such as science and technology, agriculture and infrastructure. Furthermore, after these ten years she has been renewed as an initiative by its integration into the structures of the African Union (AU), as development agency. I do not know many African initiatives that will not only last for ten years, but also that now exist in a formal, institutionalized with a mandate that focuses on issues of implementation.

The second point is that NEPAD is directly responsible for the most important development strategies in priority sectors such as agriculture (with CAADAP) or infrastructure (with PIDA). The fact that all African countries should endeavor to apply the standards and rules of these two continental strategies is a considerable success.

The third point, and yet least known is the envy of Europe and other parts of the world, it is the African Peer Review Mechanism. This is an original approach which aims to take stock of governance (economic, political ...) in countries who volunteer. During this process, an independent group of experts makes a frank and objective assessment of the country and its findings are shared with peers President whose country was considered. It's a unique experience. To date, 23 countries have volunteered. So NEPAD, especially on these three points, had a visible development work.

Yet many people, especially in Africa, wonder what NEPAD is and for what it's used?

Often the problem is that many Africans spend their time repeating what the Western media carry on the mainland and on us. It will take time to disconnect from this colonial mentality. Obviously when you look at the coverage of Africa by a major chain like CNN, retains what is that Africa is a continent of misery, ruled by incompetent, corrupt and extremely n 'absolutely no idea of the public interest. And many of us Africans repeat what CNN and others say, without hindsight and analysis needed. We seem to wallow in a kind of self-denigration. Nowhere on any other continent, is such an attitude not as prevalent. Elsewhere in Latin America, Europe or Asia, people share things. They do not denigrate themselves systematically.

So it is surprisingly rare to hear the African elite and Africans in general take about positively on Africa. We will not say African integration ahead thanks to the efforts of the African Union, we will say more often than this continental organization is useless because it could not achieve this or that.

Unfortunately, this self-denigration is negative. We cannot afford to send a perpetually negative image of Africa to our children. Put things into perspective. A country like Rwanda has made significant progress and has reduced its dependence on foreign aid. Cape Verde has become a middle-income country by mobilizing its own resources. Kenya made considerable progress in terms of governance; if one judges by including the adoption process of their new Constitution. Botswana refuses foreign aid. And many others are following suit...

Nevertheless, to return to NEPAD, the plan remains in the view of many Africans, an abstraction. Why?

NEPAD remains an abstraction because people do not know what he has done, because what has been done has not been disclosed. This raises the more general issue of information on Africa. How much effort is made to make positive things, the mass of negative information produced by the Western media makes it difficult for positive ideas. Therein lays the fundamental question...

If you see one of our recent publications, devoted precisely to the achievements of NEPAD for ten years, you will notice that we have managed many things in the areas that I mentioned earlier, for example, and many others.

All this is not well known as a result of this wave of negative information including NEPAD and other African players are the victims, that because of the tendency to self-denigration among many of us.

In this context, we need to deploy the most appropriate strategies to better know what we are doing. It is our challenge to us.

Specifically, consider two current issues: famine in the Horn of Africa and blocked political changes that sometimes lead to revolutions and North Africa. Faced with these challenges, what are the solutions of NEPAD?

On the issue of vibrations and democratization, a clarification is needed to get started: the number of African countries organizing democratic elections has increased dramatically over the last 15 years. Only seven countries have very serious problems in governance, a total of 54 countries. Unfortunately, it is often a question of seven black as successes on 40 sheep.

About the famine threatening the Horn of Africa and more generally on the issue of food insecurity on the continent, it should be remembered that most of our countries have seen their population multiplied five times in the past 50 recent years. And most of our countries have achieved higher levels of agricultural production than they were twenty years ago. Certainly there are problems famines. But again, if you take the 54 African countries, fewer than a dozen are affected.

More importantly, for six years, investment in agriculture is increasing. There are many ways to go, both in terms of policies, resources, participation of producers ... But we are on the right track.

Many, listening to you would be tempted to say that you beings too optimistic. What do you say?

I'm realistic. I'm not trying to exaggerate. I just found that this realistic view of African issues does not pass. We are trying to impose on us a different vision. It is as if we try to keep the Africans in the mentality of marginalization.

Africa has two major advantages: first the highest intensity of natural resources in the world and the world's youngest population. So this is clearly the continent of the future. And if we do not want this continent to play its role, we must instill in the elites they are incompetent, corrupt and they sow misery. This is obviously not the case.

On the ideological orientations of NEPAD, Many analysts note that it is more liberal capitalist neoliberal inspiration and even. But capitalism has been a great tool for generating wealth, but it is also generating great inequalities. Wealth and poverty, is the path on which NEPAD leads the continent?

This question, this statement I hear often, but it is not at all justified, but then absolutely not justified. Everything starts from that, when the active minority of leaders I mentioned earlier led to the creation of NEPAD, she wanted the program to be recognized by the world's major industrialized countries (G7 meeting and G8).

The result interferences on the communication map. Many felt that because the NEPAD was agreed by the G8, it was a neoliberal. Since then, the accusation sticks to the skin, so to speak.

But I say it plainly: NEPAD is not a neoliberal project. This program supports such as developing African agriculture must develop regional markets and that these markets must be protected. Therefore we demand economic dimensions as protectionism. Furthermore, NEPAD also says that for its development, Africa needs to reintroduce the concept of planning. This is not very neoliberal. Add to this that NEPAD believes that the free market has shown its limits and must be reinvented in Africa, a state of development. Which, we must admit, has nothing to do with neoliberals?

NEPAD celebrates its 10th anniversary in New York

Besides various projects and programs implemented on the continent, the New Partnership for Africa's Development (NEPAD) also aims to renew the ability to "strategic thinking" of African countries. This capability has been severely weakened by years of economic decline and austerity, said Executive Secretary of NEPAD, Ibrahim Mayaki, at a high level debate held in New York on October 7. Other speakers of this exchange on the review of the progress made by NEPAD since its adoption, there were the Under-Secretary General and Special Adviser to the UN for Africa, Cheick Sidi Diarra; Deputy Secretary-General Asha Rose Migiro; Amos Sawyer, a member of the peer review and Amos Namanga Ngongi, President of the Alliance for a Green Revolution in Africa Group of Eminent Persons of the African Mechanism.

The roundtable took place in the context of a series of activities and events organized on the occasion of the tenth anniversary of NEPAD. Of special information meetings were also held for African ambassadors and the United Nations. Over the same period, the General Assembly considered two reports of the Secretary-General on NEPAD and the causes of conflict. Finally, Mr. Mayaki attended a memorial lecture at Columbia University on the theme of changes in Africa over the past decade.

The concept was very relevant. Africa could finally speak with one voice on issues of development and present a common vision in the agricultural sector in particular. This facilitated the relationship with development partners and in particular with emerging economies. In retrospect, I believe that the Comprehensive Africa Agriculture Development Program (CAADP) was an important achievement.

At first, many saw it as a bureaucratic structure. But his opinions were serious and consistent, how to think and plan for the agriculture doubts were right. It is clear that the best proposals to the Global Program on Agriculture and Food Security (GAFSP) are those inspired CAADP. Moreover, the GPAFS recommended that non-African countries are inspired by this program.

NEPAD, how can we contribute better?

In Africa, agriculture remains underdeveloped. With appropriate policies and investments, the continent could easily feed its people and export the surplus. NEPAD could contribute by supporting international partnerships (scientific, political or in the field of infrastructure) that promote better agricultural production.

Over the past 25 years, research and scientific production related to agriculture were generally flat on the continent.

NEPAD can, based on CAADP, provide researchers with a platform at the sub regional level, for example, which would generate a critical and coherent mass. Research institutes in Africa could more easily access the expertise and available worldwide technologies. Sustainable management of land and water in the context of climate change must be a central issue for researchers. In addition, intra-African trade could be improved by efforts to modernize infrastructure and reduce barriers to cross-border trade. NEPAD should also promote and facilitate the establishment of strategic grain reserves to help mitigate the effects of food shortages caused by climate change and conflict.

Do you share the view that, for the majority of Africans, NEPAD remains an abstract and vague project?

NEPAD has become a development agency, its contribution and visibility should improve. Agriculture is of great importance in the daily lives of most Africans. By engaging in a professional manner and determined in the areas of agriculture and food, NEPAD can become a partner on issues including food security.

But to be effective, the agency will require personnel and funds. In the coming years, it is his ability to obtain and maintain the support of African governments that we will judge. The rise in commodity prices is an opportunity. The challenge for governments and for NEPAD is to allocate new resources to investments that benefit the poor, victims of famine and marginalized continent. If done effectively, there will be every reason to celebrate the second decade of NEPAD.

The Global Program on agriculture and food security is a multilateral financing mechanism for developing countries, created at the request of the G20 summit in 2009, the end of August 2011; he was endowed with $ 557 million and financed the projects in 12 countries, including six in Africa.

1 -Connect the continent

Connect African countries through high-speed Internet under the Network broadband infrastructure, NEPAD aims to connect African countries to one another and to the world. Two cable networks are being built. A submarine network (Uhurunet) and a terrestrial network (Umojanet). Uhurunet, representing EUR 515 million investments around, should be completed in 2012. NEPAD has also launched the e-Schools, to improve the quality of teaching and learning in primary schools, colleges and high schools in Africa, thanks to the information technology and communication (ICT). Sixteen African countries and more than 80 schools participated in the pilot phase. Each facility has been equipped with a laboratory of 20 computers and a server and a network and peripherals (scanners, printers, and electronic whiteboards). To date, many challenges remain. However, the NEPAD Agency and its partners make every effort to address them in order to extend the initiative across the continent.

2 -More power to women

Train women in key sectors

Established in 2007 and funded by the Spanish Government, NEPAD Spanish Fund for African Women Empowerment supports efforts to eradicate poverty and strengthen the economic capacities of women. In total, 6285 million that was disbursed as part of 46 projects implemented in 23 countries. For now, 31 projects have been completed. These projects form a greater number of women and girls in areas such as ICT in particular. They also led to the creation of jobs and various income-generating activities for women, the establishment of a system of micro-financing, a greater awareness of gender-based violence, and the establishment of a mechanism to fight against this problem. The Fund has recently allocated € 2 million to create a business incubator for women entrepreneurs to East, West and Southern Africa.

3-Feeding Africa Changing agricultural policies

Through the Comprehensive Africa Agriculture Development Program (CAADP), NEPAD advocates a radical change in agriculture in Africa. This is to help African countries to promote growth by increasing investment in the sector. The main goal of CAADP is to encourage these countries to invest 10% of their national budget expenditure on agriculture. In May 2011, 26 countries had ratified the agreement CAADP and had built their agricultural strategies. Eight countries now exceed the budget target of 10% and most others are on track to achieve this. To date, nine countries have exceeded the annual average agricultural growth rate of at least 6% CAADP set the goal.

Furthermore, NEPAD has established or supported various programs, including the Partnership for African Fisheries (PPA), which aims to guide reform of the sector across the continent. In addition to helping individual countries to develop plans for regional fisheries, PPA is implementing in Ghana and Sierra Leone a pilot project, with a budget of about € 2 million. The total budget of the PPA for 2009-2014 exceeds 8 million.

The Fertilizer Support Program has increased the number of small African farms that use chemical fertilizers to improve yields. Finally, NEPAD launched a regional initiative in 2005, Terr-Africa for better land management.

African countries must live more Actively Foreign Investments Into agriculture Medical against the transmission of AIDS from mother to child. Production of medicines in Africa is controlled by foreign players. NEPAD wants to change that.

4- Building the infrastructure of the future -Provide the continent with an overall strategy

Launched at the Summit of the African Union held in Kampala (Uganda) in July 2010, the Program for Infrastructure Development in Africa (PIDA) aims to establish a strategy for infrastructure development at the regional and continental scale the transportation, energy, cross-border water management and information technology and communication.

The PIDA will guide policies and investments in these sectors from 2011 to 2030 It brings together in a coherent program previous regional initiatives on infrastructure such as the Action Plan of NEPAD short-term, the Strategic Framework and Medium long-term and the NEPAD infrastructure Master Plan of the African Union.

The PIDA budget, estimated at € 7.8 million project ,funded by the European Union, the Islamic Bank of development, the African Water Facility and NEPAD.

5- To facilitate the production of medicines in Africa

Encourage local production

Adopted at a summit of the African Union held in 2007, the Plan of pharmaceutical manufacturing for Africa is to encourage local production of drugs. At present, the sector is dominated by foreign companies. The plan helps African countries to develop strategies and build skills to promote and Developer local pharmaceutical innovation. To do this, NEPAD has published a strategic document, Strengthening Pharmaceutical Innovation in Africa. Since the democratization wave of the 1990s, several initiatives have been launched in Africa in governance. What is the uniqueness of the Peer Review Mechanism?

It offers many things that are unique to him in the first place; it's self-assessment of the country a mechanism by itself at all levels (government, civil society, business community). Then it's a peer review, implemented by governments themselves. Peers, sit around a table with the country's leaders.

This commitment means that the criticism is constructive and it is illustrated by good practices. But it does not stop there. A program of action is formulated and the chief of the country under review is required to return to his colleagues, every two years, for an overview of progress.

This process is slow. It is non-confrontational. But the country that uses it wisely opens doors that allow the international community to support its development programs. And reinforce its governance system because even its methodology, the process requires countries to engage in dialogue with their citizens.

This process is there an implementation of the spirit of the Arusha Declaration of 1990?

Yes. The 1990 conference on popular participation involved a mobilization of human potential in the development process so that trade unions and farmer groups involved in governance. We must go beyond the thought that only concerned about the "government" to think in terms of 'governance', which allows you to interact with different classes of citizens. The peer review provides a practical implementation of these aspects.

In the Panel of Eminent Persons of the APRM, many people come from civil society, but in the end the process ends with the approval of African heads of state. Do you not see a risk of tension?

Yes indeed we are working. One of the issues raised by groups representing civil society in Africa is that the evaluation process at Head of State should be carried out with the participation of civil society, is giving way to a concurrent process that would allow civil society to provide its own conclusions on the report. I would not be surprised if things change in the future.

In some countries, civil society groups have complained that those who were allowed to participate in the peer review were mainly government-approved.

The situations are different. In some countries, civil society is well organized and is present on the political scene. In others, she did not say. I say you should ensure its participation in the political process.

Liberia is the latest to have acceded to the APRM. Countries emerging from conflict they need time to adapt before a peer review can serve them?

For Liberia, the time is right. A country emerging from conflict must first bring order to its institutions. Or when new institutions are in place, it is also a good thing that they comply with the standards required by the APRM. The legislature, for example, should not be subject to the control of the executive. Legislators must take seriously their responsibilities to the voters. The judiciary must be independent, have adequate funding and be accessible. The peer review can help.

How to know if the APRM had an impact?

Unfortunately, we know pretty quickly when the APR is not taken into account. When evaluating Kenya in 2006, four or five critical points were raised and ignored ... We remembered it in 2007-2008, during the election violence. Today, from the presidency to civil society, everyone says that if the conclusions of the report had been followed, many of these problems could have been avoided.

In South Africa, we raised the issue of xenophobia. I was not a member of the group; I was only looking for the preparation of the report. Initially, the South African government was in denial and several points of disagreement he felt that we were wrong. But the member of the group responsible for the process defended the report, which has been validated. South Africa has finally decided to address the problem of xenophobia, unfortunately after the outbreak of violence in 2008.

Thirty countries have acceded to the APRM, but only a few have been fully evaluated. Why?

Thirty countries have acceded to the APRM and 14 were evaluated. Two other evaluations are ongoing, and in January the last two assessments are completed. Another country, Tanzania, invited the Commission to intervene, what will be done. Apparently, Gabon, Republic of Congo and Liberia are preparing too. There is therefore still a significant number of countries to deal with, at least 10.

We recently decided on a strategy to encourage countries that are reluctant to participate. We have planned several visits which should enable us to see how we can persuade them to advance in their participation in the peer review process. We encourage African leaders to join their colleagues and for my part, I think that peer pressure can be more decisive than many other types of pressure.

I know that this idea of a peer review is in the context of Africa, where some leaders are seen as authoritarian and corrupt as others. If there is no denying some aspects, it seems that the idea is to engage African leaders themselves to such a process have a lot of merit.

It can produce significant results, beneficial for Africa. We need to encourage this process. We must encourage and strengthen civil society so that they become key players in this process. This is how we build our systems and democratic governments.

The African Charter for Popular Participation in Development and Transformation, known as the Arusha Declaration was adopted at a conference of 500 representatives of African civil society, governments, and donors. The conference was organized by the United Nations in Arusha (Tanzania) in February 1990.

In the poorest African countries, there are more mobile phones than bank accounts. No wonder then that telephone operators are very interested in money transfer via mobile phones. An inexpensive, effective and safe alternative that allows migrant workers to send money to their families back home without having to go through the corporate funds transfer or knowledge returnees.

Money can be sent quickly, even to the most remote areas. It is sufficient that the recipient has access to a laptop or can go to a payment center. This market should be very profitable, says Pieter Verkade, part of the telecommunications company MTN.

Technology begins to take root, especially in countries where companies transfer funds levy high fees. The operator Safaricom Kenya and Britain's Vodafone led the way in 2007 by launching M-Pesa (M for "mobile" and pesa meaning "money" in Kiswahili). Initially limited to Kenya, M-Pesa has since internationalized, especially with Kenyans living in the UK. The growth of mobile phone banking in the Kenyan market, where M-Pesa is dominant, has been rapid. In late 2010, four operators had more than 15.4 million subscribers (more than half of the adult population).

The rapid growth of M-Pesa is all the more surprising that this service has initially been "ignored by financial institutions," recalls Bernard Matthewman, CEO of Paynet, which developed M-Pesa for a software using ATMs without a map. One of the first challenges was to convince banks that rural populations were potential customers. "Above all, says Matthewman, launching the service without a map, we had to conduct an information campaign.

On the user side, few people had ever used a cash machine bank, let alone without a map. However, a transaction without a map is nothing complicated. Just send SMS to the recipient a secret code that remains active for a few hours. This ease of use may explain the immediate success of M-Pesa service. Shortly after its launch, remittances received by this method reached a total value of $ 100 million.

Alliances

The money transfer via mobile for remittances and small payments, such as school fees and utility bills, phone, spread to other African countries. In South Africa, Vodacom recently teamed up with Nedbank to offer these services within the country. "The current penetration of the target market Vodacom, its presence through distributors even in rural areas, interested us," says Ilze Wagener, an executive at Ned-bank.

Transactions by mobile phone may allow banks to access rural markets without having to open new branches. In May 2011, nine months after its launch, the Vodacom-Ned-bank partnership had 140 000 subscribers in South Africa and was established more than 3,000 M-Pesa agents and 2,000 ATMs in the country. In a country like South Africa, where customers and distributors have more varied backgrounds, "we must consider M-Pesa in very different ways," says Wagener. In his view, the service "presents opportunities and challenges unique."

In some countries, banks are forming partnerships with multiple telecommunications companies. "The network of mobile money transfer in place through partnerships with four mobile phone companies in Ghana has enabled us to expand our services to customers located throughout the country," said Africa Renewal Owureku Osare, head of banking transactions of Ecobank Ghana. The strengthening of this network in Ghana part of a broader expansion of customer strategy, has he added.

Everything indicates that traditional banking and financial adapt to new technologies and new markets. This is to attract those who do not have bank accounts. Banks that offer money transfer services via mobile phones recommend that beneficiaries have remaining some money to put it in "mobile wallets": electronic bank accounts linked to a mobile phone.

"By enabling the unbanked to keep their money in the mobile wallets linked to their mobile numbers, we hope that this money will end up in a real bank account," says Osare. In May, Ecobank has proposed to its customers in West Africa a mobile savings account that can be linked to a mobile wallet.

The case of M-Pesa is interesting in more ways than one. As part of this service, a telecommunications company and bank teamed last year to offer a savings account, known as M-Kesho. This is one of the first partnerships of this type. An M-Pesa user can move money, by mobile phone, M-Pesa mobile wallet to a savings account M-Kesho, managed by Equity Bank.

In 2010, a report by the Bill & Melinda Gates Foundation showed those three months after the launch of M-Kesho, 455,000 new accounts were opened, more than at the beginning of the implementation of the M-Pesa service. In addition to a full virtual account managed by mobile phone, M-Pesa offers the account holder can take out a micro-loan after a few months.

Expansion

In addition to the savings and micro-lending accounts, banks also offer their customers new prepaid credit cards and insurance services. Insurance policies that support funeral costs are now an important financial activity in many African markets. For now, they are usually offered only to clients of cities, says Mr. Verkade MTN.

Faced with the growing popularity of mobile financial transactions in Ghana, Hollard Insurance and Mobile Financial Services Africa joined forces in early 2011 to MTN to launch mid-Life service "micro-insurance" run by mobile phone. "These insurance services make full use of our technology, so that the entire registration process also takes place via mobile phone," says Verkade. With very low premiums, the idea is to take advantage initially of unmet demand for this type of service in Ghana, especially in underserved rural areas and then expand to other African markets like Rwanda.

Partnerships between Telco's, banks and other financial services are expected to increase in the future to serve a growing number of countries and African markets.

Another logical step is to develop so-called "cash-light" transactions that eliminate or greatly reduce instead of cash in operations remittance says Matthewman. "We are already starting to see that when a person buys a package of prepaid communication on an M-Pesa phone and send it to another user. There is then no need to pay cash, "he said. Thus, a person living abroad can send a prepaid package of communication to the recipient, who can in turn interact directly against the goods or services at participating retailers.

The six challenges of the transfer of funds

Despite the growth of international remittances by mobile phone, several obstacles remain; Limited market.

The rapid development of M-Pesa in Kenya is partly explained by the fact that the company that launched Safaricom, has benefited from its position near monopoly. Elsewhere in Africa, M-Pesa and other services of the same type do not register the same success; on the found cash.

 In rural and remote areas, services funds transfer may not have enough cash to be exchanged transfers. To remedy the problem, Owureku Osare Ecobank (Ghana) said that his bank is looking to partner "with a microfinance institution that already has a field experience to enhance the cash agents in those regions." In Kenya, Paynet service offers a different solution by offering free withdrawals map to ATMs.

Mistrust and misunderstanding

Many rural residents are wary of banks or do not have access. Building on the popularity of mobile phones, banks and phone companies send representatives on the ground, even in the most remote areas, to explain to people how to make remittances by mobile phone. Other train local agents, who receive a commission for recruiting clients,.

Technical obstacles; Although present in 30 African countries, Ecobank has still not managed to find an operator with a single platform that allows it to provide cross-border banking services via mobile phones.

Barriers; Laws and regulations on cross-border transfers of modest amounts vary from one country to another, and their application to the case of the sometimes confusing mobile phone. The Central Bank of Kenya is developing draft regulations for issuers of electronic money and electronic transfers to detail and Tanzania's central bank announced it was preparing a new draft law governing such transactions.

Control of operations; In South Africa, remittances by mobile phone are not currently inside the country, and all cross-border transactions, even a modest amount, must be subject to control. In accordance with national legislation against money laundering, only banks and authorized dealers are authorized to perform money transfers with foreign countries. This excludes retailers, which are at the heart of the strategy by the banks for money transfer via mobile phone. Meanwhile, the banks themselves are reluctant to perform a large number of international transactions by a modest amount. The cost of reporting these transactions to the authorities is generally high.

For more than 100 million Internet users in Africa, the connections are generally slow and costly. On average, only one in ten has access to broadband, faster. This can and must change, says the Broadband Commission for Digital Development Service, which aims to promote better access to the Internet worldwide. Met last October in Geneva (Switzerland), members of the UN commission set ambitious goals. In the 48 least developed countries (33 of which are in Africa) the percentage of broadband users is expected to reach 15% of the population by 2015 for developing countries, the goal is 50% and 60% for developed countries.

According to the commission, the use of broadband opens new horizons for young people, promoting women's empowerment and provides greater economic opportunities for all. To improve access to broadband, each country should have national programs and adopt a favorable regulatory expansion, advises the commission.

Although ambitious, these goals are quite similar to some forecasts for the growth of broadband Internet in Africa. Informa Telecoms & Media, a consulting firm, estimates that by 2015, Africa will have 265 million broadband subscribers (over 20% of the population), against about 12 million today.

In South Africa, aid on the line

Siboniso Hlela lives in the township of Siphumelele near Howick in KwaZulu-Natal in South Africa. Her house is located at the bottom of a hill, near a small stream. Sometimes, especially when it rains, the sewer system overflows. Wastewater invades the residence of Siboniso. In late 2010, the situation was so bad that six months, a pool of dirty water due to failure of the municipal sewer system, was prevented from opening a door from its housing. Bad smells were such that some of his friends did not want to visit Siboniso.

For many months, Siboniso tried to get help from the authorities, without success. But using social media and establishing contacts with non-governmental organizations (NGOs) and local government officials, he was able to make things happen.

Siboniso had heard of Duzi Umngeni Conservation Trust (DUCT), an NGO that deals with the management of rivers in South Africa. After being flooded with sewage again, he filmed the damage with his mobile phone. He then phoned Liz Taylor, a volunteer of the NGO. They set an appointment with him by SMS. Once there, Liz also took pictures with his cell phone. Video files are too large to be transferred via SMS; Siboniso told Liz how to transfer mobile to mobile via Bluetooth, a method for wireless short range.

On Saturday, February 14, 2011, Siboniso once again phoned Liz. Sewers overflowed again. Liz and a colleague working for another NGO took pictures of the flooding. But it was the weekend and municipal offices were closed. At 11:00 am on Sunday, Liz has sent an email and photos Sbu Khuzwayo, the District Officer of the

Municipality of UMgungundlovu, which was quick to respond a few minutes later. A response team went to the scene on Monday, less than a week later, municipal pipelines were repaired and the problem resolved.

For some African countries, the Report on the 2011 Human Development * contains good news. Published by the United Nations Program for Development (UNDP), the paper classifies countries according to three indicators of human development: life expectancy, education and income (together they form the human development index HDI). Kenya and Nigeria, extreme poverty declined thanks to advances in access to safe water, sanitation and hygiene. Ghana has made progress noticed and now ranks among the countries with medium human development.

According to the report, the HDI of the forty countries ranked lowest (many African countries) increased by 82% between 1970 and 2010; twice faster than that of most countries. If such growth continues during the next 40 years, the majority of countries misclassified reach equal or superior to those of the best countries currently classified levels, the report said.

Norway, Australia, the Netherlands, the United States and New Zealand are in the lead.

 Libya, 64th Africa's country; Followed by Mauritius at the 77th, 94th and Tunisia. Egypt ranks 113th, South Africa and Nigeria is 123rd is 159th position. Ten African countries are low on the list and that is the Democratic Republic of Congo (DRC), which occupies the 187th and last place.

The report recognizes that although many African countries have made progress, most still face various challenges: insufficient income, education levels and limited life expectancies lower than the world average because of deaths related to malaria and including AIDS.

The poor performance of some sub-Saharan African countries is partly a result of armed conflicts, as in the DRC and Liberia. And progress in poor countries could be canceled and reversed by mid-century if efforts are not made to combat the threats of climate change trend, the report notes.

The index of gender inequality, a recent indicator, lowered the classification of certain African countries, including the Central African Republic, Chad, DRC, Liberia, Mali, Niger and Sierra Leone, among all ten countries most marked by inequalities. "In sub-Saharan Africa the biggest losses arise from gender disparities in education and high mortality rates and the rate of adolescent fertility.

The Multidimensional Poverty Index (MPI), which looks at factors such as access to clean water, fuel for cooking and health services (in addition to measuring income) up the Niger in last place for the number of poor in proportion to the population. It is followed by Ethiopia and Mali.

The 2011 report covers an unprecedented number of countries (187).

In 2010, it covered only 169 countries. This means that the 2011 results are not comparable with the figures for the previous year.

According to the World Bank, the business climate is improving in sub-Saharan Africa

Between June 2010 and May 2011, the majority of sub-Saharan African countries have made life easier for businesses. Only Eastern Europe has done better. In its latest "Index of the ease of doing business", the World Bank reports that 36 of the 46 economies in the region have improved the business environment. A record that beats the one established in 2005 Six African countries (Rwanda, Burkina Faso, Mali, Sierra Leone, Guinea-Bissau and Senegal) are among the top 15 ranking in terms of improving the business climate.

In Rwanda, the African country whose economy is currently the more business, the Bank notes from the recent changes a sharp drop in registration fees for setting up a business, greater accessibility of information on credit and obligation for the company to submit forms for taxation every three months instead of every month. The Rwanda now ranks 45th overall business destinations, just behind Spain. Among the measures to improve the regulatory environment for local businesses in Africa, there are the first revision in 18 years brought to a common legal and institutional framework in 16 countries in West Africa and Central Africa.

Despite this positive trend, the World Bank notes that sub-Saharan Africa is still the region where the creation and management of a company are more complex and costly.

The whole world watched with surprise and amazement the uprisings that shook Tunisia and Egypt in late 2010 and early 2011 the North African and Middle Eastern populations, accustomed to see the slightest hint opposition harshly repressed, does not expect that these protests become revolutions. Yet close observers as those who contributed to the writing of Social

Movements, Mobilization, and Contestation in the Middle East and North Africa, felt for several years that something was up in the area and that despite formidable obstacles to freedom of expression, certain disadvantaged social groups found ways to organize establish contacts and begin to demand change. The biggest research and writing of this book was completed when the "Arab Spring" began. The authors acknowledge, not immodestly, that nothing in the book "no indication insurgencies that erupted in Tunisia and Egypt." But as the book was not yet in print, they have added an epilogue devoted to events in those countries.

Although written before the recent turmoil, the book is nevertheless the numerous social mobilization activities that have challenged the old simplistic picture of a politically immobile or region prone to irrational bouts of anti-Western terrorism. The case studies in Egypt, Lebanon, Morocco, Saudi Arabia and Turkey show that workers, unemployed managers, the rural poor, women, parents and victims of political other segments of the population actively exploring new ways to be heard. The studies are designed specifically some of the main theories of social movements, which have mostly been developed and applied to develop societies, and explain how they apply or not. Some analyzes, including that of Benin on the unrest in Egypt, confirms the old adage about revolutions: even though they are often difficult to predict, they are usually preceded by shocks, which cannot take the full measure that hindsight.

THE ECO ...

references

BAFD, OCDE, PNUD et CEA (2013), *Perspectives économiques en Afrique 2013*, Banque africaine deDéveloppement, Organisation de coopération et de développement économiques, ProgrammeDes Nations Unies pour le développement et Commission économique des Nations Unies pour L'Afrique, Éditions de l'OCDE, Paris.

Banque mondiale (n.d.), *Global Economic Monitor (GEM) Commodities*, World DataBank, http://databank.banquemondiale.org/data/ (consulté en janvier 2014).

Banque mondiale et FMI (n.d.), *Debt Sustainability Analysis: Low-Income Countries*, www.imf.org/external/pubs/ft/dsa/lic.aspx (consulté en janvier 2014).

Bosworth, B. et S.-M. Collins (2008), "Accounting for growth: Comparing China and India", *Journal ofEconomic Perspectives*, 22(1), pp. 45-66, Washington, DC.

Carmignani, F. (2010), "Cyclical fiscal policy in Africa", *Journal of Policy Modeling*, vol. 32, Issue 2,mars-avril, pp. 254, Brisbane.

Direction des statistiques du commerce du FMI (DOTS) (n.d.), rapports de données, Fond monétaireInternational, http://elibrary-data.imf.org/ (consulté en janvier 2014).

FEM (2013), *The Travel & Tourism Competitiveness Report 2013*, Forum économique mondial, Genève.

Ghazanchyan, M. et J.-G. Stotsky (2013), "Drivers of growth: Evidence from Sub-Saharan African countries", *IMF Working Paper n° 13/236*, Fonds monétaire international, Washington, DC.

Ilzetki, E. et C. Vegh (2008), "Procyclical fiscal policy in developing countries: Truth or fiction?",

NBER Working Paper 14191, National Bureau of Economic Research, Cambridge, MA.

Jangili, R. (2011), "Causal relationship between saving, investment and economic growth for India– what does the relation imply?", Reserve Bank of India Occasional Papers, vol. 32, n° 1, Bombay, été.

Leibfritz, W. et H. Rottmann (2013), "Fiscal policies during business cycles in developing countries:

The case of Africa", CESifo Working Paper 4484, CESifo Group, Munich, novembre.

Moody's Investors Service (2013), 8 octobre.

Schmidt-Hebbel, K., L. Servén et A. Solimano (1996), "Saving, investment, and growth in developing countries: An overview", in Solimano, A. (dir. pub.), Road Maps to Prosperity: Essays on Growth and Development, University of Michigan Press, Ann Arbor, MI.

Building a Common Future in Southern Africa

Mongardini, Joannes, Tamon Asonuma,

Olivier Basdevant, Alfredo Cuevas, Xavier Debrun,

Lars Holger Engstrom, Imelda M. Flores Vazquez,

Vitaliy Kramarenko, Lamin Leigh, Paul R. Masson

Oil Wealth in Central Africa: Policies for Inclusive Growth

Coorey, Sharmini et Bernardin Akitoby

The Impact of the Global Financial Crisis on Sub-Saharan

Africa

Département Afrique 2009

Tanzania: The Story of an African Transition

Nord, Roger, Yuri Sobolev, David Dunn,

Alejandro Hajdenberg, Niko Hobdari, Samar Maziad et

Stéphane Roudet

Responding to Shocks and Maintaining Stability in the West African Economic and Monetary Union

Kolerus, Christina, Aleksandra Zdzienicka, Ermal Hitaj et Douglas J. Shapiro

13/6

West African Economic and Monetary Union: Financial Depth and Macrostability

Imam, Patrick A. et Christina Kolerus

13/5

Senegal: Financial Depth and Macrostability

Imam, Patrick A. ET Christina Kolerus

13/4

Senegal: Achieving High and Inclusive Growth While Preserving Fiscal Sustainability

Kireyev, Alexei et Gaston K. Mpatswe

13/3

Banking in Sub-Saharan Africa: The Macroeconomic Context Mlachila, Montfort, Seok Gil Park et Masafumi Yabara

13/2

Energy Subsidy Reform in Sub-Saharan Africa: Experiences and Lessons Alleyne, Trevor
Managing Volatile Capital Flows: Experiences and Lessons for Sub-Saharan African Frontier Markets Cheikh A. Gueye, Javier Arze del Granado, Rodrigo Garcia-Verdu, Mumtaz Hussain, B. Jang, Sebastian Weber et Juan S Corrales

13/8

Mali: Achieving Strong and Inclusive Growth with Macroeconomic Stability

Christian Josz

Banking in Sub-Saharan Africa: The Macroeconomic Context Mlachila, Montfort, Seok Gil Park et Masafumi Yabara

13/2

Energy Subsidy Reform in Sub-Saharan Africa: Experiences Lessons Alleyne, Trevor

13/2

Boom, Bust, or Prosperity? Managing Sub-Saharan Africa's Natural Resource Wealth Lundgren, Charlotte J., Alun H. Thomas, et Robert C. York

13/1

Restoring Sustainability in a Changing Global Environment: Options for Swaziland

Basdevant, Olivier, Emily Forrest et Borislava Mircheva

Restoring Sustainability in a Changing Global Environment: Options for Swaziland

Basdevant, Olivier, Emily Forrest et Borislava Mircheva

Macroeconomic Vulnerabilities Stemming

From the Global Economic Crisis: The Case of Switzerland

Basdevant, Olivier, Chikako Babaet Borislava Mircheva

What Do Fast Job Creators Look Like? Some Stylized Facts and Perspectives on South Africa

Zhan, Zaijin

Zimbabwe: Challenges and Policy Options after Hyperinflation

Kramarenko, Vitaliy, Lars H. Engstrom,

Geneviève Verdier, Gilda Fernandez, Stefan E. Oppers,

Richard Hughes, James McHugh et Warren L. Coats

10/02

Expenditure Composition and Economic Developments in Benin

Pani, Marco et Mohamed El Harrak

10/01

Wage Policy and Fiscal Sustainability in Benin

Lundgren, Charlotte J.

09/04

The Global Financial Crisis and Adjustments to Shocks in Kenya, Tanzania, and Uganda: A Balance Sheet Analysis Perspective

Masha, Iyabo

09/03

Impact of the Global Financial Crisis on Exchange Ratesand Policies in Sub-Saharan Africa

Ben Ltaifa, Nabil, Stella Kaendera et Shiv Dixit

Case Studies on Energy Subsidy Reform: Lessons and

Implications

Document conjoint du Département des finances publiques, du Département Afrique et du Département

Moyen-Orient et Asie centrale

2012

Oil Wealth in Central Africa: Policies for Inclusive Growth

Coorey, Sharmini et Bernardin Akitoby

2009

The Impact of the Global Financial Crisis on

Sub-Saharan Africa

Département Afrique

2009

Tanzania: The Story of an African Transition

Nord, Roger, Yuri Sobolev, David Dunn, Alejandro

Hajdenberg, Niko Hobdari, Samar Maziad et Stéphane

Roudet south Africa: Macro Policy Mix and Its Effects on Growth and the Real Exchange Rate—Empirical Evidence and

GIMF Simulations

Canales-Kriljenko, Jorge Iván

11/02

Measuring the Potential Output of South Africa

Klein, Nir

11/01

In the Wake of the Global Economic Crisis: Adjusting to Lower Revenue of the Southern African Customs Union in Botswana, Lesotho, Namibia, and Swaziland

Mongardini, Joannes, Dalmacio Benicio, Thomson Fontaine, Gonzalo C. Pastor et Geneviève Verdier

10/03

Zimbabwe: Challenges and Policy Options after Hyperinflation

Kramarenko, Vitaliy, Lars H. Engstrom,

Geneviève Verdier, Gilda Fernandez, Stefan E. Oppers,

Richard Hughes, James McHugh et Warren L. Coats

10/02

Expenditure Composition and Economic Developments in Benin

Pani, Marco et Mohamed El Harrak south Africa: Macro Policy Mix and Its Effects on Growth and the Real Exchange Rate—Empirical Evidence and

GIMF Simulations

Canales-Kriljenko, Jorge Iván

11/02

Measuring the Potential Output of South Africa

Klein, Nir

11/01

In the Wake of the Global Economic Crisis: Adjusting to Lower Revenue of the Southern African Customs Union in Botswana, Lesotho, Namibia, and Swaziland

Mongardini, Joannes, Dalmacio Benicio, Thomson Fontaine, Gonzalo C. Pastor et Geneviève Verdier

10/03

Zimbabwe: Challenges and Policy Options after Hyperinflation

Kramarenko, Vitaliy, Lars H. Engstrom, Geneviève Verdier, Gilda Fernandez, Stefan E. Oppers, Richard Hughes, James McHugh et Warren L. Coats

10/02

Expenditure Composition and Economic Developments in Benin

Pani, Marco et Mohamed El Harrak

south Africa: Macro Policy Mix and Its Effects on Growth and the Real Exchange Rate—Empirical Evidence and GIMF Simulations

Canales-Kriljenko, Jorge Iván

11/02

Measuring the Potential Output of South Africa

Klein, Nir

11/01

In the Wake of the Global Economic Crisis: Adjusting to Lower Revenue of the Southern African Customs Union in Botswana, Lesotho, Namibia, and Swaziland

Mongardini, Joannes, Dalmacio Benicio, Thomson Fontaine, Gonzalo C. Pastor et Geneviève Verdier

10/03

Zimbabwe: Challenges and Policy Options after Hyperinflation

Kramarenko, Vitaliy, Lars H. Engstrom, Geneviève Verdier, Gilda Fernandez, Stefan E. Oppers, Richard Hughes, James McHugh et Warren L. Coats

10/02

Expenditure Composition and Economic Developments in Benin

Pani, Marco et Mohamed El Harrak.

www.ingramcontent.com/pod-product-compliance
Lightning Source LLC
Chambersburg PA
CBHW071410180526
45170CB00001B/45